State, Civil Society and Apartheid in South Africa

An Examination of Dutch Reformed Church–State Relations

Tracy Kuperus
Assistant Professor
Political Studies Department
Gordon College
Wenham, MA
USA

First published in Great Britain 1999 by
MACMILLAN PRESS LTD
Houndmills, Basingstoke, Hampshire RG21 6XS and London
Companies and representatives throughout the world

A catalogue record for this book is available from the British Library.

ISBN 0–333–72649–9

First published in the United States of America 1999 by
ST. MARTIN'S PRESS, INC.,
Scholarly and Reference Division,
175 Fifth Avenue, New York, N.Y. 10010

ISBN 0–312–21883–4

Library of Congress Cataloging-in-Publication Data
Kuperus, Tracy, 1967–
State, civil society and apartheid in South Africa : an
examination of Dutch Reformed Church–state relations / Tracy
Kuperus.
p. cm.
Includes bibliographical references and index.
ISBN 0–312–21883–4 (hardcover)
1. Apartheid—South Africa—History. 2. Race relations—Religious
aspects—Reformed Church. 3. Nederduitse Gereformeerde Kerk–
–History—20th century. 4. Christianity and politics—South Africa–
–History—20th century. I. Title.
DT1757.K86 1999
305.8'00968—dc21
98–46443
CIP

This book is printed on paper suitable for recycling and made from fully managed and sustained forest sources.

10   9   8   7   6   5   4   3   2   1
08   07   06   05   04   03   02   01   00   99

Printed and bound in Great Britain by
Antony Rowe Ltd, Chippenham, Wiltshire

STATE, CIVIL SOCIETY AND APARTHEID IN SOUTH AFRICA

In the loving memory of my father, Fred Kuperus (1924–98), for his deep faith, humility, and integrity

Contents

Preface

This book focuses on the interaction of dominant groups within a church, the *Nederduitse Gereformeerde Kerk* (NGK), otherwise known as the Dutch Reformed Church, and the South African state over a 60-year period within the broader context of state–civil society relations. The unique relationship between factions controlling the NGK and the South African state merits considerable attention, especially regarding the development of race policy, and large portions of this book address this relationship in depth. Special attention, however, is given to how NGK–state relations are situated within a wider state–civil society context.

State–civil society debates have re-emerged within the phenomenon of regime change that has swept across many areas of the world over the past few decades. Civil society has become an important factor in understanding regime change because many claim that it strengthens already existing democracies and/or demands democratic change from authoritarian regimes. But the use of this concept has brought with it considerable ambiguity. For example, what is civil society, what is its purpose, and is civil society necessary to the proper functioning of a democracy? An examination of these questions is the theoretical focus of this book.

Liberal or mainstream scholars provide the dominant insights concerning the purpose and function of civil society, as well as the relational dynamics between state, civil society, and democracy. Civil society is believed to be a necessary but not sufficient condition to the establishment of democracy. It is defined as a sphere of activity or conglomeration of associations that can resist an authoritarian regime, thus creating a conducive environment for political liberalization and abetting a democratic transition, *or* civil society is viewed as a particular mix of associational life that helps strengthen or consolidate democracy by fostering civility or holding an overcentralized state accountable. To be effective, civil society must be liberated from an overcentralized state, and a viable democracy can be achieved if an autonomous, properly constrained civil society is nurtured.

An examination of South Africa's state–civil society relations can enlarge our understanding of the assumptions undergirding state–civil society literature. While civil society literature adequately explains the nature, role, and purpose of civil society in a society committed to genuine pluralism, one that is basically constructed along liberal democratic lines, it has not explained extensively the role, nature, and purpose of civil society in an authoritarian regime or a limited democracy. The comparative, historical examination of state–NGK relations from 1934 to 1994 allows for the analysis of the operation of a civil society institution in a limited, race-based democracy, and it reveals that some of the active, above-ground civil society institutions resisted the development of widespread democracy because they were committed to the narrow, ethnic interests of white South Africans. Second, South African state–NGK relations will be analyzed with respect to the variety of factions contained within the NGK and state that held unique and divergent perspectives concerning race policy formation and political reform. It was the politicking among the divergent factions over material, social and political issues that explains nuanced state–NGK relations from 1934 to 1994. Finally, a survey of state–civil society relations in South Africa – or any other country for that matter – shows that state–civil society relations extend far beyond the outcomes of conflict or cooperation. In Chapter 1, I posit a typology of state–civil society relations which begins to unravel the rich variety of state–civil society relations.

According to the typology, state–civil society relations can be described in terms of cooperation, conflict, or some mix of the two. Six dominant state–civil society interactions result, which include collaboration, mutual engagement, balanced pluralism, coexisting conflict, conflictual resistance, and enforced disengagement. The six interactions are measured by policy collusion/conflict and official/unofficial interaction among leaders and groups ruling state and civil society institutions.

This continuum of state–civil society relations helps explain the different civil society organizations' interactions with the groups dominating the white minority government within the South African state over time, including the Christian Institute, Black Sash, and the Congress of South African Trade Unions. The latter interactions were basically conflictual, but what of the civil society institutions that engaged with groups dominating the white minority government within the South African state during the last 50 or 60 years? My research addresses one such civil society institution: the *Nederduitse Gereformeerde Kerk* (NGK).

Although the NGK existed primarily to meet the spiritual needs of the Afrikaner people, this church also helped legitimate the state during the years of segregation and apartheid through such things as NGK leaders' involvement in constructing 'apartheid theology' and their support for specific governmental policies. In assessing NGK–state relations, I have tried to delineate the various theological, ideological, and political perspectives or factions within both the NGK and the state. It is easy to portray the South African state and the NGK as monolithic institutions, however, I am aware that each entity contained numerous 'political' groups whose interrelationships begin to unravel the complexities of NGK–state relations, which I will try to describe and explain accurately.

This research, then, addresses two principal concerns. First, it examines how and why the NGK's relationship to the groups within the white minority government dominating the South African state changed in conjunction with the development of race policy from 1934 to 1994. Second, the case study engages with a broader body of literature on state–civil society relations that promotes discussion concerning the rise of civil society and its connection to democracy. The typology and arguments developed in this book demonstrate that state–civil society relations are more complex and ever-changing than generally realized. Additionally, civil society can and does exist in an authoritarian situation, although its function and purpose will be different from that of civil society within a democratic situation, and it can deter the establishment of democracy in the event that components of civil society identify themselves with exclusive, ethnic interests.

A variety of South African civil society organizations could have been the focus of this project. I concentrate on the *Nederduitse Gereformeerde Kerk* to the exclusion of other civil society institutions in an effort to demonstrate how powerful Afrikaner civil society was when it engaged with the state during the twentieth century, but particularly after 1948. The NGK also provides an excellent example of how components of civil society operate in divergent political contexts like a race-based democracy and a multiracial democracy.

While I incorporate the comparative method to analyze the political history of NGK–state relations, highlighting important milestones – the rise of Fusion government in 1934, the National Party's victory in 1948, the Sharpeville massacre of 1960, the Soweto uprising of 1976, and the first democratic election in 1994 – this book is not intended as a treatise covering all the intricate issues and debates in the eras covered. I am not an historian, and while my work has certainly benefited from the insights gleaned from this discipline, my intent is that the historical exposition sets the context for the particular NGK–state relation that is situated within a broader state–civil society framework rooted in the discipline of political science.

Finally, I start the in-depth examination of NGK–state relations in 1934 because this year marked the beginning of Fusion government, an important political event. Moreover, the 1930s and 1940s were years when the NGK emerged as a *volkskerk* (people's church) which led to interesting dynamics between groups dominating the NGK and the state. However, I begin my analysis of how the NGK developed as an influential Afrikaner civil society institution in 1910 (Chapter 2), the year the South African state was formed.

Concepts central to this work are state, civil society, and democracy. The state is defined as that entity, centered around legal, coercive, and administrative organizations, that contributes to the reproduction of societal relationships through formulating and implementing binding rules within a given territory. In South Africa in the twentieth-century, the state was often identified with the government or party that dominated the political establishment. Civil society refers to formal associations and institutions engaged in activities like economic and social production in an effort to preserve societal identity for the purpose of reaching collective goals and/or holding the state accountable. Civil society can incorporate trade unions, churches, families, cultural organizations, and neighborhoods. Finally, democracy refers to a political system that has established formal civil and political rights, regularly scheduled, competitive elections, representative institutions, and substantive, social benefits.

As far as 'race' terminology is concerned, South African law until the early 1990s distinguished among Africans, 'Coloureds', Asians and whites. These terms will be used when referring to these groups separately. More specifically, 'Africans' will be used to describe indigenous peoples such as the Xhosa, Zulu, or Sotho; 'Coloured' to refer to those with mixed race, San, or Khoi heritage; 'Asian' to refer to those of Indian or Asian descent, and 'whites' to describe English-speaking South Africans, Afrikaners, and others of European descent. 'Black' will be applied to the first three groups comprehensively. Throughout the century studied in this research project, the NGK and the state referred to these groups using terminology that included native, Bantu and European. These terms will be referenced when necessary for the context of the argument.

This research is based primarily on dissertation field work undertaken in the 1992–3 academic year. Interviews were conducted with 40 clergy, parliamentarians, and academics from January to May 1993.

I collected primary material from archives and libraries in South Africa, including the South African Public Library, the Government Archives, and the NGK Archives. The most important sources for my research were NGK synodical reports from 1934 to 1994 dealing with such issues as influx control, the 'poor white' problem, mixed marriages, and education policy. Documents from the *Federale Raad van die Kerken* and the *Federale Sendingraad van die NGK* were also helpful. Primary sources from the NGK were supplemented with information found in church periodicals: *Die Basuin, Die Kerkbode, Koers, Nederduitse Gereformeerde Teologiese Tydskrif,* and *Op Die Horison.* Regarding state or government information, parliamentary debates, parliamentary select committee reports, and parliamentary joint committee reports were used.

Unless otherwise noted, all translations in the text are mine. Because I was tutored in Afrikaans during graduate school, some of the translations will perhaps reflect a more literal reading of the text compared to a native Afrikaans–English translation. I have tried to be sensitive to the fact that many Afrikaans words have multiple English translations, for example, the word '*volk*' can be translated as either 'people' or 'nation'. The Afrikaans text of an English translation will be found in the footnotes.

The organization of this book is as follows: Chapter 1 includes an examination of the different debates within state–civil society literature. The substantive gaps within this literature are exposed through the enumeration of South Africa's state–civil society relations, after which I posit a state–civil society typology that represents the wide range of state–civil society interactions that can help explain the changing relations between groups dominating the NGK and the South African state from 1934 to 1994.

Chapter 2 explains the NGK's role as an increasingly influential Afrikaner civil society institution in South Africa from 1910 to 1933. It begins with a review of South African historiography and continues with an analysis of Afrikaner nationalism, the 'poor white' problem, and segregation policy as they relate to the wider debates about the relationship between economic growth and segregation.

The remainder of the book explains specific NGK–state relations in South Africa through distinct political phases. From 1934 to 1947, state–NGK relations can be described as coexisting conflict, the focus of Chapter 3. While cooperation between the NGK and the state did occur, leaders within each entity pursued slightly different agendas and held differing opinions on the formulation and implementation of race policy. The dominant factions within the NGK supported strict segregation, or apartheid, based on ideological and material factors, while the group dominating the state supported partial segregation, based on the interests and political concerns of pragmatists.

Chapters 4 and 5 focus on the era of NGK–state relations during the majority of the apartheid years. From 1948 to 1961 the NGK and the state exhibited a relationship of mutual engagement in which the leaders within each entity held similar opinions on the majority of policy issues. Church and state officials interacted closely and even held the same goal of Afrikaner supremacy in political and economic spheres, but they formulated independent policies on how to achieve this goal. The reason for discrepancies between NGK–state strategies lies in the factions that existed within Afrikanerdom which developed in relation to the political-economic environment. From 1962 to 1978, during the era of collaboration, the focus of Chapter 5, the NP-dominated state and the NGK collaborated with each other to promote the idea of separate development as a morally just racial solution for South Africa.

In the final phase of apartheid reform and democratization (1979–94), the focus of Chapter 6, NGK–state relations can again be described as mutual engagement. Most of the time, NGK leaders continued to give their unequivocal support to the state; however, situations arose periodically when the groups dominating the state and the NGK arrived at different opinions concerning policy directions and strategies. During these years, the NP-dominated state took the lead in promoting the attainment of white survival and economic prosperity through political reform while the NGK lagged behind, supporting the goals of white, but more specifically Afrikaner, survival and economic prosperity through a slower implementation of reform. Portions of Chapter 1 and Chapter 6 were previously published in the *Journal of Church and State*, for which reproduction permission was obtained.

Chapter 7 provides a summary of the book's findings. It begins with a review of the different eras of NGK–state relations, discusses the NGK's role in a post-apartheid South Africa, and concludes with broader theoretical findings. Regarding the latter point, an examination of state–civil society interactions in South Africa, other African countries, or different regions can expand and refine our understanding of civil society's impact on regime change and political-economic development. These areas of research should be pursued as civil society becomes more and more relevant to our understanding of an inclusive democracy.

Acknowledgements

I owe much to the colleagues, friends, and family members who helped me complete this book project which began as my dissertation. The dissertation fieldwork undertaken in 1992–3 was funded through a MacArthur Foundation grant awarded through the ACDIS Program at the University of Illinois in Urbana-Champaign and a Foreign Language Area Studies fellowship through the Center for African Studies at the University of Illinois. I am particularly grateful to the administrators at Gordon College who graciously awarded me a grant that included release time during the 1997–8 academic year which allowed me to complete the revisions to this book. My colleagues at Gordon College also offered helpful advice and provided a nurturing environment. Finally, I would like to thank the staff and editors at Macmillan Press who offered timely advice in the completion of this project.

I would also like to acknowledge the invaluable help of some of the people instrumental to this project in its dissertation phase. My dissertation committee, consisting of Merle Bowen, Steve Douglas, and William Martin, helped formulate the structure of the book's original arguments through insightful critiques and thorough analysis. Steve Douglas was an exceptional advisor and a steady source of encouragement. Patrick Furlong at Alma College offered hours of his time analyzing the dissertation as an outside reader and helped fine-tune the historical aspects of this study.

There were countless other individuals who helped me complete this project. André du Toit and Charles Villa-Vicencio enhanced my fieldwork experience in South Africa through meetings that restructured my research questions and developed my interview list. Many thanks to T. Dunbar Moodie who served as an 'unofficial reader' offering helpful comments on the entire rough draft of this substantially revised manuscript. Petro Terblanche and Lisa-Jo Rous worked on translations of Afrikaans texts that saved me precious time and Kimberly Bogart, a political studies student at Gordon, helped me construct the index. Finally, I would like to thank the 40 individuals I interviewed for this project who graciously gave of their time and offered insights into the NGK's role in South Africa. I have tried to remain true to the context of your statements, just as I tried to accurately reflect the many sources which provided an understanding of changing NGK–state relations. In the end, none of the scholars or individuals mentioned above are responsible for any of the weaknesses of or views expressed in this work.

I would also like to thank personally the many South Africans, or those living in South Africa, who offered their homes and hearts to my husband and me from 1992 to 1993. They include Amanda Gouws, Robert Mattes, Eddie and Sue Mees, Ishmael Mothlanke, Bernard and Rosalind Pather, and Louis Verhoef. You made our stay in South African an enjoyable one, which we will always remember with fondness.

I would also like to thank my family. Anyone who has written a book of this nature and scope knows that it is impossible to complete without moral support. My parents, Fred and Jennie Kuperus, blessed me with their constant encouragement. It is to my father, who shared my love for the Reformed tradition and South Africa that I dedicate this book. He taught me priceless lessons and showed me that integrity rather than achievement defines a person's character.

And finally I want to acknowledge the support and encouragement of my husband Matt Heun. Thank you for traveling with me to South Africa and for sharing my love of this vibrant country. You have listened patiently to my setbacks, given me encouragement when I needed it, and shared the joy of my advances. Without your constant support, I could never have completed this book.

List of Abbreviations and Acronyms

AB	*Afrikaner Broederbond* (Union of Brothers)
APK	*Afrikaanse Protestantse Kerk* (Afrikaner Protestant Church)
AHI	*Afrikaanse Handelsinstituut* (Afrikaner Institute for Commerce)
ANC	African National Congress
AS	*Algemene Sinode* (General Synod of the NGK)
CODESA	Convention for a Democratic South Africa
COSATU	Congress of South African Trade Unions
CP	Conservative Party
CPSA	Communist Party of South Africa
DEIC	Dutch East India Company
DRC	Dutch Reformed Church (or *Nederduitse Gereformeerde Kerk*)
FAK	*Federasie van Afrikaanse Kultuurverenigings* (Federation of Afrikaner Cultural Organizations)
FRK	*Federale Raad van die Kerken* (Federal Council of the Churches)
FSR	*Federale Sendingraad* (Federal Mission Council)
GNP/PNP	*Gesuiwerde Nasionale Party* (Purified National Party)
HNP	*Herenigde Nasionale Party* (Reunited National Party)
IFP	Inkatha Freedom Party
LP	Labour Party
NAD	Native Affairs Department
NGK	*Nederduitse Gereformeerde Kerk* (or Dutch Reformed Church)
NGKA	*Nederduitse Gereformeerde Kerk in Afrika* (Dutch Reformed Church in Africa)
NGSK	*Nederduitse Gereformeerde Sendingkerk* (Dutch Reformed Mission Church)
NHK	*Nederduitsch Hervormde Kerk*

NP	(Afrikaner) National Party
OB	*Ossewa Brandwag* (Ox-Wagon Guard)
PAC	Pan-Africanist Congress
PFP	Progressive Federal Party
RCA	Reformed Church in Africa
RDB	*Reddingsdaadbond* (Rescue Action Society)
SA	South Africa
SAAU	South African Agricultural Union
SABRA	South African Bureau of Racial Affairs
SACC	South African Council of Churches
SACP	South African Communist Party
SADCC	South African Development Coordination Conference
SADF	South African Defense Force
SAIRR	South African Institute of Race Relations
SANAC	South African Native Affairs Commission
Sanlam	South African National Life Assurance Company
Santam	South African National Trust and Assurance Company
SAP	South African Party
UDF	United Democratic Front
UP	United Party
WCC	World Council of Churches

1 State–Civil Society Relations within South Africa

Beginning in 1989, South Africa experienced an unprecedented political transition from authoritarianism to liberal democracy. This process culminated in the elections of April 1994. The consolidation of democracy in South Africa is far from certain, but it is a notable success in that the majority of South Africans who were denied their basic civil rights under the apartheid state have been embraced by the new regime.

The road to South Africa's present political condition has been long and arduous. It has been the history of a white minority ruling over the lives of a black majority. The white minority government's construction and implementation of race policy explains much of South Africa's past. Although the National Party, which dominated the South African state, was regarded as the main protagonist of apartheid, countless other societal organizations were engaged in its formulation and legitimation. My research addresses one particularly influential societal institution, the *Nederduitse Gereformeerde Kerk* (NGK).[1] I will examine how the NGK's relationship to factions dominating the South African state changed in conjunction with the development of race policy from 1934 to 1994.

This chapter introduces concepts and debates central to this book. It begins with a discussion of church–state literature concerning the NGK. While the historical, comparative examination of NGK–state relations remains the empirical focus of this work, the case study is placed within a wider context of state–civil society relations, and the sections that follow include the elaboration of recent debates concerning state and civil society, state–civil society relations within South Africa's divided society, and the enumeration of a state–civil society typology.

CHURCH–STATE LITERATURE CONCERNING THE NGK

The NGK merits special attention as a civil society institution that was intimately involved with the development of apartheid. Dubbed 'the

1

National Party in prayer', the NGK has been linked to the rise and fall of race policy in South Africa. It is also the largest and most influential of the three Afrikaans-reformed churches in South Africa with 1.3 million members and about 60 per cent of the Afrikaner population.[2]

The NGK played an important legitimizing role concerning the South African state throughout the apartheid years. An elaboration of the NGK's relationship with white minority governments dominating the South African state will be addressed in much greater detail in the chapters that follow, but a brief summary of the NGK's history and involvement with race policy provides useful information concerning how the case study of the NGK connects with this research project's theoretical foundations.

The NGK is South Africa's oldest Christian church. Its involvement with the spiritual and material needs of the white settlers began shortly after 1652 when Jan van Riebeeck, representing the Dutch East India Company, landed with about 200 people at the Cape to establish a provisioning station for ships sailing to the East.[3] Reformed ministers cared for these Dutch settlers in the mid-1600s, and the first NGK congregation was established in 1665. In the 1700s, the NGK's membership grew mainly, if not exclusively, among the white population in the Cape, and, despite some serious schisms which arose after the Great Trek of 1836, the Reformed church had spread out to the Transvaal and Orange Free State republics by the late 1800s. This book does not contain a detailed analysis of the relationships between the NGK and the Afrikaans people or between the NGK and governmental structures prior to the 1900s, however important they may be,[4] yet the consideration of a prominent debate concerning the NGK's early involvement with race policy illuminates recent analyses of the NGK.

Scholars concentrating on the history of the NGK disagree over the origin of race ideology in the church and the prominence of religion in shaping race policy. Jonathan Gerstner and J. Alton Templin, for example, promote a version of the 'primitive Calvinist' paradigm which stresses the ideological and socio-political factors behind the NGK's development of a coherent race policy.[5] This perspective suggests that the first colonial settlers in the Cape brought with them the basic tenets of seventeenth-century Calvinism. Calvinism survived and developed among uneducated *trekboers* in the frontier society for about one hundred years, and it was this 'primitive Calvinism' that re-emerged in the 1800s during the Great Trek and the founding of the Republics in reaction to formative events.[6] Afrikaners relied on

Calvinist notions including divine election, predestination, and the 'chosen people' to challenge British colonialism and African encroachment in the late 1800s. Vestiges of 'primitive Calvinism' and racial ideology were at the root of the exclusive thought which permeated South Africa after the Afrikaners came to power in 1948.

André du Toit, Irving Hexham, and others challenge this paradigm and argue that the Calvinist idea of a 'chosen people' was not part of eighteenth-century Afrikaner consciousness.[7] Early accounts of white settlement (1700–1850s) do not reveal the existence of a 'mission ideology'. Although the use of providential language and evidence of racial or ethnic superiority emerged among some white settlements in the 1700s, this is not proof of a specifically Calvinistic tradition, since other Christian traditions resorted to providential language and racial preferences in these years as well. Additionally, many of the racial attitudes displayed by frontiersmen were evidence of the *lack* of traditional religious beliefs. Du Toit disputes the idea that racial segregation in South Africa can be attributed to the influence of the NGK's Calvinist theology and argues that the economic and social practices of the settler years were a more powerful influence on the development of racial prejudice than the NGK's theology.

Du Toit argues that it is incorrect to posit religion as *the* decisive factor shaping race prejudice, no matter how important religion was in shaping the norms, values, and institutions of later Afrikaner society. Evidence for this belief is found in the church's treatment of 'non-whites' in the early years.[8] According to the official stance of the NGK, baptized and Christianized slaves were entitled to their freedom and certain rights. This practice suggests that it was culture, not race, that divided the Cape Colony inhabitants. Of course, this does not negate the fact that the NGK rarely evangelized, baptized or embraced blacks due to the pressures placed on clergymen from slave-owners in their congregation who wanted to maintain their ownership of slaves, but the official practice of the NGK suggested that early settlers regarded blacks as culturally, not racially, inferior. The division of society ran along culture and caste lines more than race, with whites being 'on top' because of their education, religion, and civilization. Racial differences emerged on account of personal segregation which was practiced widely among the social classes, but it was only later, in the late 1800s, when Afrikaner leaders in institutions like the NGK and the Afrikaner Broederbond formulated an ideologically driven form of Calvinism to justify racial differences.

Hexham's work affirms Du Toit's when it suggests that the fusion between Calvinism and Afrikaner nationalism developed in the late 1800s/early 1900s, long after the era suggested by advocates of the 'primitive Calvinism' thesis. Additionally, the NGK's contribution to the development of the 'theology of apartheid' was not as crucial as the small, but theologically powerful, *Gereformeerde Kerk* (GK) because of the evangelical and pietistic influences within the NGK.[9] Other scholars who support André du Toit's and Irving Hexham's analysis regarding the origin and development of race policy in the NGK point to the structural factors peculiar to the Afrikaner people, not an innate sense of Afrikaner ethnicity or Calvinist mission, which undergirded the NGK's involvement in the development of a coherent race policy. For example, Johann Kinghorn, A.J. Botha, and Susan Rennie Ritner point to socio-political factors including British imperialism, the 'poor white' problem, and the 'black threat' faced by Afrikaners in the late 1800s and early 1900s which explain the NGK's 'ideological-politicization' in the 1900s.[10]

Although scholars disagree on the presence of primitive Calvinism among the members of the early NGK and on religion's influence in shaping race policy, they do coalesce on one point. Racial prejudice affirmed by biblical and theological interpretations became more commonplace in the late nineteenth century when Afrikaner nationalism emerged. Afrikaners developed a neo-Calvinist, ideological world view as Afrikaner nationalism developed in the late 1800s and early 1900s through the influence of individuals like S.J. du Toit, the leader of the first generation of Afrikaner nationalists in the 1870s, Paul Kruger, president of the South African Republic from 1881 to 1900, and Abraham Kuyper (1837–1920), a Dutch philosopher, prime minister, and theologian.[11]

The NGK, which helped develop and rationalize this neo-Calvinist, nationalist world-view in the 1930s and 1940s, used it to legitimize earlier decisions on pre-existing race policy within its church structures as well as later apartheid policy. For example, during the mid- to late 1800s, many white members complained to their pastors of the 'uncivilizing manners' of black converts. Differences in language, culture, and tradition caused whites to become intolerant of black worshipers. Some members supported separate church structures for different race groups; others called for separate communion services. In 1857, white members of the Stockenstrom district in the eastern Cape petitioned the church council for separate communion services. The complaint was taken to the synodical level, where NGK leaders succumbed to the desires of these members. The decision read as follows:

> The Synod considers it desirable and according to the Holy Scripture that our heathen members be accepted and initiated into our congregations wherever it is possible, but where this measure, as a result of the weakness of some, would stand in the way of promoting the work of Christ among the heathen people, then congregations set up among the heathen, or still to be set up, should enjoy their Christian privileges in a separate building or institution.[12]

Although separate churches for different race groups were not expected in this decision (it only established separate communion services), in 1881 the *Nederduitse Gereformeerde Sendingkerk* (NGSK) was formed for the 'Coloured' population. NG churches for Africans and Asians were formed after the NGSK's formation. NGK leaders did not accept the 1857 and 1881 resolutions as correct in principle. These decisions occurred, they thought, because of the practical concession to the 'weakness' of white members. However, these decisions to separate communion services and churches by race played a prominent role in later developments when influential NGK theologians justified these events theologically and biblically. In fact, while nineteenth-century NGK leaders appeared to reluctantly embrace church separation, NGK leaders and theologians who followed them argued that their forefathers had anticipated the tradition of separation which South Africa needed for the survival of whites.[13]

Indeed, by the 1930s and 1940s, NGK theologians had developed a 'theology of apartheid' which used biblical texts (Genesis 11:1–9; Acts 2:1–12; Revelation 7:9) and theologically-based ideas, for example, the themes of calling, election, and God-willed diversity, to legitimize race policy. Beginning in the 1930s then, the NGK, undergirded by its 'theology of apartheid', promoted political and religious agendas that coincided with the perceived needs of the Afrikaner people, and throughout these years, the NGK found its interpretation of Afrikaner needs generally accepted by the race-based state. The NGK became one of the dominant Afrikaner civil society institutions, along with the Afrikaner press, the Afrikaner Broederbond, and various cultural organizations, which 'represented' the concerns of the Afrikaners, despite the divisions within Afrikanerdom.

Revisionist scholars surveying the NGK's involvement in the development of race policy and the promotion of Afrikaner interests would disagree with the analyses made by many of the NGK scholars mentioned above because they overlook the centrality of materialist concerns to the Afrikaner people. Too many scholars assume that the racist, backward views of a socio-economically threatened Afrikaner people triumphed momentarily over the rationalism of the free market and capitalism. A more accurate perspective on the development of race policy, according to revisionists, has to take into account the material contributions of capitalist development or the growth of class orders. Although he does not focus on the NGK, Dan O'Meara presents the classic neo-Marxist treatise on the development of Afrikaner nationalism and race policy. For O'Meara, Afrikaner nationalists justified race policy because of economic, rather than ideological, factors. O'Meara's work will be covered in much greater detail in the chapters to follow, but he argues that the material contradictions, conditions, and struggles of capitalism best explain the behavior of Afrikaner nationalist institutions; ethnic or socio-political factors were subsumed under the class struggle.[14]

In my understanding of state–NGK interactions in the 1900s, I will examine how and why the NGK's relationship to the South African state changed vis-à-vis the development of race policy throughout different political eras including race-based limited democracy (1934–47), Afrikaner-dominated limited democracy (1948–78), and apartheid reform and democratization (1979–94). I have chosen to begin the detailed exploration of NGK–state relations in 1934 rather than 1910 because by the 1930s NGK leaders had become distinctly aware of the social, material, and religious needs of Afrikaners and instrumental in promoting those needs collectively to the government and political parties.

In explaining the NGK's development of a coherent race policy, I have tried to adopt a perspective that incorporates factors of race, class, and ethnicity because an awareness of all these factors offers the richest analysis and gives proper credit to the variety of forces contributing to the important nuances of NGK–state relations.[15] I have also tried to delineate the various theological, ideological, and political perspectives within the NGK and the state. While easily portrayed as monolithic institutions, the South African state and the NGK contained different and important groups whose interrelationships begin to unravel the complexities of NGK–state relations.[16]

While the NGK's relationship with the state through key periods of transition is the empirical focus of this book, the dynamic interaction of state and Afrikaner civil society in the creation of South Africa's race policy applies to broader theoretical questions concerning state–civil society relations. For example, what is the state and civil society? Is civil society necessary to the proper functioning of a democracy? Finally, what is the relationship between state and civil society in an authoritarian context and how different will this relationship be in a democratic context? The examination of these questions will be the theoretical focus of this book.

CIVIL SOCIETY AND DEMOCRACY DEBATES

Civil society has become an important factor in understanding regime change related to 'democracy's third wave'.[17] Many scholars claim that civil society strengthens already existing democracies and/or demands democratic change from authoritarian regimes, thus helping to build a strong society and an accountable state.[18]

While 'civil society is suddenly all the rage in social science and comparative politics circles',[19] the philosophical and historical context of this term is rich, rooted mainly in European developments. John Keane provides a thorough review of the meaning of civil society in European philosophy, and many scholars today adopt definitions of civil society based in these philosophical contexts.[20] Liberal or mainstream scholars provide the dominant insights concerning the proper definition, function, origin or historical status, and the Western specificity of civil society.[21]

The liberal approach generally argues that civil society is a necessary, but not sufficient condition, to the establishment of democracy. Democracy is defined as 'a system of institutionalised competition for power (with broadly inclusive political participation and effective guarantees for civil and political rights)'.[22] Civil society is noted as a sphere of activity or conglomeration of associations that can resist an authoritarian regime, thus creating a conducive environment for political liberalization and abetting a democratic transition; or civil society is viewed as a particular mix of associational life that helps strengthen or consolidate democracy by fostering civility or holding an overcentralized state accountable. To be effective, civil society must be liberated from an overcentralized state –- it must be relatively autonomous and independent from the state. On the other hand, civil society cannot be 'a substitute for state power, as an alternative to effective state democracy, or as a new form of non-state direct democracy'.[23]

Scholars Larry Diamond, Guillermo O'Donnell, and Donald Rothchild grapple with the relational dynamics between state, civil society, and democracy.[24] Dealing with liberal democratic transitions and consolidation, Larry Diamond defines civil society as 'the realm of organized social life that is voluntary, self-generating, (largely) self-supporting, autonomous from the state, and bound by a legal order or set of shared rules'.[25] Democratic transitions are based mainly on the strategic choices made by elite actors and the negotiating that follows, but civil society is credited with providing some of the stimulus for democratization. The liberal approach sees the primary function of civil society as restraining the power of the state in the process of consolidation. It is also engaged in fostering tolerance, generating a democratic political culture, enhancing the freedom of association, and providing an outlet for marginalized groups. This perspective cautions against anti-statist, romantic perspectives of civil society rooted in the Lockean tradition where the state is viewed as a suspicious institution that must be countered by a democratic civil society. Some scholars have stated that relations between state and civil society can go beyond conflict to include cooperation or a mix of the two;[26] however, conceptual clarity on this continuum of relationships has been lacking.[27] Moreover, while state–civil society literature has made great strides in explaining the role of civil society in democratic societies, considerable debate remains concerning the attributes of civil society in an authoritarian context. How does the nature and purpose of civil society differ in an authoritarian context relative to a democratic context? Must civil society always support universal norms like tolerance and civility? For example, does civil society include all associational life and interest groups that take part in rule-setting activities, even those as 'undemocratic' as the Klu Klux Klan or the Afrikaner Broederbond (Afrikaner Brotherhood)? Or, can civil society actually discourage the establishment of democracy?

Michael Bratton, in a case study of Zimbabwean farm unions, demonstrated that 'associational life does not always pluralize the political environment and generate a set of alternative values and practices which can be a force for the democratization of African politics'.[28] Bratton concentrated his study on the Zimbabwean government's effort in the 1990s to create one agricultural union out of the three existing unions representing large-scale commercial farmers, black smallholders, and peasants on land resettlement areas. Over time an agricultural union developed among the later two organizations, but the union leaders who agreed to the merger did so in an effort to bolster their interests through the possibility of well-paid positions and access to material spoils. The ties of neo-patrimonialism superseded broader political interests; the result being reduced participation for smallholder farmers in Zimbabwe. Bratton's conclusion showed that, 'the institutions of civil society in Africa do not always provide protection against autocracy'.[29]

Africanist scholars have also questioned whether civil society can actually contribute to the consolidation, not the mere emergence of, democracy in Africa. Although the second wave of democratization in Africa arose in part due to the vibrancy of civil society, some analysts are pessimistic about the ability of African civil society to consolidate and sustain democracy. In the words of E. Gyimah-Boadi, 'Civil society remains too weak to be democracy's mainstay.'[30] Peter Lewis makes a similar argument when stating that Africa lacks the historical conditions that would foster a vibrant civil society, namely a legitimate state, political inclusion, and political engagement.[31] Further investigation into the political context and the kind of institutionalization that coexists with the varieties of associational life is needed to clarify how civil society can help give rise to a strong state and democracy as well as the consolidation of a democratic regime.

In sum, scholars who analyze civil society generally agree that civil society can play a key, but not leading, role in fostering democratization and consolidating democracy, and they agree that civil society arises when a variety of autonomous 'mediating' institutions exist, distinguishable from but interacting with the state, that mobilize, aggregate, and define opinions vis-à-vis public policy.[32] However, considerable ambiguity exists concerning conceptual clarification on state–civil society relationships. Moreover, civil society literature more than adequately explains the nature, role, and purpose of civil society in a society committed to genuine pluralism, one that is basically constructed along liberal democratic lines, but it has not explained *extensively* the role, nature, and purpose of civil society in an authoritarian or weak democratic context. An examination of state–civil society relationships in South Africa enlarges these ongoing civil society debates.

STATE–CIVIL SOCIETY RELATIONS IN SOUTH AFRICA's DIVIDED SOCIETY

Civil society has become a catch-word among South African politicians. Leaders like Nelson Mandela and Thabo Mbeki suggest that civil society can help usher in development and democracy for South Africa, and political reports consistently reference the government's appreciation of a vibrant civil society that can build a stronger society. Additionally, conferences are devoted to the role and status of civil society in a post-apartheid South Africa.[33]

The status of civil society in South Africa today cannot be understood apart from the nature and purpose of civil society in South Africa before and during the apartheid years which is related to the nature and purpose of the South African race-based state. The state is defined, according to Joel Migdal, as the entity 'composed of numerous agencies led and coordinated by the state's leadership (executive authority) that has the ability or authority to make and implement the binding rules for all the people as well as the parameters of rule making for other social organizations in a given territory, using force if necessary to have its way'.[34] The South African state emerged in 1910.[35] The South African state went through a variety of transformations in the 1900s, including the attainment of full sovereignty in 1933, republican status in 1961, and the establishment of a second republic in 1984, and it contained numerous governments and one substantial regime change,[36] but through these alterations, what undergirded the state was a racially exclusive form of rule. The nature of South Africa's state, to be explored below, and its 'white settler' status often defined the country's unique state–civil society relations.

'White settler' rule was a form of colonialism that entailed European settlers gaining an independent control of the state (e.g. Zimbabwe). The white settler state in South Africa was synonymous with racially oppressive laws, although exceptions did exist. Until 1936 male Africans and Coloureds in the Cape could vote if they met a particular property requirement, and until 1960 Cape African representation occurred through four white representatives,[37] but generally, white political parties and citizens believed in severely limiting, if not removing, civil and political rights from the majority of blacks who suffered under the implementation of segregation and apartheid. White settler states also used influx control policies and land ownership laws to exploit black labor and secure capitalist development.[38]

Besides constitutionally entrenched racism and economic exploitation, white settler colonialism was premised on the idea that European settlers needed to be coddled and protected. The state assumed intervention on their behalf. This was evident in the state's protection of industry, in its provision of services for farmers, and in its maintenance of a comfortable lifestyle for whites. Colin Stoneman and Lionel Cliffe suggest that, 'The settler colonial state was a "corporatist" state, providing a structured place for a set of interests of the whites.'[39] This is not to say that the settler state was homogeneous in its class and economic interests. Indeed, power plays resulted among the various factions of capital, for example, national versus domestic, industry versus agriculture, but the settler state implemented policies that appeased white interests within a capitalist mode of production.

South Africa's 'white settler' state contained its own unique features. For example, South Africa's history reveals a highly influential, ethnic political party, the National Party, in power from 1948 through 1994 which forwarded an exclusive, nationalistic agenda.[40] Throughout the years of apartheid, it was difficult to distinguish the party, regime, and state from one another as they often commingled to form a single hegemonic unit of control favoring whites, but more particularly Afrikaners. This work acknowledges that outcome, but it also points to the reality of the state not being captive to the interests of a single class. The South African state *was* a hegemonic unit of control, but it *was not* a monolithic entity. It contained a variety of institutions and a variety of factions divided by opposing interests. Finally, the South African state contained complex European and indigenous heritages.[41] A bitter rivalry between English-speaking South Africans and Afrikaners persisted into the early twentieth century which coincided with the variety of conflicts that arose among and between indigenous groups and South African whites throughout the 1900s.

When one accounts for the majority who were excluded from the political and social process, the nature and/or type of the South African state would have to be identified as authoritarian; however, it did not resemble a military dictatorship, or a one-party state. Instead, it was an oligarchical, racist 'democracy' – a democracy for minority whites, beginning especially in 1930 when white women received the right to vote. The South African state adequately met the needs of its white citizenry, and the white electorate overwhelmingly viewed the state as legitimate and voluntarily supported it. However, the vast majority of South Africans were excluded from participating in South African society. Their rights were denied or reduced through the extensive racial, ethnic, and class stratification that the segregationist and apartheid state propagated.

Because the South African state catered to white South African needs in a highly partisan fashion, particularly after 1948, it lacked a relative measure of autonomy. State autonomy refers to 'the state's ability to formulate interests of its own, independent of or against the will of divergent societal interests'.[42] The South African state was unable to act on its own preferences or formulate interests of its own due to its widespread commitments to the interests of dominant white societal-based groups. Even though its autonomy was severely limited, the South African state, during the segregation and apartheid years, was relatively strong. It had the capacity to achieve domestic, societal hegemony through enforcing a set of rules and standards on the majority of people living within its borders.[43] The South African state's strength can be measured by the extensive application and enforcement of apartheid laws as well as the high levels of compliance and legitimacy from the white population. State strength diminished considerably in the 1970s and 1980s due to domestic resistance, external pressure, and schisms within white minority rule, but the state was unparalleled in its legal control of society until that time. Taking into consideration the unique nature of South Africa's authoritarian state and its 'white settler' status, how did the state in general 'relate to' South African civil society?

As a result of white settler colonialism and South Africa's extremely divided societal arrangement, civil society arrangements were markedly limited.[44] The term civil society in this book will refer to the formal associations, societal spheres, and institutions engaged in activities like economic and social production, civic education, family maintenance, or religious training in an effort to preserve societal identity, reach collective goals, demand government responsiveness, and/or hold the state accountable.[45] Civil society can incorporate trade unions, churches, cooperatives, families, cultural organizations, and neighborhoods. The uniqueness of South Africa's race-based state and divided society led to the situation of a relatively healthy, vibrant white civil society within a broader uncivil society.

A rich variety of civic institutions existed for white South Africans that included neighborhood associations, cultural groups, churches, trade unions, and women's groups. Specific examples of civil society institutions that were primarily available to and dominated by whites included the *Afrikaanse Handelsinstituut* (AHI) or the Afrikaans Commercial Institute, *Christelike Kultuuraksie* (CKA) or Christian Cultural Action, the NGK, the Urban Foundation, and the South African Chamber of Business. These civil society institutions interacted with the state, but did not try to control it, and they promoted virtues like tolerance and civility among whites. These arrangements met the 'litmus test' for voluntary civil society institutions, that is, they generally involved 'citizens acting collectively in a public sphere to express their interests and ideas, achieve mutual goals, make demands on the state, and hold state officials accountable'.[46]

Despite the vibrancy of civil society among white South Africans, in truth, South African associational life, even among whites prior to the first non-racial, democratic election, rarely developed into healthy, autonomous, pluralistic civil society institutions. This is because South African white civil society institutions often sought to 'monopolise a functional or political space in society, crowding out all competitors while claiming that it represents the only legitimate path'.[47] Many white civil society institutions thwarted the creation of a democratic political culture that included all South Africans; they represented narrow ethnic interests that excluded others on the basis of racial or ethnic distinctions; and they legitimated a racially exclusive authoritarian state. This meant that certain civil society institutions, like the NGK from 1934 to 1994, held the state accountable to white and Afrikaner ethnic interests, but they did not hold the state accountable to widespread, inclusive democratic norms. Certain white civil society institutions in South Africa were able to maintain a measure of autonomy from the state and promote wider reform efforts, for example, the Black Sash and the Institute for a Democratic Alternative for South Africa (IDASA), but civil society institutions like the NGK were unable to promote general reform because of their connections with and commitments to ethnic, parochial interests.

Civil society institutions that acknowledged the interests of black South Africans were either limited, excluded from participation in society, or banned and forced underground. For example, the activities of the Christian Institute were seriously constrained in the 1970s until the organization was banned in 1977. The South African Council of Churches, an organization that was never banned, was limited by threats that included the detention or house arrest of its leaders. Debates among South African scholars today focus on the origin and health of civil society among black South Africans in the apartheid years. Some believe that South Africa's long liberation struggle helped form vibrant and diverse associational organizations by the 1980s. The state disenfranchised the majority of citizens and banned national movements, but civil society was nourished within the struggle. Steven Friedman points out that scholars like Mark Swilling believe that 'during the 1980s, resistance activity was led by social movements, professional groups, churches and unions operating within the country, many of whom coalesced in the United Democratic Front.'[48] Work by

Swilling and Fitzgerald suggests that even though these 'civil society institutions' were not created in ideal situations, they were voluntary organizations that existed to temper and replace state power in an effort to establish full-scale democracy.[49]

But many scholars argue that the apartheid era of South Africa hardly modeled a vibrant civil society. Khehla Shubane states that a healthy, democratic civil society did not exist in South Africa among the black population during the apartheid years. 'Evidence' of civil society constituted popular movements involved with the liberation struggle that wanted to replace the state and co-opt 'civil society' once apartheid passed away.[50] Shubane argues South Africa's oligarchical, racist government disenfranchised millions of South Africans. The majority, then, were excluded from forming civil society and instead joined the liberation movement which arose out of force. According to Shubane, liberation movements lacked the plurality and autonomy that civil society assumes. The tension between these two positions is significant, and although an independent, strong civil society did not exist until the 1990s among black South Africans because of the restrictions placed on it by the state, I would argue that activity among *weak* civic bodies *did exist* and was vibrant in anti-apartheid South Africa throughout the 1900s. These civic bodies, including churches, familial associations, and student organizations, formed the basis of South Africa's diverse, vibrant civil society today.

To repeat, during most of the twentieth century, many of the most active, above-ground civil society institutions resisted the development of widespread democracy because they identified with the narrow, ethnic interests of white South Africans. In this book, I will concentrate on how the NGK related to the South African state, through focusing mainly on governmental politics, in conjunction with the development of race policy from 1934 to 1994. I will be looking at *one* component of white, Afrikaner civil society. I will not be examining how white minority governments within the state related to or discouraged black civil society or other types of white or mixed civil society institutions, however important such analyses may be. Instead, I have chosen to concentrate on a narrow slice of Afrikaner civil society because such Afrikaner political and civil society institutions have witnessed tremendous political change – from racial oligarchy to multiracial democracy. The NGK provides an excellent case study of how components of civil society within a partisan state responded to the establishment of democracy. This can enlarge our understanding of collaborative and engaged civil society institutions within state–civil society literature.

I recognize that the NGK was much more than an institution of 'politicized' civil society. It served mainly as a religious (civil society) institution meeting the spiritual needs of its members. However, the NGK's spiritual and political roles overlapped considerably beginning in the 1930s (*volkskerk*). This work concentrates on the NGK's active promotion of Afrikaner interests to political, economic, and social spheres for the purpose of reaching collective needs and reproducing societal relations that benefited the Afrikaner people. As mentioned above, this focus on the NGK's more 'politicized' civic activities shows that it was the NP-dominated state, rather than visible civil society institutions like the NGK, that led the effort toward negotiating change in the 1980s and 1990s.

Some, of course, would argue that the NGK's minimal role in encouraging democracy's development in South Africa is not surprising considering the ethnic interests it represented and protected during the apartheid years. However, important nuances of NGK–state behavior show that both the NGK and the state contained a variety of factions that displayed considerable independence concerning race policy formation and political reform such that the NGK could have led the way in promoting political reform throughout the last few decades of the apartheid state.

Indeed, South Africa's unique state–NGK relations must be examined with respect to the reality of divergent policy formations and the diversity of white interest groups. As mentioned above, this work does not assume that the state was captive of the interests of a single group. The same assumption holds for the NGK. Both the NGK and the state were comprised of a variety of factions divided by opposing interests. It was the politicking among the divergent factions over material, social and political issues within the South African state and the NGK that explain the nuanced state–NGK relations from 1934 to 1994.

Finally, studies of state–civil society relations often contain dichotomous views of state–civil society relations. State and civil society are viewed as conflicting entities engaged in a zero-sum game over scarce resources or cooperating entities engaged in a properly balanced liberal-democratic framework. A dichotomous perspective of state–civil society relations does not allow for the continuum of relations that can exist between state and civil society institutions. In the section that follows, I posit a typology of state–civil society relations that can enlarge our understanding of state–civil society relations in both authoritarian and democratic contexts.

STATE–CIVIL SOCIETY TYPOLOGY

The complexity of state–NGK relations can be displayed in a typology that incorporates a continuum of state–civil society relations. According to the typology (Figure 1.1) state–civil society relations can be described in terms of cooperation, conflict, or some mix of the two. Six dominant state–civil society interactions result which include cooptation or collaboration, mutual engagement, balanced pluralism, coexisting conflict, conflictual resistance, and enforced disengagement. These six interactions range from extreme cooperation to extreme conflict.[51]

These six state–civil societal interactions can be measured by the similarity or differences on the positions taken by state (but often governmental) and civil society leaders or factions on policy matters and the official (and unofficial) interaction between state–civil society leaders. The greater the amount of policy collusion and official interaction, the greater the amount of engagement and the possibility of cooptation or collaboration. Likewise, the greater the amount of policy conflict and the lesser the amount of official parlay, the greater amount of disengagement and likelihood of enforced disengagement.

Both factions dominating the state and the NGK held strong opinions on race policy that changed over the eras studied in this research project. When discussing general race policy, I will also refer to particular issues, for example, migrant labor, influx control, the 'poor white' problem, and education policy, as they relate to the historical context of state–NGK relations. The discussion of both general and specific race policies will clarify the points of agreement and disagreement between the factions dominating the NGK and the South African state. The six state–civil society interactions or ideal-types are defined in the following manner:

Cooptation or collaboration involves a situation of extensive state–civil society interaction where policy collusion and official interaction are high. Groups dominating the state and certain sectors of civil society collaborate to pursue nearly identical goals, policies, and political preferences, or state leaders coopt certain sectors of civil society institutions to follow governmental dictates. Because of their similarity in goal attainment and policy preferences, the two entities appear indistinguishable. In situations of collaboration or cooptation, other sectors of the population and civil society are purposefully left out of participation in the political and social sector, leading to significant unrest and disengagement among this excluded societal sector.

Mutual engagement is a situation where policy similarities are commonplace and official interaction moderate to high among groups dominating the state and civil society institutions. Leaders within state and civil society institutions cooperate to pursue similar goals and preferences, but situations arise periodically where state and civil society leaders maintain varying preferences that lead to disagreements. Mutual engagement is a situation where groups dominating state and civil society are more similar in goal attainment and policy preferences than dissimilar, but differences between state and civil society occasionally emerge.

Balanced pluralism is a situation of moderate policy collusion and moderate to high official interaction between groups dominating the state and civil society sectors. State and civil society leaders cooperate in ways that allow both state and civil society institutions to hold preferred or independent goals and policy desires. Balanced pluralism can involve situations where groups dominating the state and civil society sectors concur on policy preferences. In this event, state and civil society leaders often work together to implement the policy preference, and a relatively clear dialogue exists concerning the differentiated spheres of state and civil society institutions.

Coexisting conflict is a situation of moderate policy collusion and low to moderate official interaction between groups dominating the state and civil society institutions. As with balanced pluralism, coexisting conflict allows state and civil society leaders to interact in ways where both entities maintain a degree of independence regarding the formulation of policy preferences. State and civil society leaders may cooperate over goals and policy preferences, but there are situations of considerable conflict as well. At times, leaders within civil society who feel their goals and policy preferences are not being listened to and enacted by the state will develop mistrust for state institutions or leaders, looking for a time when their policy preferences can dominate the state through the rise to power of a particular group, political party, or government within the state.

Conflictual resistance is a situation of policy conflict and moderate official interaction between groups dominating the state and civil society sectors. Leaders within the state and civil society sectors hold divergent views concerning the country's goals and policy preferences. In this environment, societal movements will typically arise that actively promote the overthrow or transformation of the state apparatus. The state will attempt to contain this dissatisfied section through a variety of repressive tactics. Both state and civil society have little respect for the leaders within the opposing entity. The outcome is civil unrest which may or may not lead to a new political era.

Finally, *enforced disengagement* is a situation of state–civil society separation. It involves policy conflict and low official interaction between the groups dominating state and civil society institutions. It arises in two circumstances. First, groups within civil society may desire to disengage from the state. They may feel that a weak state, lacking resources, is powerless to fulfill their needs. Such groups of civil society look for informal outlets within their own community to meet their needs. Second, the state may refuse to deal with certain elements and leaders of civil society. State leaders may feel threatened by certain civil society institutions and they may repress civil society in a way that does not allow it to voice its preferences.

This continuum of state–civil society relations can begin to explain the different civil society organizations' interactions with the South African state over time, including the CCSA/SACC, Christian Institute, Black Sash, COSATU, AHI, FAK, and NGK, although I will only concentrate here on NGK–state relations. The six state–civil society positions demonstrate the possibility of characterizing state–civil society relations, like the SACC and the state, in a variety of contexts. All the state–civil society relationships, for example, can be found in democratic and authoritarian regimes; however, one will find more instances of collaboration and conflictual resistance in authoritarian regimes.

This state–civil society typology will facilitate my exploration of how the NGK's relationship to the state changed over time vis-à-vis the development of race policy. (Regarding the state, I focus mainly on the factions and leaders dominating the agencies and institutions that make up the state.) In the different political periods studied, NGK–state relations can be described as coexisting conflict, mutual engagement, or collaboration. The variables of nationalism, external pressure, and political-economic environment can be used to explain why and how these state–NGK relationships evolved, although I will be concentrating mainly on the political-economic environment and the rise of Afrikaner nationalism. Nationalism refers to movements, organizations, and ideas that contribute to goals of political dominance and national self-determination. External pressure refers to international organizations and policies that condition a nation's response to a crisis. The political-economic environment refers to political and economic events that lead to a stable or unstable environment. A stable environment is one in which the event of a political revolution or dire economic depression is absent or highly unlikely. An unstable economic and political environment would be the converse, but it could also include economic hardship and significant challenges to the political system. Political challenges would include recurring mass protests, underground activity, and widespread illegitimacy of the government.

These variables, it is important to point out, influence state–civil society relations but state–civil society relations also influence them. For example, the NGK's relationship with groups dominating the state influenced the direction and development of Afrikaner nationalism, just as Afrikaner nationalism shaped the NGK's relationship to the state. Additionally, each of the variables is interactive. Afrikaner nationalism was influenced by the political-economic environment and the political-economic environment was shaped by Afrikaner nationalism.

The following chapters are devoted to explaining NGK–state relations vis-à-vis the development of race policy in South Africa from 1934 to 1994 using the state–civil society relations depicted in the typology above. Figure 1.1 shows how NGK–state relations from 1934

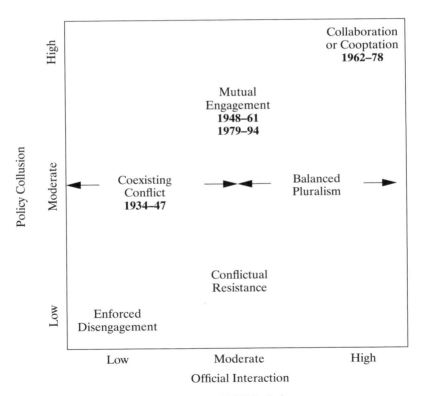

Figure 1.1   State–NGK Relations

to 1994 changed from coexisting conflict to mutual engagement to collaboration to mutual engagement again.

During the establishment of Fusion government and United Party domination (1934–47), the focus of Chapter 3, NGK–state relations can be described as coexisting conflict, characterized by moderate policy collusion and moderate to low official interaction. While cooperation between the two entities did occur, groups dominating the state and the NGK pursued different agendas and held differing opinions on the formulation and implementation of race policy. NGK leaders promoted vertical or totalist segregation while state leaders rejected the NGK's vision of race policy. State leaders, favoring partial segregation, felt that total segregation was an impossibility because whites depended on a black labor force to guarantee profits in manufacturing and mining.

During the early years of apartheid (1948–61), the subject of Chapter 4, the NGK and the state exhibited a relationship of mutual engagement in which the groups dominating each institution held similar opinions on the majority of policy issues. Most of the time, the NGK continued to give its unequivocal support to the state; however, situations arose periodically when the state and the NGK leaders arrived at different opinions concerning strategies related to race policy. More specifically, church and state officials interacted closely and even held the same goal of Afrikaner supremacy in political and economic spheres, but they formulated independent policies on how to achieve this goal. The reason for discrepancies between NGK–state strategies lies in the factions that existed within Afrikanerdom which developed in relation to the political-economic environment.

During the height of apartheid (1962–78), NGK–state relations were one of collaboration, the focus of Chapter 5. The relationship of collaboration between a state and civil society institution rests on a high degree of official interaction and policy collusion. Groups dominating the state and NGK were committed to the maintenance of three goals: (a) white (mainly Afrikaner) supremacy in the political and social arena, (b) economic prosperity through Afrikaner 'capitalism', and (c) the justification and implementation of a racial policy that maintained ethnic purity and overcame the criticisms of 'negative' apartheid.

In the final phase of apartheid reform and democratization (1979–94), the focus of Chapter 6, the NGK and the state displayed a relationship of mutual engagement. Mutual engagement meant that groups dominating each entity held similar opinions on the majority of policy issues. Most of the time, the NGK continued to give its unequivocal support to the state, as it had during the first three decades of apartheid rule; however, situations arose periodically when state and NGK leaders arrived at different opinions concerning policy directions and strategies. During these years, the NP-dominated state took the lead in promoting the attainment of white survival and economic prosperity through political reform, while the NGK lagged behind, supporting the goals of white, but more specifically Afrikaner, survival and economic prosperity through a slower implementation of reform. Sociological upheaval within Afrikanerdom explains the differences between the NGK and the state in this era of mutual engagement, or differences between the NGK and the state's position on reform can be attributed to the class and ideological interests they each represented in the 1980s.

Chapter 2, which follows next, concentrates on the development of the NGK as an influential civil society institution in the early years of the South African state. The topics of South African historiography, Afrikaner nationalism, the 'poor white' problem, and segregation policy are discussed.

2 The NGK's Development within Afrikaner Civil Society (1910–33)

In 1910 the South African state was formed. The establishment of the Union of South Africa represented a new phase of white minority rule because it was accompanied by the implementation of extensive segregation laws. These political changes coincided with significant transitions in the economy. South Africa's political economy entered a period of increased industrialization in the 1910s and 1920s that intensified class and race rivalries.

Throughout these changes, the NGK was developing into a socioreligious institution that identified with the Afrikaners and their cause. As Afrikaner nationalism grew and matured in the dynamic political-economic environment from the early 1900s through the Second World War, Afrikaner civil society institutions, such as the NGK, the *Federasie van Afrikaanse Kultuurverenigings* (FAK), and the South African Bureau of Racial Affairs (SABRA), presented Afrikaner interests to the public sector. This chapter provides an overview of the historical debates and events that led to the NGK's development into a more politically aware civil society institution in the early 1900s. The emergence of the NGK as a civil society institution identifying with the religious, social and political needs of Afrikaners provides a backdrop to the variety of specific state–NGK relations that are the main focus of this book.

SOUTH AFRICAN SCHOOLS OF HISTORICAL THOUGHT

This book concentrates on the events between 1910 and 1994, a span of time that incorporates such milestones as the establishment of the Union of South Africa in 1910, the National Party's victory of 1948, the Sharpeville massacre of 1960, and the first democratic election of 1994. Different schools of thought have arisen in the course of interpreting important events in South Africa, with the liberal and revisionist perspectives dominating.[1]

In its most simplified form, the classic liberal perspective promoted the view that South Africa's problems, politics, and history could be explained largely, if not exclusively, in racial or ethnic terms.[2] Liberals argued that racial fears and segregation policies had a long history in South Africa, developing as early as the 1650s; however, racism matured in the context of the South African frontier. Because of its emphasis on the frontier, Afrikaners (or Boers) were blamed more than the English for the development of racism in South Africa.[3] It was the Afrikaners who developed an exclusive, ethnically-based nationalism that permeated all areas of South African society, purposely oppressing black South Africans. Finally, the liberal view argued that economic growth and segregation were incompatible. Economic growth was viewed as rational, modern, and progressive in contrast to archaic race policies. Liberals argued that the civilizing mission of capitalism would overcome the oppressive aspects of and the inherent economic distortions involved in apartheid.

The classic revisionist perspective argued that class differences were at the core of South African society, not race or ethnicity.[4] Revisionists disagreed with liberals that Afrikaners were the main proponents of racist thought and policy. They argued that segregation reached a new and more radical phase in the late 1800s and early 1900s when capitalism encroached upon South African society. British imperialists worked *with* Afrikaner settlers to impose race policy on South African society in a way that benefited capitalist interests. The oppression of blacks in modern South Africa was better explained by the exploitation of black labor in a racially structured capitalism than by ethnic fears.

Revisionists also believed that segregation and economic growth were compatible. Racial domination was a functional and integral component of South Africa's economic growth. Apartheid was conceived in a rational fashion to deprive black South Africans of any rights or advancements so that capitalists could obtain cheap labor and high profits. The reproduction and regulation of this cheap labor market was a key factor of apartheid and capitalism. Early revisionists studied the segregation policies and the industrial production of the late 1800s and early 1900s for proof that industrial capital shaped the new racial order of segregation and that cheap labor was at the root of capitalist profits. To these early revisionists, racism had to be explained in relation to the changing material base of society. The frontier tradition was not sufficient.

Revisionist scholarship changed as new scholars incorporated different frameworks into their analyses. Belinda Bozzoli, Robert

Davies, Dave Kaplan, and Dan O'Meara among others carried into their work the structural Marxism of Nicos Poulantzas. Much of their work focused on state, capital, and labor relations in the twentieth century among whites. Those who followed structural revisionists included Philip Bonner and Jeffrey Pieres, who studied pre-capitalist South African society and/or explored the contributions of popular groups in the shaping of apartheid policy. The overwhelming pessimism and determinism of earlier revisionist work was replaced by the understanding that Africans were not the inevitable victims of the overwhelming power of capitalism.

The liberal perspective was also modified in the 1980s through the insights of scholars such as Heribert Adam, Merle Lipton, and David Yudelman. Apartheid was viewed as compatible with certain economic sectors, but not others, for example, high-technology manufacturing and commerce. The desire to disaggregate monolithic conceptions of race, gender, class, and ethnicity has been the overwhelming mark of revision within liberal and revisionist scholarship. Although scholars today may base their work in one school, there has been a considerable integration of perspectives. The relationship between capitalism and apartheid was never so clearly marked, and recent works by Saul Dubow, Deborah Posel, and John Lazar demonstrate the interdependencies between the different sectors and groups involved.

The exploration of South African historiography is relevant to any study that examines the formulation of race policy among state or church leaders and in institutions like the National Party or the NGK. Although this book does not intend to rewrite the history of these institutions, I will be sensitive to the various interpretations of historical events from the years between 1910 and 1994 as portrayed within revisionist and liberal scholarship. Moreover, I will attempt to highlight the important nuances within the NGK and the state, although the breadth of eras covered and the theoretical focus emphasized means that class and regional differences within the NP and the NGK will not be examined as thoroughly as they are in works by scholars such as Saul Dubow, John Lazar, Dan O'Meara, or Deborah Posel.

HISTORICAL OVERVIEW (1910–33)

Events in the late nineteenth and early twentieth centuries are integral to an understanding of evolving NGK–state relations in the 1900s.

Beginning in the 1870s, Britain increased its hold over the interior of South Africa by conquering land held by Afrikaners and Africans. Scholars have advanced plausible theories to explain why the British engaged in these activities; these range from European colonial rivalry to humanitarian concerns for Africans in the Boer Republics.[5] However, the emphasis on external factors is not as convincing as the significance of regional factors, namely, the discovery of diamonds. The profits related to the mining of diamonds attracted Britain to the interior.[6]

The mineral revolution helped develop South Africa into a capitalist, industrial society. Monopolistic controls over enterprises, the emergence of a ruling class, and a racially divided labor force all characterized the economy of the late 1800s.[7] In an effort to secure economic profit, Great Britain sought territorial gain, primarily from Africans. By the 1890s, South Africa's geography was defined by the political demarcations of settler colonies and Boer Republics. Tensions between the colonies and the republics led to the Anglo-Boer War.

The war occurred after economic and political differences between English-speaking whites and Boers concerning the discovery of gold could no longer be contained through negotiation.[8] Gold, discovered near Johannesburg in 1886, proved to be more valuable than diamonds because it was the basis of the world's financial system. But the gold deposits in South Africa posed a problem. They lay deep below the surface in alluvial deposits that required sophisticated and expensive extraction methods. Although large amounts of capital were available for the mining of gold (coming from capitalists who had invested in diamond mining), the mines could only be made profitable if there was a cheap labor force, effective political administration, and favorable business policies. Britain felt the Boer Republics were not providing a conducive environment for lucrative profits. For example, it suspected the Transvaal government was discriminating against English-speaking residents (*uitlanders*), giving precedence to Afrikaner farmers over mine owners, and implementing disadvantageous transportation policy. In order to meet Britain's interests, the Transvaal Republic needed to be annexed. It was under these conditions, and after the Jameson Raid débâcle, that the Anglo-Boer War broke out.[9] The war united the settler colonies and the Boer Republics, but at the cost of thousands of lives and considerable hardship, particularly for Afrikaners.

After the war, Britain promised self-government for the Boer Republics in the future; the republics were also given generous financial packages toward the restoration of their economies. Additionally, Britain ceded to Afrikaner demands that the issue of political rights for blacks, namely the franchise, would be addressed only after self-government was introduced.[10] These actions solidified white rule against the political demands of blacks. But the Anglo-Boer War was also followed by the policies of reconstruction and anglicization implemented by High Commissioner Alfred Milner. Despite the indignation many Afrikaners felt toward British rule, economic and political circumstances in the post-war years drove Afrikaans-speaking and English-speaking South Africans together.

Britain realized it needed to compromise with the more numerous Afrikaner population if it was to be successful in dominating South African mining profits. Additionally, political union would mean the alleviation of economic rivalry between regions over customs tariffs and railway policy. The policy of reconciliation between English-speaking whites and Afrikaners gained widespread support when former Boer generals and leading Afrikaner politicians, amongst them Jan Smuts and Louis Botha, adopted its goals. Smuts and Botha believed that the ill-feelings between Dutch and English-speaking South Africans needed to be replaced by reconciliation if the colony was to move forward. Moreover, Smuts and Botha suppressed their calls for republicanism as they were attracted to the possibility of governing the colony.[11] Political elites organized negotiating forums in 1908 and 1909 aimed at the establishment of a political union.

In 1910 the Union of South Africa was formed. Characteristics of the Union government, 'built on a racially exclusive form of the Westminster model of British parliamentary democracy',[12] included a unitary government, a restricted black franchise, British responsibility for the Union's foreign affairs, and disproportionate political power for rural constituencies.[13] White minority rule essentially stifled the possibility of freedom and opportunity for the black majority.

The first Union government was led by Louis Botha of the South African National Party (SANP). The SANP was a merger of four parties, the *Het Volk*, the *Oranje Unie*, the South African Party, and the *Afrikaner Bond*. It represented the interests of white farmers, white workers, and the petit-bourgeoisie, a rather large sector of society, but the SANP's political voice did not go unchallenged. There were two opposition parties in the first election – the Unionist Party, a pro-British party appealing to English-speakers sympathetic to mining and merchant interests, and the Labour Party, a pro-worker party representing English-speaking white workers.[14]

The SANP also faced challenges from within its ranks on two issues – white ethnic policy and South Africa's international status. On the issue of relations among whites, the SANP promoted the policy of conciliation, that is, the unity of English and Afrikaner interests in the belief that South Africa's future lay with British-Afrikaner cooperation. Botha and Jans Smuts, a prominent deputy within Botha's government, pursued an 'integrationist' pattern of political organization that encouraged the creation of a nation where whites had equal rights.[15] On the issue of South Africa's international status, the SANP did not pursue the independent, sovereign status of South Africa. Botha knew that the imperial connection could be beneficial for South Africa if Great Britain allowed it to incorporate Swaziland and Rhodesia. South Africa's Union status meant that it was 'bound by the decisions of the King, acting on the advice of his British ministers of state, on questions of war and peace.'[16]

J.B.M. Hertzog, the Minister of Justice, challenged Botha's goal of achieving the reconciliation of English and Afrikaner interests. Hertzog believed that 'the most stable white South African state would be a poly-ethnic one, in which patriotic loyalty to the common fatherland would be mediated through separate nationalisms ... Thus Hertzog insisted that the separate language and cultural traditions of the two white groups must be maintained.'[17] The Afrikaner's fear of anglicization would be alleviated if the 'two-stream policy' were implemented.

Hertzog was also committed to the autonomous (not necessarily independent) status of South Africa. In 1912, at a gathering in Smithfield, Hertzog announced that South Africa's priorities needed to be recognized by Great Britain, and he criticized the imperial leanings of the English-speaking Unionists. These actions led to a cabinet crisis in which Botha asked for Hertzog's resignation. In 1914 Hertzog created the National Party (NP), which represented Afrikaner nationalist interests. Meanwhile, Botha and Smuts took the majority of SANP members and formed the South African Party (SAP).

The political developments within South African white society impacted on the majority of South Africa's population negatively. Blacks faced two interrelated problems in the early twentieth century. First, industrialization and urbanization forced many blacks to move to the cities where they lived in utter poverty. Second, the interwar years in South Africa represented the height of segregation, an issue that will be described at length below. From 1910 to 1924, the SAP enacted a variety of segregationist legislation, but three Acts stand out for their lasting significance: the Mines and Works Act of 1911, the

Natives Land Act of 1913, and the Natives Act of 1923. These Acts discriminated against blacks in employment opportunities, land purchasing, and residential areas, respectively.

The negative effects of industrialization and segregation caused a rising national consciousness among blacks. Ever since the establishment of the Union of South Africa and the implementation of the oppressive legislation that followed, black leaders realized that one of the most effective ways to combat white supremacy was through countrywide organizations. One of these, the South African Native National Congress (SANNC), was established in January 1912 to challenge the repressive legislation being passed by the government.[18] Reverend John Dube was elected its first President General.

The SANNC fought for the political rights of black South Africans. In its early years, it worked within constitutional structures to achieve its ends. Its aims included the extension of the Cape franchise to the other republics in South Africa, the propagation of black political rights to parliament, and the education of blacks regarding their rights and duties. The SANNC provided a forum in which blacks could protest against racist legislation and actions, but many of its efforts were ignored or suppressed by the government. Organizations representing 'Coloured' (African Political Organization) and Indian (Natal Indian Congress) interests were also present in the early 1900s, but as a whole, nationalist organizations were not effective because of the lack of widespread support, the tactics of moderate protest, and an overpowering state.[19]

In 1914 the First World War broke out, bringing political turmoil to South Africa. The SAP declared that South Africa would side with the Allies. Afrikaner nationalists, on the other hand, opposed this decision. They resented the British annexation of their republics and the devastating effects of the Anglo-Boer War. The National Party called for a policy of neutrality and opposed the SAP's acquiescence to Britain to lead an invasion into South West Africa, the colonial territory of Germany. A contingent of Boer generals resisted the call to back Great Britain and led a small rebellion in 1914. They were crushed easily, but the event stimulated feelings of nationalism among Afrikaners and the generals were viewed as heroic martyrs.

In 1915 the Federal Council of the NGK churches organized a special meeting to discuss the rebellion at which church leaders decided they could not explicitly support the rebels. In fact, the Council affirmed its support for the government in the following words:

The Conference wishes clearly to state that according to God's Word the Government is ordained of God ... The Conference further wishes emphatically to declare its serious conviction that, when one takes the wider considerations into account, genuine peace and lasting unity in the country will not return, and cannot exist if resistance against the government is countered with violence alone.[20]

But the NGK also identified itself with the Afrikaner people when it stated:

That our Church ... has also received from God a more specific calling with regard to the Dutch-speaking Afrikaner people to whose existence she is intimately bound ... It is further to keep alive among the Afrikaner people an awareness of national calling and destiny, wherein lies the spiritual, moral and physical progress of a people.[21]

Furthermore, the NGK left the door open to political involvement:

That our Church will best be able to fulfill both her task regarding God's Kingdom, and regarding our Afrikaner existence as a people, when the Church, and her preachers in their official positions, remain strictly outside of the party political struggle, *unless religious or moral principles are at stake, or the concerns of the Kingdom of God explicitly justify such actions.* (italics mine)[22]

The Federal Council of the NGK recognized what was at stake in an atmosphere of rising Afrikaner unity and ethnicity. The NGK encouraged Afrikaner cohesiveness, and although it did not openly support the Afrikaner rebellion, it did leave its political options open for the future. In sum, the NGK supported the growing sense of Afrikaner identity which was evident after the Afrikaner rebellion.

By the end of the First World War, the SAP's support had weakened even further among the Afrikaner constituency. Afrikaner farmers and workers were disillusioned with the SAP because, they argued, it supported imperial interests. Afrikaner workers also experienced economic competition from blacks, and they turned to the National Party which articulated a more stringent race policy that favored white workers.

Not only did the SAP face Afrikaner nationalist disillusionment, it also confronted rising urban worker unrest in the interwar years. On the Rand, conflict arose between mineworkers and owners, but it was complicated by race divisions. Whites argued their jobs were being given to cheap black laborers. From 1915 to 1922, African workers united at various times to protest against low wages, non-existent union rights, and oppressive pass laws.[23] Any concessions the state made to black workers were viewed as a threat to white laborers. For example, the state's relaxation of the official color bar after the 1920 strike gave Africans access to semi-skilled jobs, which traditionally had been reserved for whites. In response to the concessions made to black workers, white workers launched a prolonged strike in January 1922 known as the Rand Revolt. The government used force to halt the action, in which more than 200 strikers were killed. It also backed the mine owners' demands.

White workers took their revenge against the SAP when they supported Hertzog's National Party and his alliance with the Labour Party in the 1924 election. The alliance won the election, and Hertzog became the Prime Minister of the 'Pact' government. The electoral base of the NP–LP pact was composed of workers, farmers, and intellectuals who were opposed to the domination of mining capital in South Africa. Afrikaner voters assumed Hertzog's economic policy would favor Afrikaner agricultural and manufacturing interests, or national capital, over English mining interests, or imperial capital.

Indeed, the 1924 Pact government appeared to signal a gain for national capital. The new government pursued policies beneficial to farmers, mine workers, and 'poor whites'. Domestic agriculture was protected, color bars were enacted, high protectionism was supported, state corporations were created, and the 1927 Immorality Act and Native Administration Act were passed. These policies helped diversify the economy, support industrialism, and reduce favoritism toward British commodities.[24] However, as Ben Fine and Zavareh Rustomjee argue, state economic intervention in the interwar years did not follow a coherent pattern. Although the power of imperial capital eroded in these years so that national capital could be supported, there was compromise and conflict, or an interdependency, among the capital sectors because the success of national capital depended on the strength of imperial capital.[25]

Mining interests maintained their hold in economic sectors, influencing political power and causing discontent among Afrikaner nationalists. Some Afrikaner nationalists felt that as South Africa was becoming economically advanced, Afrikaner farmers and unskilled workers were growing poorer at the expense of government policy which served British interests. Hertzog's original economic vision was for South Africa to be an industrial nation, not one based solely on primary production, that is, minerals. But even Hertzog's support for local industries and higher tariffs could not eradicate the continued dominance of mining capital in the political and economic arenas.

Nationalist Afrikaners used the Pact government's economic policy as 'evidence' that Hertzog was siding with mining interests over national, Afrikaner interests. Another issue to which the National Party eventually lost the support of nationalist Afrikaners was independence. Hertzog was engaged with and supported the Balfour Declaration of 1926 which granted South Africa independence as a British Dominion. Hertzog's claims of South Africa's independence were not accepted by Afrikaner nationalists who wanted all ties with Great Britain to be severed and republican status granted. In fact, soon after the Balfour Declaration was adopted, the Broederbond became involved in a campaign to end Hertzog's leadership of the NP. Nevertheless, Afrikaner nationalists generally maintained their support for Hertzog rather than for Smuts throughout the 1920s because Hertzog's perspectives on race policy coincided with theirs.

In 1929, the Great Depression caused an economic crisis in South Africa. South Africa's reluctance to abandon the gold standard led to an overvalued currency and overpriced products which caused huge decreases in profits for South African mines and industries. Because of the pressures placed on Hertzog by mine and manufacturing owners, he abandoned the gold standard in 1931 and eased protectionist measures. South Africa's currency was devalued, its economy boomed and the economic crisis was averted.[26] White political alignment between the NP and the SAP occurred soon after. The era of 'Fusion Government', to be analyzed in the following chapter, signalled a unique political dispensation for South Africa.

In sum, when Hertzog came to power in 1924, he pursued a number of policies that appeased his nationalist constituency, for example, enacting strict color bars and race segregation, introducing a new flag, and promoting bilingualism. However, his support from the Afrikaner community diminished over time as he compromised on the republican status of South Africa, supported general capitalist interests instead of Afrikaner-nationalist economic interests only, and agreed to a government of 'national unity' with the SAP. In order to understand the NGK's response to these changes, the issues of Afrikaner nationalism, general segregationist legislation, and the 'poor white' problem will be examined. An analysis of these issues shows the development of the NGK as a leading civil society institution identifying mainly with Afrikaner interests.

AFRIKANER NATIONALISM

The political-economic events of the interwar years cannot be analyzed in isolation from the growing influence of Afrikaner nationalism.[27] The early development of Afrikaner nationalism occurred in the late 1800s through the efforts of intellectuals in the western Cape. For example, in 1875, the *Genootskap van Regte Afrikaners* (Society of True Afrikaners) was founded in Paarl to promote the Afrikaans language and cultural traditions. In 1878, the *Boere Beschermings Vereeniging* (Farmers Protection Society) was established to promote Afrikaner farmer interests, and in 1879, the *Afrikaner Bond* (Afrikaner Association) was formed to give political expression to Afrikaner interests.

These efforts to create an organized, ethnic consciousness occurred as Afrikaners were beginning to overcome the internal class divisions and regional rivalries that had thwarted efforts in previous decades. In the western Cape, for example, wine growers and grain farmers united to promote their interests after they experienced economic difficulty in the 1870s.[28] They called for 'protectionist policies to aid farmers, a national bank to counter the imperial banks, and equal status for the Dutch language as a buffer against English merchant and commercial classes.'[29] These farmers also supported the political efforts of Afrikaner political associations like the *Afrikaner Bond* which helped to combine economic and political interests among Afrikaners in the western Cape. Regional differences between northern-based Afrikaners and Cape Afrikaners also lessened in the 1870s when the British annexed Basutoland (1868), the Diamond Fields (1871), and the South African (Transvaal) Republic (1877).[30] Afrikaners felt Britain had wronged them and they mobilized temporarily around the cause of republicanism with the success of the Transvaal revolt in 1881.

The awakening of Afrikaner nationalist notions in the late 1800s arose as petit-bourgeois Afrikaners realized they needed to stress ethnic cohesion in the light of an increasingly modern, industrialized society. However, the awakening of Afrikaner nationalism in the late 1800s did not lead to its maturity.[31] Afrikaner nationalism failed to sustain its momentum due to the persistent problems of class cleavages and regional rivalry among Afrikaners. In terms of regional divisions, the Cape Afrikaners reluctantly embraced political visions that challenged the status quo. While leaders in the Boer Republics held to their goal of republican independence, leaders in the Cape associations like the *Afrikaner Bond* stressed conciliation between English-speakers and Afrikaners and remained loyal to the vision of common nationhood among the two white groups. Additionally, Cape Afrikaners did little to promote economic links between the Cape and the Republics that would benefit northern Afrikaner interests independent of their own.

Class divisions among Afrikaners also intensified in the late 1800s and early 1900s due to increased urbanization and industrialization. In the Cape, there were self-evident differences between the interests of lower-class farmers and the upper classes, namely, the well-educated petit-bourgeoisie (teachers, clergy, intellectuals) and wealthy farmers. Similarly, the rapid commercialization of farms in the Boer Republics led to a growing gap between low-class Afrikaners (tenants, landless) and landed, commercial farmers.

Beginning in the 1910s, however, the persistent class and regional differences among Afrikaners diminished. The Botha–Hertzog differences and the formation of the National Party in 1914 allowed Afrikaner nationalists the political leverage and support they needed to pursue their interests, and a variety of self-help, nationalist organizations emerged.[32] An aid movement (*Helpmekaar*) was formed in 1915, the newspaper *Die Burger* (The Citizen) was launched in 1916, the Poor White Alliance (*Arme Blanke Verbond*) was created in 1917 to help poor whites find jobs, and Santam and Sanlam were formed in 1918 for Afrikaner insurance and investment purposes.[33]

One of the most significant developments that aided the growth of Afrikaner nationalism was the establishment of the Afrikaner Broederbond (the Afrikaner Brotherhood) or AB, in 1918, originally named 'Jong Suid-Afrika'. The Broederbond began as an above ground organization that propagated the Afrikaans language and united Afrikaners.[34] It developed into a secretive nationalist organization uniting the economic, cultural, religious, and political interests of Afrikaners across classes. The purpose of the AB was the preservation of the Afrikaner culture and the attainment of economic and political power. Its members believed that the Afrikaner nation was special, destined to live and survive in South Africa.[35] They also believed Afrikaner economic interests needed to be given special consideration by a government that had long neglected their interests. The Broederbond developed a national consciousness among Afrikaners, and it effectively organized nationalist organizations to protect and promote the Afrikaner language, culture, and industry. Most of the members of the AB were strategically located, powerful individuals, and included clergymen, politicians, civil servants, teachers, business leaders, and other professional men.[36]

Because the Broederbond was dedicated to the promotion of Afrikaner interests, it infiltrated Afrikaner institutions, whether they were churches, schools, businesses, or political parties. The question about how much control the AB had over Afrikaner institutions is much debated. Some argue that the organization was all-domineering and all-pervasive, controlling South African society.[37] Others argue that the AB was merely a cultural organization protecting Afrikaner interests.[38] Because the AB was secretive, it is difficult to verify the extent of its influence over South Africa. It is true that the AB guided the direction of policy in areas such as education, sports, and race relations. Additionally, the overlapping memberships of leaders in all Afrikaner nationalist organizations eliminated the conflict of interest that would have emerged if the organizations had not been so closely interconnected. However, it is also true that the AB's influence varied over time according to the needs of Afrikaner nationalism and the leadership in nationalist organizations. In sum, the Broederbond is essential to any study focusing on Afrikaner nationalism. Its presence cannot be ignored, and although this research does not focus directly on the organization, I do not doubt its significant influence on the NGK and the political establishment over the years covered by this book.

The growth of Afrikaner nationalism in the years between 1910 and 1933 could not have occurred without the proliferation of prominent institutions like *Helpmekaar* and the Broederbond which brought Afrikaner concerns to the public level, but Afrikaner nationalism also benefited from the activity of long-established institutions like the NGK. The NGK was one of the most respected institutions within Afrikaner society, and its involvement in the propagation of Afrikaner ideals helped spread the goals of nationalism to many people.

Many studies focusing on the historical development of the NGK emphasize the NGK's involvement in Afrikaner nationalist efforts in the 1900s because of the growing threat Afrikaners felt from black encroachment and British anglicization. From the Anglo-Boer War to the 'poor white' problem to the rise of the NP in the late 1940s, the NGK took a leading role in providing justification for the Afrikaners' existence and rebuilding Afrikaner morale and social welfare. The NGK became 'the major bulwark of the Afrikaners in the struggle to preserve their language, culture, religion'.[39] As Afrikaner nationalism grew in strength, preachers became more sensitive to political matters; some even entered the nationalist arena in pursuit of Afrikaner needs (e.g. D.F. Malan). Moreover, T. Dunbar Moodie's work shows how the church helped develop an Afrikaner civil religion in the 1930s, that is, a 'sophisticated theological interpretation of God's acts in Afrikaner history' which denoted the 'religious dimension of the state'.[40] As John de Gruchy states, 'The Afrikaner churches fulfilled a central role not just in this struggle for identity, but also in providing a theological base upon which nationalism could flourish.'[41] The ideological underpinnings of ethnicity and race are key to understanding the NGK's relationship to Afrikaner nationalism and its response to race problems,[42] but along with the NGK's concern with ethnic and racial purity, its activities in the 1900s can also be explained by economic concerns which arose when a large section of the Afrikaner people were being threatened by British-dominated capitalism and unskilled black labor, as will be shown in the analysis of the 'poor white' problem and racial segregation.

The NGK's involvement in Afrikaner nationalist concerns was rising in the early 1900s, but the church's role within Afrikaner civil society was not as clearly defined as it was in the 1930s and 1940s. Afrikaners were beginning to solidify their identification along class and social lines in the years between 1910 and 1930, and significant differences arose among Afrikaners and within the NGK concerning Afrikaner nationalism's goals. Some Afrikaners sought vertical segregation, others horizontal; some sought republican status for South Africa and others sought greater autonomy. Within the NGK, different theological traditions existed which corresponded to the specific positions related to the Afrikaner nationalist cause.

T. Dunbar Moodie points to three distinct groups within the NGK in the early 1900s – the pietist tradition, the *volkskerk* (people's church) Calvinists, and the neo-Kuyperians.[43] The pietist strain within the NGK, associated with the work of Andrew Murray, emphasized revivals, Christian witness, and a more personal relationship with God. It believed that the church stood apart or even above the political apparatus. Instead of concentrating on the socio-economic concerns of the people or emphasizing national identity above other concerns, the church was called to unite people and lead individuals to personal salvation.[44] While the pietist element within the NGK was greatly strengthened by a series of revivals that swept the Cape colony in the 1860s, two groups emerged out of and 'surpassed' the pietist tradition in numbers by the early 1900s, namely, the evangelical and missionary groups. These latter two groups were also preoccupied with the believer's relationship to God, but while the evangelical Reformed group primarily committed itself to the concerns of the Afrikaner people (explained below), the missionary group kept alive the belief that whites had to minister to the spiritual, but not necessarily material, needs of black South Africans.[45]

The neo-Kuyperian faction was influenced by the work and ideas of Abraham Kuyper (1837–1920), an influential Dutch scholar-statesman who articulated a comprehensive vision of Calvinism as a way of life. Kuyper highlighted the importance of God's sovereignty, the belief in a systematic Christian worldview to combat secular modernism, and biblical norms that instruct the 'governing' of unique societal spheres. South Africa's Potchefstroom University was significantly affected by Kuyper's ideas, and key 'representatives of this South African Kuyperianism were Professors H.G. Stoker in philosophy, J.D. du Toit (the poet Totius) in theology, J.A. du Plessis and L.J. du Plessis in political science, J. Chris Coetzee in education and A.J.H. van der Walt in history'.[46] Neo-Kuyperian Calvinism emphasized the respect for plurality and ethnic diversity as God not only willed the separation of societal spheres but the uniqueness of each people and culture too. Neo-Kuyperianism provided theological justifications for apartheid policy, and it incorporated civil-religious themes into its theological worldview.

The intermediate position between neo-Kuyperians and pietists became known as the *volkskerk* (people's church) group, 'with its view of the Church as an institution separate from the state yet at the same time supportive of the nation'.[47] *Volkskerk* predikants like J.R. Albertyn, J.D. Kestell, A.F. Louw, D.F. Malan and William Nicol, were trained in the revivalist strain of Scottish Calvinists, but they responded to the social and material needs of the 'poor whites' within their midst because they believed that a vertical relationship with God included a desire for horizontal, caring social relationships. *Volkskerk* pastors of the evangelical Reformed tradition were persuaded by some of the elements within neo-Kuyperianism and drawn into the Afrikaner nationalist struggle. They perpetuated the ideas within Afrikaner civil religion, and they took up the cause of '*volkspolitiek*' (people's politics) while distancing themselves from party politics. In T. Dunbar Moodie's words, 'Because the N.G. was a People's church, concerns such as Afrikaans-medium education, Afrikaner poverty, and the Afrikaner People's unity (*volkseenheid*) were relevant issues for the N.G. pastor. On the other hand, he could not directly tell his parishioners how to vote …'[48]

The development of the NGK as a prominent white civil society institution representing Afrikaner interests, but also articulating the general concerns of white South Africans, occurred in the interwar years as demonstrated in the church's positions on segregation policy and the 'poor white' problem (to be explored below). Although the NGK's positions on race policy were not yet developed due to the continuing maturation of the Afrikaner nationalist movement, the NGK's identification with the Afrikaner people was becoming more apparent.

THE 'POOR WHITE' PROBLEM AND THE NGK'S RESPONSE

The 'poor white' problem refers to the situation among Afrikaners who suffered extreme poverty in the urban areas of South Africa from the 1900s through the 1930s.[49] The emergence of 'poor whites' coincided with the Rand's industrialization. Many Afrikaners in the late 1800s and early 1900s sold their land, unable to compete with commercial farmers who supplied growing urban areas with the necessary foodstuffs. The land devastation associated with the Anglo-Boer War, droughts, and pestilences also forced many Afrikaners off their land. Still committed to farming, they became tenants (*bywoners*) of wealthier farmers. But as capitalism developed, turning agriculture into a more capital-intensive industry, *bywoners* were evicted and forced to move into the towns in search of work. What made their situation worse was their refusal to engage in unskilled work because this was reserved for 'the natives'. Much of the segregationist legislation enacted in this period was a response to the concerns of poor whites and the fear that intermingling between races would diminish the racial superiority of whites.

The NGK, in its role as a *volkskerk*, a church of the people, was actively involved with the 'poor white' problem. The church was concerned with the urban threats facing poor whites, threats which included liberalism, anglicization, and racial mixing. The emergence of poor whites also meant Afrikaners had become second-class citizens among the white population, coming perilously close to the low-class status of blacks. In its effort to avoid the racial and economic fears facing Afrikaners, the NGK initiated and organized a series of *volkskongresses* (peoples' congresses) that dealt with the 'poor white' problem.[50]

In 1916, the Cape NGK organized a congress to discuss the situation of rural Afrikaners who had migrated to the towns. Many prominent NP and clergy officials attended. Some of the speeches were dedicated to the fear of Afrikaner survival in the face of an economically dominant English-speaking group. D.F. Malan, in his keynote speech, argued that the greatest factors contributing to poverty among Afrikaners were natural disasters, poor education, and rivalry between the two white groups. Anglicization needed to be halted through the efforts of Afrikaner nationalist organizations. If this happened, the 'poor white' problem could be alleviated. But the fear that poverty would erase race and class differences among blacks and whites was also evident among certain leaders of the congress. Professor A. Marais suggested that 'in order to eliminate this unequal competition between black and white, or to limit it to a minimum ... the principle of industrial segregation, insofar as this was possible, should be implemented.'[51] These leaders also stressed that the ultimate fear of the Afrikaners, that is, racial-mixing, would be realized if the 'poor white' problem was not addressed. Participants at this congress believed the 'poor white' problem posed a serious threat to Afrikaners. 'Poor whites' not only represented the reality of diminished ethnic purity; they also represented the reality of a low-class status which was accompanied by economic powerlessness.

Further attention was given to the 'poor white' problem in the 1920s through opinions expressed in NGK periodicals, but the next conference on the issue took place in 1923. The NGK convened another *volkskongress* on the 'poor white' problem in Bloemfontein of this year.[52] Delegates recommended that the government establish a committee to combat the competition that unskilled white workers were facing from black laborers. It was clear to the delegates that the greatest threat to Afrikanerdom was the Afrikaners' competition with black labor; the way to solve this problem was urban and industrial segregation.

Eventually, the government took action on this demand. It allowed a country-wide investigation of the 'poor white' problem in 1929 to 1932 by the Carnegie Commission which offered analysis of and solutions for the 'poor white' problem. Many of its solutions were subsequently adopted by the state. The NGK's rising concern for poor whites showed that it recognized the racial and economic fears facing Afrikaners in the years between 1910 and 1933. As Piet Meiring, former NGK minister, noted, 'especially in the depression years when Afrikaners were poor and were far behind the English in culture and politics ... it was the church which helped them to find their feet again.'[53] The NGK's visible involvement with political issues of national significance gave rise to its 'civic' organizational efforts, in this case, on the part of the Afrikaner. On the issue of segregation, the NGK demonstrated its concern for meeting Afrikaner, but also general white, interests.

SEGREGATION POLICY AND THE NGK'S RESPONSE

Segregation, 'a complex amalgam of political, ideological and administrative strategies designed to maintain and entrench white supremacy at every level',[54] developed into a cogent, systematic ideology in South Africa in response to the changes accompanied by industrialization from 1900 through the 1930s.[55] Before moving on to an elaboration of the segregation Acts implemented in the early 1900s and the different individuals who gave segregation policy its legitimacy, it should be noted that segregation policy and apartheid policy, though interrelated, are distinct. In fact, different interpretations exist concerning the distinction between segregation and apartheid, with liberals arguing that apartheid represents a fundamental break from the past and revisionists asserting that apartheid was merely an extension of segregation.

The relationship between apartheid and segregation is exceedingly complex. It is difficult to argue that apartheid represents a dramatic break with the past because the ideology of apartheid was built on the model and edifice of segregation. Additionally, both segregation and apartheid policy were formulated in response to rising industrialization and growing African proletarianization. These race policies were intended to counteract the haphazard implementation of previous race policy which could not respond to increased race and class demands. Finally, there were clear ideological links between the two forms of race policy, from their emphasis on diversity to their justification of white guardianship.[56] It is incorrect, then, to posit a sharp break between segregation and apartheid policy.

But it is also incorrect to see apartheid as an extension of segregation.[57] Real differences in ideology and content exist. Apartheid policy was based on the dogmatic notion of cultural separation. Much of its ideology rested on romantic nationalism and Kuyperian Calvinism.

Segregation policy of the 1920s and 1930s was not based on Christian-National ideologies; it used Darwinian evolutionary thought or an anthropological rationale which emphasized cultural differences. Saul Dubow, a scholar who analyzes the ideology of apartheid and segregation, points to the difference in the following words: 'Whereas the hallmark of segregation was its ambiguity and ideological flexibility, apartheid ideology was unremitting in its zeal and logic.'[58]

In sum, both segregation and apartheid meant the concentration of power in the hands of a white minority. However, apartheid was different from segregation in its grand notions of vertical separation along race lines. It sought the separation of races in all areas of life, hiding this in the shroud of equality among cultures, while segregationist proponents were still wondering how far cultural segregation needed to go. The unique aspects of apartheid policy will be clarified in the following chapters, while the remainder of this chapter will concentrate on the evolution of segregation policy.

The first vestiges of a systematic segregation policy emerged from the South African Native Affairs Commission, or SANAC (1903–5), a committee appointed by Lord Milner to devise policies affecting the administration and livelihood of Africans. It proposed segregated residential areas, the regulation of African labor through the use of passes, differentiated wage structures, and race stipulations for land ownership. From 1910 to 1924, the SAP enacted a significant amount of segregationist legislation, much of it modeled on the SANAC's recommendations. Three Acts stand out for their lasting influence.

The first piece of legislation was the Mines and Works Act of 1911 which reserved certain skilled jobs for whites only.[59] The second was the Natives Land Act of 1913, a response to the demands accompanying increased industrialization. After the mineral revolution, mining companies realized that peasant activity was keeping Africans from working in the mines. Additionally, commercial farmers and poor white farmers in the Transvaal and the Orange Free State were facing increased encroachment from black peasant agriculture. A series of laws were passed restricting African peasant production, the most notorious of which was the Natives Land Act of 1913 which established land segregation by prohibiting Africans from purchasing lands outside designated reserve areas.[60] The Act met the needs of commercial and white-owned farms, and it halted the efforts through which Africans had resisted working in the mines.

With Africans being squeezed off the land, cities and towns experienced increased urbanization. The Natives (Urban Areas) Act of 1923 was a response to increased urbanization. Prior to the 1920s, each municipality created independent segregation policies regarding the living arrangements of Africans. As more and more Africans moved into the cities, tensions mounted. White workers feared labor competition, and many others feared the political protest that was inevitable in crowded, cramped conditions. The recommendations of the Stallard Commission were adopted in the Natives Act which 'laid down the principle of residential segregation in urban areas and reinforced the doctrine that Africans had no permanent rights in the towns and no justification in being there unless needed by the whites as units of labour'.[61] The Natives Act rejected the more lenient recommendations of the Godley Committee, which suggested that Africans could be exempt from pass controls and labor movement restrictions if they were property-holders, skilled workers, or educated. The government's adoption of the Stallard Commission signified a victory for white workers over industrialists who were more open to a stratified urban community and a permanent black labor force.

Although these acts were passed under the Smuts government, Hertzog continued to implement segregationist policies during his reign in office. The 1926 Mines and Works Amendment tightened the color bar, reserving many jobs for whites in private industry. Differential wage rates were justified by 'race civilization' standards, that is, wage rates could be lower for blacks because they represented an underdeveloped people whose work expectations were not high.

In addition to segregating the labor front, Hertzog introduced bills in 1926 which limited black franchise and representation. The Representation of Natives in Parliament Bill sought to remove Africans from the Cape common roll. Africans would be represented in Parliament by seven white representatives who could vote only on affairs relating to Africans. The Union Native Council Bill tried to set up a council of 50 people, some appointed by the government, others directly elected by Africans, that would serve as a liaison between the government and African peoples. Hertzog also introduced bills that clarified the Cape Coloured franchise and extended governmental authority over Africans in every province.[62] Despite Hertzog's efforts to push through the bills, they could not muster the necessary two-thirds majority in Parliament until 1936 when they passed in an amended format.[63]

Meanwhile, the reserves and townships remained impoverished and overcrowded. Hertzog's government successfully passed the 1927 Native Administration Act which enacted a uniform system of administration of Africans in the reserves. 'Tribal' connections were stressed as the Hertzog government desired accessible control of ethnic groups. For example, chiefs were expected to collect taxes and control the people under their tutelage. This piece of legislation resembled the Shepstonian system of segregation of nineteenth-century Natal, rejecting any form of African assimilation.

Although the core elements of segregation policy were laid by 1920, segregationist ideology only developed in the 1920s and 1930s when it became clear that segregation was supported as government policy and when it was implemented in a more consistent manner.[64] Segregation legislation resonated with policy officials and the white citizenry in the 1920s because it was seen as effective in limiting African worker militancy and rural resistance that grew out of rapid industrialization.[65] Segregation also appealed to many whites because it offered the 'middle ground' between assimilation and overt repression. Political leaders portrayed it as policy that preserved African traditions, at the Africans' request, against the onslaught of Western industrialization, which would in turn maintain white privilege. Such a cohesive policy drew its support from a diverse class base, including white workers, mine owners, and white farmers.[66]

While the majority of white South Africans comfortably supported segregationist ideology, different segregation positions arose among political leaders, ranging from those who promoted accommodationist segregation to those who promoted a more exclusive form of segregation. J.C. Smuts, Prime Minister in 1919 and leader of the opposition from 1924 to 1933, represented the accommodationist perspective on segregation. Smuts was not willing to embrace unrestrained assimilation, but he believed in the possibilities of benevolent trusteeship and accommodation. This position did not 'entirely rule out the possibility of gradually incorporating an emergent African peasantry or urban elite into the structures of white power'.[67] Smuts also presented a more ambiguous position on race policy when he vacillated between different factions within the SAP on race policy to preserve party unity.

Hertzog and his supporters provided a stricter 'native' policy than the accommodationist position of the Smuts government.[68] Hertzog made it clear that he viewed blacks as culturally, if not biologically, inferior to whites; Europeans needed to be the guardians of blacks in all areas and there was no possibility of assimilation between whites and blacks. Instead of benevolent paternalism, Hertzog's segregation stressed domination. Hertzog's segregationist policy 'was strident, it was racist in character and it emphasized the economic and political exclusion of African from a common society'.[69] Afrikaner nationalists supported Hertzog's views because they offered a solace to the economic and political encroachment Afrikaners felt was occurring by blacks.

As segregation policy developed, NGK leaders tried to devise a position regarding how segregation should be implemented. However, the existence of various factions within the NGK's leadership over the goals of segregation policy limited the coherence of the church's perspective. A large majority of the NGK's clergy in these years promoted a conciliatory view of black–white relations. Segregation was necessary, but not necessarily permanent, and segregation policies had to be implemented in a manner that uplifted the 'native'. This group also promoted partial segregation; it admitted that social and political segregation were needed for South Africa but not economic segregation. Another NGK group promoted a strict view of segregation between blacks and whites in all areas of life – social, political, and economic. The evidence of two factions within the NGK meant that NGK pronouncements incorporated ideas from both sides, although generally, official NGK documents supported a just, partial segregation policy.

The first substantive statement concerning race policy was published by the NGK in 1921. The document affirmed the policies that the state was promoting, namely, that whites and blacks should remain separate because of cultural differences, and whites should remain the dominant race. But the NGK also acknowledged this policy's weaknesses and faults when it said that 'the European race must look upon the natives as a sacred trust ... The native has a claim – the claim of the weak and the defenceless in all times and places – to protection, impartial justice and righteous treatment at our hands. We confess with shame that he has not always enjoyed these elementary rights.'[70] It also pointed out that

> Segregation, strictly interpreted, implies that all intercourse between natives and Europeans must wholly cease. This is an unattainable ideal. The European does not want the native near him in his social capacity, but he wants him very badly in his economic capacity.[71]

The NGK's dominant position on race policy indicated an awareness that segregation could hurt black South Africans. It promoted the 'fair' implementation of race policy. The NGK also felt that segregation was necessary, but it did not need to be complete, essentially because white economic hegemony depended on the supply of cheap, black labor. Essentially, the NGK, in these years, admitted that race policy could hurt blacks, but, in the end, segregation was needed to protect the white race and to maintain white economic privileges.

The NGK's position on segregation policy, that is, its support for a just, partial implementation of segregation, continued throughout the 1920s in church conferences and official statements. In 1923, the Federal Council convened a multiracial and interdenominational conference to discuss race policy. Delegates discussed a wide range of issues including the plight of urban blacks, 'native' education, the land question, and segregation. Concern was expressed that the problems of blacks were being ignored, and delegates argued that blacks needed to be consulted before laws were passed affecting them. On the issue of segregation, the delegates unanimously approved the following statement proposed by Edgar Brookes, an English-speaking intellectual who became one of the leading interpreters of segregation policy:

> This Conference is in favour of the principle of the differential development of the Bantu, so far as such differentiation is based on Bantu traditions and requirements, and is not used as a means of repression. So far as this general differential development can be described as 'Segregation', the Conference is in favour of segregation. Understanding 'Segregation' in its limited geographical sense, the Conference believes that complete segregation is neither possible or desirable.[72]

The ideas associated with partial segregation were reiterated at conferences held in 1926 and 1927 which were organized by the NGK to discuss the race legislation that Hertzog introduced in 1926. The following resolution was adopted by an ecumenical conference scheduled by the Federal Missionary Council in 1926:

> It is the opinion of this conference that the general principle applicable to all Christians concerning the relationship between Whites and Blacks today, is one of *co-operation* between them for the good of *the fatherland*. From this follows: 1) that it goes against Christian principles to put general constraints on the progress of natives; 2) that it does not necessarily conflict with such principles to attempt to uplift Blacks apart from Whites; 3) but it nevertheless remains the responsibility of Christians to scrupulously monitor such divisions in order to ascertain that all sections of the population be treated fairly.

This conference, in obedience to the teachings and Spirit of Christ, emphatically emphasizes the divine dignity of natives as men and women created in the image of God. Thus, they shall never be used as instruments to be exploited in order to enrich others.[73]

Although the differences between NGK delegates and representatives from English-speaking churches and African communities prevented agreement on a resolution concerning African franchise rights, the official opinion of the NGK until the late 1920s mirrored other churches in that there was a support for partial segregation if it was implemented fairly. The government was urged to seek gradual solutions that created healthy relations among the races. The official leaders of the NGK approved Hertzog's and Smuts' race policy in their support for segregation, but they made it clear that they did not support integration or full segregation. More pointedly, the NGK generally supported the ideals of the SAP's accommodationist race policy, regardless of the harsh policies that were implemented when Smuts was in power. Additionally, the NGK recognized that economic segregation would be harmful to the development of white civilization. J. du Plessis, Mission Secretary of the NGK, made this point when describing the 1927 conference:

The South African native has an ineradicable place in the economic framework of the Union; both as a skilled and unskilled worker he is indispensable to us. We must not lose sight of this fact. At the conference there was one lone voice advocating that the native should be returned to the reserve, there to work out his own salvation, but the majority concluded that however attractive the segregation plan might appear, the time had long since passed since such a policy could be considered within the realm of practical politics.[74]

The church recognized that in order for white economic hegemony to be maintained, cheap, black labor was necessary; thus, a more limited, partial segregation policy was needed. At least with regard to race policy, this 'moderate' faction, perhaps influenced by the missionary tradition within the NGK, was dominant. The church emphasized 'the equivalence and rights of individuals in their relationship with God rather than on the *volk* as a collectivity'.[75] However, it would be incorrect to argue that the *volkskerk* tradition or those promoting total separation of races were absent; indeed, the more ideological, nationalistic minority was rising in the latter part of the 1920s. This minority promoted more stringent ideas concerning white supremacy and the strict separation of races which would meet the racial and economic concerns of threatened whites, but mainly Afrikaners. A.B. le Roux, a younger clergyman, expressed these ideas when he wrote: 'The social destiny of the native differs from that of the white man. He is and shall remain in a great measure a worker for the white man. His position is and ought to be that of a contented subordinate citizen of our State, in which whites dominate.'[76] Some who abided by this dogmatic strand of racist thought proposed the territorial separation of races. J. Reyneke, another clergyman, wrote:

> The method proposed to maintain White culture is through the gradual implementation of a system of ... territorial segregation. Anyone who thinks about this matter will realize that it is impossible to maintain the interests and needs of White and Black equally without this resulting in the ultimate mixing of the races, unless we mark off separate spheres in which each group can develop separately.[77]

In sum, 'moderates' defined the NGK's official position on race policy in the interwar years, but nationalist church leaders like H.P. van der Merwe, A.L. Fick, and A.F. Louw were rising to the top. Or, during the years between 1910 and 1933 the NGK supported the state's segregationist legislation, but stricter segregationists who felt the government should implement stronger versions of race policy were gaining power.

CONCLUSION

The entrenchment of segregation, the strengthening of capitalism, the emergence of nationalistic parties, and the growth of African and Afrikaner nationalism all affected NGK–state relations between 1910 and 1933. Throughout the interwar years, the NGK rose to become a prominent civil society institution among Afrikaners, and from the 1920s, the NGK formulated its first extensive statements on race policy. As Afrikaner nationalism matured from 1934 to 1948, the focus of Chapter 3, the NGK's pronouncements on race policy became more strident and ideological. The church was an important and respected institution within Afrikaner society as it continued to identify with the interests of the Afrikaner people.

3 NGK–State Relations during UP Governance (1934–47)

The year 1934 marked a turning point for South Africa. The rise of Fusion government coincided with key changes in the political-economic environment. The doubling of the gold price after 1932 made it possible for the mining industry to finance industrial diversification, but the impact of urbanization and the demands of industrial capitalists led the government to relax its implementation of race policy. The latter changes intensified the Afrikaner nationalists' opposition toward the Fusion government. Tensions between leaders dominating the NGK and the state grew during the 1930s and 1940s as the NGK increasingly expressed its solidarity with the Afrikaner community.

The situation of coexisting conflict between groups leading the NGK and the UP-dominated state was characterized by moderate policy collusion and low to moderate official interaction. Coexisting conflict meant that the individuals and groups dominating the NGK and the political establishment were relatively autonomous from one another regarding the formulation of race policy. Although cooperation between the two entities did occur as they desired policies that benefited white interests, they held divergent opinions concerning the formulation of race policy. In the end, the differences between leaders dominating the NGK and the state became so acute that the NGK became mistrustful of state institutions because they did not support the objectives of Afrikaner nationalism broadly conceived. This chapter examines the situation of coexisting conflict between the NGK and state, a form of conflictual state–civil society relations that represents relative, not thorough, disengagement, and assesses the variety of factors that explain this relationship, including socio-ideological developments, class interests, and material concerns.

POLITICAL-ECONOMIC ENVIRONMENT SURROUNDING COEXISTING CONFLICT

In 1929 South Africa experienced economic hardship because of the worldwide Great Depression. The value of its exports dropped, commercial and manufacturing activity decreased, and wages fell. Economic hardship continued when Great Britain abandoned the gold standard in September 1931. J.B.M. Hertzog resisted devaluing South Africa's currency in order to prove the country's independence, but this led to capital flight and falling exports. By December 1932 South Africa had abandoned the gold standard.[1]

During this economic crisis, a government of national unity was considered by the National Party (NP) and the South African Party (SAP) to alleviate some of the distress the country was facing. In 1933 the NP and the SAP established a coalition government, and in 1934, the two parties amalgamated to form the United Party (UP). The so-called Fusion government addressed the rising discontent felt by its constituents. First, there was growing disillusionment from Hertzog's constituents over his government's response to the economic downturn. NP leaders believed that a coalition government could provide a clear economic policy which would diminish dissatisfaction and avert election losses. Second, both Smuts and Hertzog wanted to avoid 'divisive politicking' over race policy in order to create an overarching, consistent race policy. Any significant changes in racial policy required a two-thirds majority vote in parliament, and this meant that the major parties had to be allied in such efforts. Finally, a government drawing off the resources of both parties could resolve the constitutional relationship of South Africa within the British empire.[2]

Fusion between Hertzog's National Party and Smuts' South African Party occurred in 1934 because time had assuaged some of the animosities between Afrikaners and English-speaking South Africans. Some Afrikaners were now willing to reconsider their attitude toward the British.[3] Moreover, Hertzog, who had appealed to Afrikaner interests in the early twentieth century, was committed to broad-based Afrikaner and English interests by the late 1920s. Hertzog softened his earlier 'two-stream policy' because he saw Afrikaners standing on an equal footing with English-speaking South Africans, and he felt many English-speaking South Africans were dedicated to South Africa's interests first and foremost. Hertzog believed that Afrikaner and English interests should receive equal attention, with neither dominant over the other.

Additionally, Hertzog's political and economic goals for South Africa had merged with Smuts' by 1933. As mentioned in the previous chapter, the Pact government's policies were neither anti-capitalist nor anti-imperialist, even though Hertzog's election slogans may have emphasized these themes. For example, the protective tariffs enacted by Hertzog were no higher than those of Australia, a British dominion within the Commonwealth which was comparable to South Africa. Hertzog did not abandon the British sterling system and his financial policy was always responsive to British financial planners. Hertzog did obtain some victories that appeased whites desiring a break from imperial rule, for example, there was a new flag, a new national anthem, and bilingualism, but these gains were primarily symbolic. Moreover, 'since 1926 Hertzog had moved toward Smuts and away from the ardently republican wing of the National Party in his inter-pretation of the Union's constitutional position.'[4]

Soon after Fusion in 1934, minorities from both parties broke away. Colonel Stallard, a strong supporter of British imperialism, formed the Dominion Party in 1934, while D.F. Malan, a leader within Hertzog's NP, formed the *Gesuiwerde Nasionale Party* (Purified National Party or PNP).[5] Malan's party represented the more extreme Afrikaner nationalists who felt fusion with a British sympathizer like Smuts was a betrayal of the republican ideal for South Africa. For this reason, among others, Afrikaner nationalists joined Malan's 'ortho-dox' National Party.[6]

The establishment of the PNP gave Afrikaner nationalists another forum to express their political dreams. In fact, the year 1934 marked a watershed for Afrikaner nationalism. Ever since the 1920s, Afrikaner nationalism had been growing in strength, carried forward by the petit-bourgeoisie who were active in organizations such as the Afrikaner Broederbond (AB), the *Federasie van Afrikaanse Kultuurverenigings* (FAK), the Broederbond's front organization catering to cultural inter-ests, the *Nasionale Pers*, and the *Afrikaanse Nasionale Studentebond* (ANS).[7] Afrikaner nationalists were slowly widening their web throughout society, drawing in Afrikaners across class lines. Hertzog's decision to fuse the NP with the SAP indicated to Afrikaner national-ists that Hertzog was sacrificing Afrikaner nationalist interests for the 'glory' of British capitalism. After 1934 the organizational skills and financial backing of the AB and the FAK switched from Hertzog's party to Malan's. Malan's initial support was restricted to the agricul-tural and finance capital base in the western Cape. He also had the support of intellectuals and clerics in the northern Orange Free State and Transvaal PNP aligned with the AB and the FAK. To gain political power, Malan needed to mobilize Afrikaners (workers, farmers, industrialists) across class and regional differences who were facing competition from English commerce and industry.[8]

Dan O'Meara argues that Malan's National Party and the Afrikaner nationalist movement gained strength in three ways. First, the Broederbond actively promoted Afrikaner culture through the FAK.[9] The FAK organized cultural activities, including the centenary celebration of the Great Trek in 1938, through its coordination of the nationalist programs of youth groups, religious associations, and educational institutions. Second, O'Meara argues that nationalists depicted English-dominated trade unions as exclusively materialistic and under foreign control in an effort to draw Afrikaner workers away from these unions. A noticeable shift by workers toward Malan's National Party occured in the 1940s.[10] Finally, nationalists promoted Afrikaner financial and economic activity in an effort to challenge the domination of English capital. Afrikaner capital was based primarily in the western Cape through the savings that had been mobilized and invested by Santam and Sanlam since 1918.[11] But by the late 1930s, the AB-controlled *Volkskas*, based in the Transvaal and OFS, had developed into a private commercial bank. The Broederbond also encouraged cooperatives in the northern republics. The economic entrepreneurs of the Cape-based organizations and the cultural ideologues of the northern-based Broederbond joined to promote Afrikaner capital after 1934. An economic strategy devoted to uniting different Afrikaner classes was developed at the *Ekonomiese Volkskongres* (Economic People's Congress) in 1939, an historic conference attended by nationalists from many different fields.

The economic strategy devised at this *volkskongres* was straightforward – capital gathered from Afrikaners and invested into productive enterprises would create a capitalist society beneficial to Afrikaners. Through hard work and individual entrepreneurship, Afrikaners could mobilize their savings and create a *'volkskapitalisme'* or people's capitalism. Organizations central to this endeavor were the *Ekonomiese Instituut* (Economic Institute), the *Afrikaanse Handelsinstituut* (Afrikaner Institute for Commerce), and the *Reddingsdaadbond* (Rescue Action Society). The development of *'volkskapitalisme'* was indeed a promising program for the PNP, but it had to wait until the 1940s before it saw measurable success (economically and politically). For now, not even the growing strength of Afrikaner nationalism could stifle the accomplishments of the Fusion government.

The Fusion government was successful in achieving two goals. First, it clarified the constitutional relationship of South Africa within the Empire. In the compromises made between Smuts and Hertzog before Fusion, Hertzog promised to respect South Africa's responsibilities to the Empire in times of foreign crisis. He also promised to refrain from making statements supporting republicanism that would threaten South Africa's status in the Commonwealth. Fusion government assumed the 'legal freedoms offered by the Statute of Westminster' (1933), which clarified South Africa's autonomy and the sovereign status of the parliament, and 'ensured that all acts of the state, even the making of war and peace, even secession from the Commonwealth, could now be performed legally on local authority alone.'[12]

Fusion also opened the door for the passage of Hertzog's 'native bills'. The first bill, entitled the Representation of Natives Bill, destroyed the Cape franchise for Africans, relegated African political representation to a few white representatives in Parliament, and created a Natives Representative Council intended to advise the government on African needs. The second bill, the Native Trust and Land Bill, increased the percentage of land reserved for African occupation to 13 per cent. African farms outside the reserves could be occupied by whites through forced removals. These laws appealed to white South Africans who feared black encroachment and they met the needs of Afrikaner farmers who wanted to maintain their economic power through the control of a cheap labor force.

Laws which restricted African land ownership and free movement from 1890 to 1940 have been part of a debate concerning the cheap labor power thesis. Frederick Johnstone and Harold Wolpe argue that laws regarding land ownership and influx control in South Africa were designed to secure capitalist profits by providing farmers, mine owners, and industrialists with a cheap black labor force.[13] The cheap labor power thesis links capitalist development and racial policies. It suggests that an oppressive system of labor reproduction, such as South Africa's mining sector, can maintain low wages because some of the costs of reproduction are met through pre-capitalist production, like subsistence farming in the South African reserves. The cheap labor power thesis provides much explanatory power for the era preceding the second industrial revolution in South Africa. It can be argued that two modes of production existed from the late 1800s to the 1920s, with the capitalist mode (i.e. mining and industrial sector) depending on the existence of a pre-capitalist mode (i.e. subsistence farming) for exploitative profits.

Beginning in the 1920s and 1930s, however, state laws and regulations, like the 1926 Master and Servant Amendment Act which gave farmers extended control over their tenants, were forcing more and more Africans into the towns, leading to the termination of the pre-capitalist mode of production. Mines and commercial farmers demanded cheap labor, and laws were provided which channelled Africans into these activities. Additionally, the reserves were depleted of any possibility of productive activity, diminishing the possibility that they could provide supplementary income for Africans working in urban areas. By the late 1930s, then, it was becoming more difficult to maintain pre-capitalist economic activity as the country was embracing full-scale capitalism.

Changes in the production structures coincided with an extremely prosperous economy. The economy expanded from 1933 to 1939 due to increases in the price of gold. As manufacturing and mining profits rose, the GNP grew and industries diversified. The commanding position of mineral and agricultural exports was replaced by a high level of industrialization. The UP government followed the course of industrial capitalism without losing sight of mining interests.

South Africa's expanding economy attracted overseas investment on a large scale. For example, private capital and state investment from Great Britain and the United States increased in this period.[14] British investors especially saw South Africa's mines and industries as lucrative markets, and they did not hesitate to get involved. Western governments were aware that the South African state exploited black labor, but they did not call for changes that challenged South Africa's racial order because of the profits they received:[15] South Africa's racist segregation policy was ignored. They argued that white rule under Hertzog and Smuts was getting more liberal, and that it would change over time. More pointedly, segregation was so entrenched throughout the world that Western governments paid little heed to South Africa's race problems.

Because of persistent and oppressive discrimination, some black South Africans organized to protest racist legislation. However, resistance to the racial and economic order in the 1930s was limited because of ethnic, class, and social barriers. The leaders of the three most active resistance organizations in the 1930s, the African Political Organization (APO), the South African Indian Congress (SAIC), and the African National Congress (ANC), were Western-oriented, middle-class individuals. Their goal was to gain rights for middle-class blacks which would be extended to all black South Africans. These groups worked within the system to try to convince the white electorate that discriminatory legislation was harmful to blacks.

An example of the ineffectiveness of black protest was the outcome of the All African Convention. The All African Convention was organized to oppose Hertzog's 'native bills'. The Convention attracted over 400 delegates from the ANC, the APO, the SAIC, the Communist Party, rural organizations, and local organizations. Although the delegates agreed that Hertzog's bills needed to be defeated, their protests were ineffective against the white power structure. Black leaders confined themselves to very mild forms of protest. They sent delegations to meet Hertzog, declared a national day of conciliation, and emphasized the importance of remaining within the boundaries of the Commonwealth's appeal process.[16] Overall, black leaders resisted the economic and political power structures of the racist regime, but they lacked widespread populist appeal because of their promotion of moderate protest within the system. Even if black associational life could have gained widespread populist appeal, it would have faced an uphill battle to have its interests heard by the white minority government. Blacks were essentially excluded from any real participation in electoral politics, and white leaders generally ignored their demands.

The election of 1938 was the first major test of the Fusion government's strength. The UP fared well, winning the majority of parliamentary seats. For the PNP, the election was a disappointment. It won only 27 seats compared to 111 won by the UP. Since its restructuring in 1934, the PNP had not established a support base outside its traditional strongholds of the rural Cape Province and the Orange Free State. One of the major differences between the UP and the PNP in the 1938 election was their view on the constitutional status of South Africa. The UP felt the Commonwealth offered South Africa security and privilege because South Africa's association with the British Empire made it part of a significant worldwide civilization. The PNP believed that independence was the only solution for South Africa.

Another area of disagreement between the UP and the PNP concerned nationalist issues. The PNP was much more exclusive than the UP on cultural issues.[17] While the UP held that the two segments of white society could be unified for South Africa's good, the PNP believed that assimilation would mean the domination of English-speakers over the Afrikaners. The rhetoric of anti-Semitic, anti-Coloured and anti-Indian sloganeering in the PNP also hurt its efforts in the 1938 election although the PNP's nationalist messages made steady gains among the white populace as the years progressed. The political repercussions of the Second World War also helped Malan's National Party gain electoral support in the 1940s.

The outbreak of the Second World War (1939) splintered the cohesion of the Fusion government. Hertzog and his supporters promoted neutrality, while Smuts and his followers supported Great Britain and the Allies. Hertzog and Smuts reacted differently to the rise of German aggression, with Smuts seeing Germany's actions as an international danger and Hertzog viewing the actions as understandable due to the humiliation Germany experienced after the First World War. Hertzog also believed that South Africa's right to neutrality needed to be upheld within the Commonwealth due, in part, to the negative events that followed South Africa's participation in the First World War.[18] The UP split when Smuts and his followers, including the Labour Party and the Dominion Party, won the parliamentary vote on joining the war on the Allies' side. Hertzog left the UP, merging briefly with the *Herenigde Nasionale of Volksparty* (HNP) or the Reunited National Party in 1940.

The ramifications of these party changes due to the 'war vote' meant that the UP was stripped of almost all its Afrikaner support. With Smuts at the helm, it became the primary party of English-speaking South Africans. The HNP, on the other hand, represented Afrikaners. For some Afrikaner nationalists who were influential in the HNP after 1939, South Africa's entry into the war not only reawakened resentments against the British, it also fostered a growing attachment to national socialism.[19] Nationalist socialism's emphasis on race, the glorification of the nation, respect for leadership, and the supremacy of the community merged with Afrikaner nationalist messages. Prominent Afrikaners who dabbled in fascist thinking included G. Cronje, a German-trained sociologist who taught at the University of Stellenbosch, N. Diederichs, a German-trained philosopher who chaired the Afrikaner Broederbond from 1938 to 1942 and became State President from 1975 to 1978, Piet Meyer, a philosopher who chaired the Broederbond from 1960 to 1972 and the state-controlled South African Broadcasting Corporation from 1959 to 1981, and John Vorster, a leader in the Ox-Wagon Guard and later prime minister of South Africa from 1966 to 1978.

In the 1940s, organizations like the *Ossewa Brandwag* (Oxwagon Sentinels), a paramilitary, pro-German group, and the New Order, a group committed to a South African version of fascism, put pressure on the HNP to adopt forms of far-right thinking. At first, the HNP was sympathetic to the pro-Nazi sentiments of these radical right organizations. Over time, however, the New Order and the *Ossewa Brandwag* (OB) challenged the HNP's leadership within Afrikaner nationalism. Bitter personal rivalries tore the HNP apart in the early 1940s. In 1942 Malan ended the factionalism by forcing all HNP members to resign from the OB.

HNP factionalism weakened the party in the 1943 general election. Other factors that diminished the HNP's appeal were its position of neutrality on the war (when the Allies were clearly victorious) and the party's support for an autonomous Afrikaner republic. Nevertheless, the HNP became the official opposition party after the 1943 elections, winning 43 seats to the UP's 89.[20] The Reunited NP also received a greater percentage of votes in 1943 than ever before as UP and LP voters began to shift their allegiance to the HNP.

Meanwhile, the period of the Second World War coincided with an economic boom. The need to supply troops with large quantities of manufactured goods diversified South Africa's economy even further. Although South Africa welcomed the industrial revolution, problems arose. The economic boom created a large demand for cheap labor, causing a greater influx of black laborers into the urban areas. Social problems of overcrowding, poor housing, and deteriorating health developed. The government tried, but could not stop increased African settlement into the towns. Racial tensions increased as black South Africans began to mingle with whites in residential areas and as blacks filled semi-skilled positions in industrial posts which had previously been taken by whites.[21]

The Smuts government responded to the rising racial tension by making adjustments to segregation laws that accommodated industrial needs. Some of the changes softened stringent segregation rules. Color bars were relaxed which allowed blacks to take positions previously reserved for whites; pass laws were also relaxed to accommodate the growing influx of black labor; and laws relating to African trade unions were eased to allow for increased membership.

Despite the relaxation of segregation laws, black political activity increased in the 1940s due to a rising nationalist consciousness. Blacks were becoming increasingly conscious of their oppression and their need to organize as workers against exploitative owners. Demands for higher wages and better living conditions became commonplace among black trade unions. Their demands met with some success as wages increased among African workers in the 1940s. From 1941 onward, African workers organized themselves primarily through the Council of Non-European Trade Unions (CNETU). The largest of the CNETU unions was the African Mineworkers' Union. In August 1946, the African Mineworkers' Union launched a well-organized strike which halted production at 12 mines.[22] The government met this protest with savage repression, but its actions only increased the solidarity among workers.

The radicalization of trade unions affected the activity of black political organizations in the 1940s as well. The ANC Youth League was formed in response to the timidity and moderation of the ANC. It adopted a more militant stance concerning African identity and national freedom by highlighting African organizational efforts over cooperation with whites. In 1944 the Non-European Unity Movement was formed to seek democratic rights for blacks. It refused to work within government structures and rejected single-issue campaigns. In 1946 the Indian National Conference launched a passive resistance campaign against the Pegging Act (1943) and the Land Tenure and Indian Representation Act (1946) – Acts that were designed to force Indians to live and work in designated areas only. The radicalization of black movements alarmed the white electorate, who believed the masses were becoming uncontrollable, a fear that was often expressed by Afrikaners as the '*swart gevaar*' (black danger). The rising racial divisions between 1939 and 1948 led whites to call for more cohesive 'native' policy from the UP and the HNP.

The 1948 election was one such test of the electoral parties' 'native' policies. In February 1948, the UP issued a report, commissioned by Justice H.A. Fagan, which proposed mild reforms along accommodationist segregation lines.[23] The report's underlying tone encouraged the stabilization of African labor in urban areas by discouraging local authorities from returning unemployed Africans to reserves and keeping a steady supply of Africans in urban areas for industrial needs. On the other hand, the Fagan Report also entailed the centralization of the labor reserve process, suggesting that migrant labor could be streamlined into particular industries through the use of labor bureaus. The Fagan Report, overall, contained measures that both eased and tightened control over migratory labor, but what was most worrisome to the white electorate was its notion that the urbanization of blacks was a permanent and irreversible trend.[24] These beliefs seemed to encourage policy measures that would ease segregation, such as relaxing color bars, and increasing black wages and work benefits for Africans. Such policies, associated with the UP more than the HNP, worried whites who feared the threat of black encroachment. The HNP's perspectives on race relations were summarized in the Sauer Report, released in 1946.[25] Some of its conclusions promoted a much stricter form of segregation than the Fagan Report. It stated, for example, that Indians were an alien people in South Africa; it favored the consolidation of reserves and tighter influx control; and it called for the removal of the Natives Representative Council. The Report, however, contained a considerable measure of ambiguity on the issue of economic segregation. It suggested that economic segregation was necessary, but not if farming and manufacturing interests depended on economic integration, and it recognized that the implementation of apartheid would have to proceed gradually to safeguard white interests. Nonetheless, the simplicity of the 'apartheid slogan' (segregation of all races), outlined in the Sauer Report, offered security to many Afrikaner nationalists and the white electorate at large.

Malan exploited the issue of race in the 1948 election campaign. The relaxation of the color bar and the emergence of the Fagan Report were criticized by the HNP for appeasing African demands and promoting race equality in South Africa. In reality, the HNP's apartheid program was not substantively different from the UP's policy in terms of its aims and goals. However, it appeared much more consistent and thorough regarding the maintenance of white civilization and economic prosperity.

In addition, by the late 1940s, the HNP appealed to and consolidated Afrikaner classes across different regions through the efforts of the Broederbond which advocated and successfully achieved its goal of an Afrikaner 'people's economy'. The support of four groups – farmers, workers, the petty-bourgeoisie, and financiers – greatly aided the HNP. Additionally, the differences between regional or provincial parties and groups that had splintered nationalism in previous years, namely, the Orange Free State/Transvaal HNP versus the Cape HNP, were diminished by the election of 1948. The HNP was able to win the 1948 election by consolidating white voters under two main planks. First, its anti-British, monopolistic rhetoric appealed to Afrikaners with economic ambitions. Second, its apartheid slogan drew various classes together by promising that white culture would be protected and that black labor would be channeled where it was needed for purposes of economic prosperity.[26] The National Party, in alliance with the Afrikaner Party, won the May 1948 election. Although they polled only 39.4 per cent of the vote compared to the

United and Labour Party alliance's 53.3 per cent, the single-member district system, which 'loaded' rural constituencies, allowed the HNP to emerge victorious with 79 seats compared to the 65 seats won by the UP–LP alliance.[27]

In sum, the political-economic environment from 1933 to 1947 was unsteady but stable. There was a change in government, political infighting concerning the Second World War, increased entrenchment of segregation laws, rising black protest, growing urbanization, and increased proletarianization. These events were significant, causing widespread dissatisfaction among Afrikaners and black South Africas. Regarding NGK–state relations, this environment was conducive to a state–civil society relationship of coexisting conflict, which we will examine next.

THE UP-DOMINATED STATE'S POSITION ON RACE POLICY (1934–47)

Before addressing the factors that lay behind the era of coexisting conflict, it is important to make a disclaimer. I am well aware of the tendency to portray the South African state and the NGK as monolithic entities regardless of their differentiated nature. In the years under examination, the NGK's Cape and Transvaal synods, for example, contained different leaders, classes, factions, and issue foci. Similar divisions appeared within South African parties such as the HNP and UP. The South African state also encompassed a multitude of 'natures' due to the existence of different leaders, classes, bureaucratic divisions, political parties, and so forth, so it would be impossible to talk about *the* South African state's position on general race policy or any other issue. Besides, the South African state cannot maintain a position on race policy; only leaders and groups within the state can do so. While I have tried to be sensitive to the important divisions within the South African state and the NGK, the focus of this study is an overview of state–NGK relations which focuses on the broad patterns of race positions that evolved within these entities due to the positions held by dominant groups, individuals, and/or institutions.

With reference to this era of coexisting conflict, the NGK and the UP-dominated state promoted noticeably different views of general race policy. Neo-Kuyperian ideas began to provide the basis for NGK leaders' conceptions on race policy by the 1930s such that the church promoted a totalist apartheid position, while the political establishment promoted a guardian-segregationist view, based on the merged ideas of J.C. Smuts, J.H. Hofmeyr, and G.N. Heaton Nicholls. NGK–state differences on general race policy were based on the class interests and political concerns they represented or identified with, with NGK leaders identifying with conservative Afrikaner nationalist, petit-bourgeois and working-class concerns, and state leaders, related to the prominence of the UP government, representing the interests of pragmatic industrialists. Both views on general race policy maintained the interests of white South Africans, and both were aimed at capitalist reproduction, but the ideologies behind them were distinct.

The UP-dominated state contained numerous groups that held distinct positions on race policy. The NGK and other institutions committed to Afrikaner nationalist causes responded mainly to the policies enunciated and practices implemented by the faction associated with J.C. Smuts, but three other significant positions on general race policy existed within the political establishment from 1934 to 1947.

Hertzog, the Prime Minister or Premier of the South African state from 1934 to 1939, promoted a stricter 'native' policy than the accommodationists and liberals within the United Party government. As pointed out in Chapter 2, Hertzog made it clear that he viewed blacks as culturally, if not biologically, inferior to whites. Hertzog supported territorial and political segregation among the races, conceived as beneficial to blacks, but he also made it clear that whites, in any industrial or economic undertaking, had first priority. He supported the industrial color bar, the abolition of the Cape franchise, and the establishment of 'native' councils to represent black interests. Hertzog's defense of amendments to the Riotous Assemblies Act (1930), which placed limits on labor strikes and meetings and increased police powers in measures of enforcement, and his support for the Native Administration Act (1929), which brought all black workers under the mantle of pass laws and movement control, and the Representation of Natives Bill and Native Trust and Land Act (1936), described above, indicate Hertzog's belief in the stricter enforcement of segregation.[28] Hertzog's position on segregation resonated, in part, with SAP/UP/DP members like Colonel Stallard and G.N. Heaton Nicholls who championed a stricter implementation of segregation policy.[29]

The political establishment also contained a more liberal position on general race policy associated with individuals like J.H. Hofmeyr, F.S. Malan, E. Brookes, and Margaret Ballinger. Beginning in 1938, Brookes and Ballinger served as 'native' parliamentarian representatives. While they could not erase or soften the segregation-ist legislation that had been passed, they were able to transform par-liamentary debates on 'native' legislation in ways that focused on the long-term welfare of Africans rather than white fears.[30] F.S. Malan and J.H. Hofmeyr, SAP/UP stalwarts who served in a variety of min-istries during their long political careers, also represented the liberal, benevolent segregationist position among whites in the South African state. J.H. Hofmeyr, for example, believed that the starting point of race policy needed to be differences among races, not discussions about racial superiority or inferiority. Hofmeyr believed that segregation was necessary, but he also believed that the economic dependence of whites on blacks was undeniable. He supported measures that improved the welfare of black South Africans, he denounced fears of race mixing as illogical, and he refused to vote for Hertzog's Representation Bill because it denied Africans their constitutional rights.[31]

The racial policies enunciated and the practices implemented by the faction associated with J.C. Smuts dominated the political establishment from 1934 to 1947. J.C. Smuts supported an accom-modationist form of segregation.[32] He was a committed segregation-ist who believed that the differences between races were substantial and policies needed to be constructed to preserve the security of whites. But he did not necessarily support total segregation; he mainly supported political and territorial segregation. Smuts believed that partial segregation would meet two goals: the mainte-nance of white privilege and economic growth. Total segregation was too exclusive. At a public lecture in 1942, Smuts made clear that he had certain misgivings about the economic ramifications related to total segregation. In his remarks about complete segregation he said:

> We have tried to carry out this policy ... The high expectation that we entertained of that policy has been sadly disappointed. How can it be otherwise? The whole trend both in this country and through-out Africa has been in the opposite direction. The whole movement of development here on this continent has been for closer contacts to be established between the various races and the various sections of the community. Isolation has gone in South Africa and segrega-tion has fallen on evil days, too.[33]

Smuts continued by offering another policy that solved race problems. He called it 'trusteeship'. Trusteeship was a harmonious, cooperative race policy based on two positions – guardian and ward. The guardians (whites), who had more political and economic security, were to help the wards (blacks), who had little. This was promoted as an ethical, religious policy, one that built trust between the races.

Smuts was not a liberal when it came to the development of race policy. He did not dismiss segregation, only strict segregation or apartheid. In fact, he supported segregationist legislation throughout his term, and he objected to the mixing of races on a general level. However, a variety of events in the 1940s gave fuel to the Afrikaner nationalists' fire that Smuts was promoting the cause of black South Africans. As a result of the shortage of cheap labor in South Africa, Smuts approved the relaxation of segregation measures including the systematic enforcement of influx control and pass laws. Segregation also slowed down after 1938 because of the lobbying efforts of white 'native' representatives in parliament, Margaret Ballinger and Edgar Brookes among them, who forced parliamentarians to reassess segregation's implementation in the 1940s. In 1942, the government appointed councils and committees to investigate the socio-economic concerns of urban Africans. As a result of these reports, the government undertook a variety of reforms which included improvements in public health, secondary education, and wage levels. Finally, the Fagan Report's publication in 1948 signaled an opening by the Smuts government for the eventual incorporation of Africans in urban areas. These measures, none of them aimed at the restoration of full rights for Africans, were regarded as liberal giveaways by the HNP. Afrikaner nationalists associated with the HNP were the final major faction within the political establishment. They regarded apartheid policy as superior to segregation.

The concept of apartheid emerged in the 1930s among Afrikaner nationalists who desired a more stringent, vertical form of separation.[34] Afrikaner nationalists instrumental in the formulation of apartheid ideology included right-wing sympathizers like G. Cronje, N. Diederichs, and P. Meyer as well as conservatives influenced by neo-Kuyperianism within the NGK, NHK, and GK – J.D. du Toit, E.P. Groenewald, A.B. du Preez, L.J. du Plessis, and F.J.M. Potgieter. HNP political leaders who supported apartheid included D.F. Malan, leader of the Cape HNP, N.J. van der Merwe, a prominent Free State Malanite, J.G. Strijdom, hardline Transvaal HNP leader, C.R. Swart, leader of the Free State HNP, and H. Verwoerd, editor of *Die Transvaler*.

A 1944 *Volkskongres* helped expose the general principles underlying the Afrikaner nationalist conception of race policy and apartheid in particular. These principles included the idea that apartheid needed to be implemented because it benefited *'volk'* development through concentrating on the organic needs and interests of each people-group; whites needed to act as guardians over blacks until they could minister to their own needs; whites needed to maintain full control over all areas of government; and any effort toward denationalization that cut individuals off from their *volk* were to be deplored.[35]

In general, the HNP developed the policy of apartheid because it offered a clearer alternative to the more integrationist racial policies of their opponents. The HNP called for stricter separation along cultural lines. The party presented apartheid as a more coherent race policy than the indifference and ambiguity of the UP's race policy. Apartheid meant the elimination of the Natives Representation Council, the abolition of African representatives in parliament, the recognition of 'native' homelands, strict control of Africans into urban areas, labor quotas to restrict the numbers of African workers, and the separation of races in all areas whenever possible.[36]

However, Deborah Posel convincingly argues that apartheid policy, as portrayed in the Sauer Report, was not an entirely coherent racial 'blueprint' due to the array of attitudes Afrikaner nationalists held toward race policy in the 1940s and 1950s.[37] Apartheid had a variety of meanings within the Afrikaner nationalist alliance depending on particular economic and class interests. The leaders who dominated SABRA, the NGK, and the FAK advocated the total segregation of races in political, economic and social arenas, while the individuals who dominated the AHI and the SAAU promoted political and social segregation only, allowing for the possibility of economic integration. Those who advocated total apartheid were typically the petty bourgeoisie and working classes, whose livelihood or interests were more connected to the advancement of total race separation, while those who promoted partial segregation were the Afrikaner industrialists, financiers and large-scale farmers. The policy of apartheid won Afrikaner support because it was ambiguous enough to meld these conflicting views concerning apartheid. For example, it appealed to workers through its promise of strict influx control, and it appealed to Afrikaner industrialists through its commitment to slowing the implementation of economic segregation if business profits were affected.

Posel's work is significant because the multitude of perspectives on race policy within Afrikaner nationalist institutions existed among political groups within the state. Some elements within the state presented a more totalist apartheid vision like HNP supporters, no matter how divided its constituents were, and other factions supported a more benevolent form of segregation based on their links with industrialists who supported an easing of segregation measures. The UP government, for example, which dominated the state, promoted an accommodationist form of segregation. Smuts' supporters recognized that Africans were a permanent part of South Africa's population. It would be impossible to implement strict segregation in all societal realms, especially the economic arena, because white businesses depended on the steady supply of a cheap labor (that is, black) force. This position clashed with the NGK's more stringent race policy perspective, which led to a situation of coexisting conflict.

THE NGK'S GENERAL POSITION ON RACE POLICY (1934–47)

A situation of coexisting conflict between factions dominating the NGK and the state meant that the two entities pursued different agendas and held different opinions on key issues, in this case, the formulation and implementation of race policy. In general, the NGK, dominated by leaders influenced by neo-Kuyperianism and other world-views, supported strict segregation, or apartheid, while the state, dominated by the ideas formulated by and policies promoted under Smuts, supported partial segregation.

Despite the different opinions held on the particular implementation of race policy, it is important to note that both church and state leaders held similar views on the broad outlines of race policy. Leading groups within the NGK and the state opposed 'race-mixing' and the 'de-nationalizing' of blacks, and they promoted race policies based on paternalistic ideas, that is, natives had to be protected by more advanced whites until they reached an adequate level of development. While claiming to support the upliftment of black South Africans, in reality, leaders within the NGK and the state supported policies that disadvantaged blacks for the benefit of whites. On the basis of these similarities, situations of conciliation, even genuine cooperation, between the NGK and the state can be found.[38]

While similar interests existed between the NGK and the state regarding race policy, a closer examination of the positions taken by leaders within the NGK and the state over general and specific race policy show significant differences. First, the ideological basis of the UP-dominated state's accommodationist segregation policy was the notion of cultural relativism within contemporary anthropology, while the ideological basis of the *volkskerk* NGK apartheid policy was Christian Nationalism. Second, the end goal of accommodationist segregation was to exclude Africans from direct participation in political affairs and to continue implementing segregation in social spheres. The purist faction within the NGK in the 1940s envisioned a stricter segregation affecting all areas of life – political, economic, and social. Finally, accommodationist segregation served the interests of white South Africans because it maintained their economic and political privileges, while apartheid served the interests of white South Africans, but more so Afrikaners, in their desire to maintain ethnic purity and to ensure economic security.

It is the perceived and real differences between the factions dominating the NGK and the state over race policy that explains the relationship of coexisting conflict as the NGK developed a mistrust toward state leaders for promoting unsatisfactory socio-economic and racial policies. In contrast with the earlier period from 1910 to 1933, when the NGK basically supported benevolent segregation pragmatically, the climate of opinion within the NGK changed in the 1930s and 1940s due to three events – an increasingly uncertain political-economic environment, rising Afrikaner nationalism, and internal church affairs – which led the church to formulate an ideological 'theology of apartheid' which contrasted with the UP-dominated state's support for accommodationist segregation.

By the 1930s, Afrikaners had become more conscious of their ethnic identity and the threats to the privileges they experienced as one of the dominant white groups.[39] Afrikaner identity had been shaped by a variety of socio-economic events in the early twentieth century as well as by the leadership within Afrikaner nationalist circles who fostered ideas of Afrikaner identity and strategies to safeguard Afrikaner privileges. By the 1930s Afrikaners had experienced the humiliation of the Anglo-Boer War and their people's internment in British concentration camps; they were aware of the brief exhilaration related to the Afrikaner Rebellion of 1914 and the Hertzog victory of 1924; and they were dealing with the disorienting effects of the Great Depression, expanding industrialization, and rapid urbanization.

Industrialization and urbanization caused the migration of Afrikaner poor whites and Africans into the urban areas. As noted in Chapter 2, many Afrikaners found themselves in competition with cheap African labor. In the midst of black encroachment and in order to maintain Afrikaner cultural purity and economic privileges,

Afrikaner nationalists realized that the 'poor white' problem needed to be addressed. Afrikaners also felt threatened in the 1930s by the fact that they could not seem to 'catch up' with English-speakers economically. Afrikaners who moved to the urban areas not only competed with unskilled or semi-skilled black laborers, but entered the job market far behind the skilled English-speaking worker.[40] Nationalist Afrikaners viewed the situation of vast economic gaps between the Afrikaner and English as a disturbing trend. The establishment of the UP in 1934 was equally significant to Afrikaners because 'fusion' signified the possibility of further material losses. Followers of Malan's NP assumed that imperial capital would dominate South Africa, with English-speaking mining and industrial capitalists preferring unskilled black labor to semi-skilled Afrikaner workers. Petty bourgeois leaders within Afrikaner nationalist circles, fearing that Afrikaner workers would become denationalized to the point of losing their support in a nationalist Afrikaner party alignment, tried to retain the backing of Afrikaner laborers by promoting Christian-National labor unions.

Afrikaner nationalism's rise as a political-national force was the result of cultural fears among Afrikaners as well as material fears. Afrikaners were anxious and alienated in the urban, industrial environment which seemed to diminish their ethnic homogeneity. Political developments in the 1930s also frightened Afrikaners. Fusion assumed the 'equalization' of a young, weak, Afrikaans culture with the rich, domineering, British culture. Nationalists argued that Afrikaner culture would inevitably be crushed under the weight of British culture. Moreover, Afrikaner nationalists were not ready to 'reconcile' with English-speaking South Africans until they had 'proved themselves' equals in cultural and economic terms. Finally, a Fusion government did not appeal to Afrikaner nationalists who could not identify or were still repulsed by the imperial symbols and slogans that it incorporated. The Afrikaners' pride was hurt by the fact that South Africa could not take actions independent of the Commonwealth's desires.

It was the middle-class or petty bourgeois leaders among Afrikaners, who themselves were seriously threatened by the imperial values and goals of the UP, that combated the social and material insecurity felt by Afrikaners in a disorientating, frightening socio-economic environment. These leaders, many of them associated with the Afrikaner Broederbond, promoted an ethnic consciousness and an ethnically based solution, that is apartheid, that attracted and mobilized Afrikaners across classes and regions.

The FAK, the *Afrikaanse Handelsinstituut*, the *Reddingsdaadbond*, the PNP/HNP, and the NGK were but a few of the institutions to which Afrikaners could turn to for economic and political advancement in the 1930s. The PNP/HNP, for example, tried to mobilize Afrikaners by pointing to the Afrikaners' group rights and their special calling within South Africa. The HNP called for republicanism, the unity of whites within an Afrikaner-dominated cultural context, the joining together of Afrikaners economically to challenge the dominance of English-speakers, and apartheid's implementation.[41] The NGK's role within the growing movement of Afrikaner nationalism involved its renewed commitment to resolving specific issues like the 'poor white' problem as well as providing theological and biblical justification for the policy of apartheid.[42] Its specific actions and its theological 'discoveries' offered solace to Afrikaners feeling threatened by the loss of their cultural distinctives and their uncertain economic situation.

The NGK's promotion of a stricter application of segregation emerged after an important event within the church. Johan du Plessis, a Stellenbosch theologian, was suspended by a high-level synodical committee in 1930 after a heresy trial. Du Plessis advocated a moderate stance on segregation policy, and while his racial views were not the basis of the charges, his expulsion did strengthen the neo-Kuyperian group within the NGK, and this promoted the elaboration of the 'theology of apartheid'.[43]

As mentioned in Chapter 2, various theological traditions existed within the NGK which corresponded to particular positions taken on church–state relations and race relations. During the 1930s and 1940s tensions emerged between the pragmatic missionary-minded evangelicals who had been influenced by Andrew Murray's work, and the more conservative, *volkskerk* Calvinists who were influenced by Abraham Kuyper's ideas.

The pietist strain within the NGK, associated with the work and thinking of Andrew Murray, emphasized righteous lifestyles, personal redemption, and the hope of salvation for all who could be saved through hearing the message of the Gospel. Pietist NGK clergy were increasingly alarmed in the 1930s and 1940s by certain NGK leaders who became more ideologically dogmatic over the years on race policy and who cooperated with Afrikaner nationalist leaders to develop a singular ethnic consciousness in the 1940s because they saw the church's responsibility as first and foremost, ministering to everyone's, not just Afrikaners' spiritual, and not necessarily social, needs.

Missionary-minded NGK evangelicals emerged out of this pietist tradition and promoted the belief that whites had to minister to the spiritual needs of black South Africans as well as whites. Some of these missionary-minded NGK clergy also took a pragmatic position on race policy, reacting against the 'theology of apartheid'. NGK leaders J. du Plessis, B.J. Marais, and A.H. Murray tried to remind others within the NGK that race policy needed to be applied with the 'native's' needs in mind. Segregation could never solve South Africa's race problems if the policy meant maintaining white superiority. A healthy public regard for Africans, benevolent guardianship, and the just application of laws were necessary for race policy to be carried out properly.[44]

Neo-Kuyperian Calvinists like J.C. Rooy, H.G. Stoker, and J.D. du Toit, based mainly within the *Gereformeerde Kerk*,[45] differed from the pragmatic pietist and missionary-minded evangelicals by emphasizing opposing themes, for example, divine election, common grace, God-willed diversity, and sphere sovereignty, derived from the ideas of the Dutch theologian and statesmen Abraham Kuyper.[46] Kuyper believed, first and foremost, that all of creation was under God's sovereignty. God created different spheres, like the family, associations, and the church, and each sphere was created for a specific purpose with a biblical norm that directed its activities. In addition, each sphere had its own authority or sovereignty that could not be encroached upon by the others. Society was seen as an organic whole of spheres, not as an aggregate of individuals. Another idea Kuyper promoted was the emphasis on diversity. Kuyper defended diversity at all levels of society against the uniformity promoted in an increasingly industrialized and commercialized modern world. Within the Netherlands, he upheld diversity through the implementation of policy that established separate schools and churches for distinct communities. Unity on this earth could only be attained *through* the recognition of diversity.

Neo-Kuyperian Calvinists within the NGK and GK adopted Kuyper's ideas of diversity and separate structural spheres in their explanation of racial and ethnic separation.[47] According to churchmen influenced by Kuyper, diversity was the norm defining the world. Different nations or peoples were willed by God and needed to maintain their separateness, otherwise this God-willed pluriformity of peoples would disappear. Kuyper's antipathy to modernism, liberalism, and equality also resonated with theologians who believed an industrialized, liberal society threatened their existence. Finally, his vision of a 'Christian-National' community found a nurturing home among clergy who were looking for a model to build South African society. F.J.M. Potgieter was one of many prominent NGK clergymen who devised the following neo-Calvinist framework of separation using neo-Kuyperian logic applied to the South African situation:

> If this presupposition is applied in our circumstances in this multiracial land, then it is quite clear that no-one can ever be a proponent of integration on the basis of the Scriptures. It would be a direct contradiction of the revealed will of God to plead for a commonality between Whites, Coloureds and Blacks .... It is now abundantly clear that God himself has ordained that the ... pluriformity of the peoples as well as that of the churches should continue to the consummation ... The true unity in all its glory and blessedness will be revealed for the first time in the glory kingdom.[48]

It should be noted in passing that another ideological influence on the NGK's development of a 'theology of apartheid' in the 1940s, working parallel to but sometimes clashing with Kuyperianism, was the secular, Germanic, neo-Fichtean ideas of romantic nationalism. The writings of J.G. Herder and J.G. Fichte glorified authoritarian nationalism and presented an idealized notion of the *volk* as an organic entity that was God-willed with a unique historical destiny. Afrikaner intellectuals like G. Cronje and N. Diederichs, who studied in Germany and were exposed to these ideas, brought neo-Fichtean ideology to South Africa in the 1930s.[49]

Neo-Kuyperian Calvinism and neo-Fichtean ideologies influenced the development of Christian-Nationalism, Afrikaner nationalism, and apartheid through their notions of culture, nation, sovereignty, and a host of other ideas. These ideas did not arise in a vacuum. They appealed to nationalists within the NGK who were trying to respond to the massive dislocation experienced by Afrikaners due to industrialization, the crisis in agriculture, the diminution of Afrikaner culture, the poverty of 'poor whites', and so forth. Leaders within the church were trying to understand the changes and provide Afrikaners with definitive strategies that would give them hope in dealing with the change that threatened their lives. More pointedly, due to the dislocation caused by urbanization and industrialization, the NGK contextualized its theology (the theology of apartheid) in ways that responded to the social and material fears of the Afrikaner people.

This leads to the third tradition within the NGK, namely, the *volkskerk* adherents who believed that the church needed to respond to the economic and social needs of the Afrikaners. *Volkskerk* predikants, like P.K. Albertyn, E.P. Groenewald, J.D. Kestell, D. Lategan, W. Nicol, and E.E. van Rooyen, were trained in the revivalist strain of Scottish Calvinists but influenced by neo-Kuyperianism. They responded to the social and material needs of the 'poor whites' within their midst because they believed that a vertical relationship with God demanded caring social relationships; thus, the church had to play a more active role in the lives of their *volk* who were suffering. These NGK leaders were committed to the cultural purity of the Afrikaner ethnic group, and they responded to the negative impact that anglicization, miscegenation, and/or poverty had on the lives of their laity. For example, the NGK's active involvement in the promotion of Christian-National education, the passage of anti-miscegenation laws, and the support for strict segregation combated the negative impacts of anglicization and poverty and kept the Afrikaans-speaking community alive and well. In the words of D.A. du Toit, an NGK theologian associated with Stellenbosch seminary,

> Physical survival was the goal. The long period of British imperialism, economic imperialism (after 1910), and the vast black continent. Between these powers (British and black), the Afrikaner did not want to languish ... It wasn't just a question of political survival but economic survival. So typically Afrikaner institutions were formed, you know, the FAK, Volkskas, Sanlam. All these things developed. It was very difficult for the DRC to be anything else but an Afrikaner church.[50]

By the 1940s, the NGK pragmatic evangelical position on race policy had become a minority position within the church, while a more 'purist' position, one advocating total apartheid, had grown in strength. The 'purists' within the NGK advocated an ideological stance on apartheid that included the total segregation of races in economic, political, and social realms which appealed to Afrikaners who were experiencing the threat of black encroachment and the continued domination of British culture. Many of the NGK 'purists' were *volkskerk* leaders who had been heavily influenced by neo-Kuyperian ideas. In fact, while it was possible to distinguish neo-Kuyperian Calvinists from *volkskerk* Calvinists within the NGK in the 1940s, it can be argued that they worked so closely in developing the 'theology of apartheid' that their commonalities outweighed their differences.

The tenets of the 'theology of apartheid' included the following: (1) Although the Bible upholds the unity of humanity in a spiritual sense, God purposefully divided humanity as a consequence of the fall. God allowed for the diversity of peoples, languages, and races (Genesis 11, Deuteronomy 32: 8, Acts 27: 26). (2) Since God willed diversity, humans must facilitate the continuation of separate nations. (3) The nation has a God-given structure and character, along with a divine mission which should be fulfilled.[51]

The NGK's 'purist' position on general race policy in this era of coexisting conflict was exhibited using the following logic. First, the NGK lamented the assimilation of nations that was occurring. The current race policy was too integrationist. Nations were losing their culture, language, and history. A new policy needed to be implemented that would halt this denationalization process. Second, the new policy needed to be a Christian one, based on ethical/normative principles, such as the development of one's nationality, self-determination, and fairness. Third, the policy of apartheid was the solution to South Africa's race problem. Apartheid would combat any equalization that was occurring in social, economic and political areas by separating the nations. It would also promote the survival and self-determination of all nations. Fourth, this policy was supported on historical, scriptural, and scientific grounds.

Examples of the 'theology of apartheid', in contrast to the political establishment's promotion of partial segregation, can be found throughout the era of coexisting conflict. Articles in church periodicals demonstrate the 'purist' NGK faction's call for stricter segregation or apartheid.[52] Purists argued that assimilation among races was occurring on a significant scale, thus, apartheid was needed. Strict segregation was 'fair' because it allowed each nation to reach its own goals of self-determination and development. Borrowing from Kuyperianism and romantic-nationalist ideology, the typical defense of strict segregation was expressed in the following words by J.G. Strydom, an NGK clergymen noted for using the word 'apartheid' in church circles for the first time,

> Assimilation means the two races shall become one, one in language, one in social areas and one in every way ... We speak of a Christian-national perspective and we believe that God willed separate nations and languages, and that the destruction of the welfare of these concerned nations does not serve well. Assimilation then is a superficial and also dangerous view ... [Differentiation] is not

oppressive. It recognizes the separate races and offers to each rights and privileges in the future but the differentiation and segregation are in the actual interests of both races.[53]

Official documents produced by the NGK also demonstrated the church's support for a stricter implementation of segregation. In 1935, the *Federale Raad van die Kerken* (FRK), a unitary body representing the various NGK white and black churches, adopted a 'Missionary Policy' produced by NGK clergy that signaled a decisive shift away from pragmatic understandings of segregation:

> The traditional fear among the Afrikaner of 'equalization' of black and white stems from his abhorrence of the idea of racial admixture and anything that may lead to it ... while the Church rejects social equality in the sense that the differences between races are negated in the normal run of things, the Church would like to promote social differentiation and spiritual or cultural segregation.[54]

This Missionary Policy clarified the NGK's position on equalization and introduced some of the key concepts that later crystallized into apartheid ideology. For example, 'The concept of nationalism was invoked for the first time in a Christian context and the burden of emphasis upon man as an individual was shifted towards man as part of a collective, organic unit.'[55] The church also supported the idea of racial separation on pragmatic and historical grounds.

Other reports and conferences throughout the 1940s promoted the NGK's ideological and biblical justification for apartheid. For example, at a 1944 *Volkskongres*, organized by the NGK and the FAK, the total separation of races, or apartheid, was promoted as the only policy that would solve South Africa's race problem. The resolutions of the congress included the adoption of apartheid for the interests of all cultural groups, the rejection of any policy that resulted in the denationalization of nations, and the maintenance of white rule so that guardianship could be continued.[56] J.D. du Toit, the Afrikaner poet and theologian, offered a speech that justified apartheid on scientific, scriptural, and historical grounds.[57] Du Toit began by arguing that the whole Bible demonstrated the biblical proof of apartheid. Numerous passages were cited as prooftexts, including Genesis 11, the Tower of Babel story, which 'proved' that God was the great Divine Separator. What God separated, no human should unite. Du Toit argued, like others at the congress, that apartheid was the most favorable race policy for South Africa because it would separate races, allowing each nation to develop to its full potential.

The NGK, as early as 1943, had approved the biblical basis of apartheid. At the Council of Dutch Reformed Churches in 1943, the following statement was made:

> This meeting took note of the increasing agitation for equality of colour and race in our country, but wants to point out that according to the Bible God actually called nations into existence (Gen 11:1–9; Acts 2: 6, 8, 11) each with its own language, history, Bible and Church, and that the salvation also for the native tribes in our country has to be sought in a sanctified self-respect and in a God-given national pride.[58]

The ideological and scriptural culmination of the NGK's race policy occurred in 1947 when E.P. Groenewald released the document 'Die Apartheid van die Nasies en Hul Roeping Teenoor Mekaar' (The Separation of the Nations and their Calling Concerning Each Other). Groenewald's report, submitted to the FRK, embraced total apartheid on scriptural grounds. It referenced all the 'theology of apartheid' tenets mentioned above, and it stated: 'Apartheid stretches over the whole area of people's lives ... The principle of apartheid between races and peoples, also separate missions and mission churches, is well maintained within Scripture. From the rich diversity of people which all together serve the Lord, may His name be brought further (Revelation 7: 9f.; Philippians 2: 9–11).'[59]

Other evidence of the NGK's involvement in the promotion of strict segregation exists in the records of the *Federale Sendingraad* (FSR), an organization formed in 1942 for the purpose of creating a unified missionary policy toward 'natives' among the various Dutch Reformed Churches but dominated by the NGK. The organization had dialogued with the state concerning native policy since its formation.[60] Throughout the 1940s, the Executive Commission of the FSR lobbied the state for specific legislation on mother-tongue instruction, separate residential areas, and the prohibition of mixed marriages. Dutch Reformed clergymen would meet with high-level governmental officials, including Smuts, Hertzog, and Minister of Native Affairs Major Piet van der Byl to discuss 'native policy'. Although their demands were not met instantaneously, NGK leaders were an effective lobbying voice for Afrikaner nationalist concerns.

Finally, the examination of specific policy issues like education or anti-miscegenation laws exposes the differing approaches to race relations and social policy between the factions dominating the NGK and the state.[61] In a book of this length, I am severely limited in my analysis of such issues, but these policy issues also bring attention to the NGK as a *volkskerk* and a prominent Afrikaner civil society institution responding to the social and economic needs of its laity, the Afrikaner people, in the 1940s.

For example, regarding education policy, the purist faction which dominated the NGK felt that the goal of black education was the production of controllable black laborers who would work for the benefit of whites *until* they could be educated to suit the needs of a black community separate from whites. The NGK believed that segregation in all areas of life could be supported theologically and biblically; this did not exclude the educational realm. In fact, the total separation of races in all spheres was beneficial to the development of all people-groups, preserving distinct cultures and customs.

More specifically, purists within the NGK in the 1930s and 1940s promoted the idea of Christian-National education, a particular form of education that included clear and stringent educational aims and goals for black and white instruction. Christian-National education sought the separate instruction of ethnic groups for the purpose of maintaining cultural standards. The ideological basis of Christian-National education allowed Afrikaners to maintain their ethnic purity within the domains of a society facing unrest and race-mixing as a result of rapid industrialization and urbanization; it also helped to combat the threats Afrikaners faced from educated, skilled blacks; finally, it countered the anglicized system of education administered by the state.

The UP-dominated state, in contrast, advocated a more moderate, less ideologically-based opinion concerning the aim and scope of education than the NGK in these years because it promoted the interests of financiers and industrialists who demanded an educated, cheap black labor force that could handle semi-skilled and unskilled jobs. The goal of black education was the production of a responsible labor force which could provide for the needs of an industrialized society. Leaders within the state acknowledged that while churches had done a lot of good for Africans by providing their education, denominational bickering had resulted. A more inclusive Christian curriculum needed to be implemented. Moreover, the educational curricula should be suited to African environments until the time when Africans could be assimilated into European environments. The UP-dominated state's positions regarding education presumed not only that blacks were inadequately trained, but also that they should be taught the appropriate work ethic and attitude that accommodated economic development. The state's education policy coalesced with its perspective of partial segregation.[62]

If one compares the aims of NGK Christian-National education and state education in the 1930s and 1940s, both perspectives sought to develop a system where blacks would be responsible citizens within society. Both educational views were paternalistic and racist, and both the NGK and the state supported policies that affirmed the division between classes and color. However, clear tensions existed between the two perspectives. The NGK perceived the state as too liberal, integrationist, and humanistic. The state did not take segregationist education as seriously as Afrikaner nationalists, who were trying to safeguard the livelihood of their *volk*. The state was viewed as insensitive to the needs of the Afrikaner people. Meanwhile, the state looked at the NGK's vision of Christian-Nationalism as too extremist and impractical for the political and economic interests of South African society. These differences were at the root of the situation of coexisting conflict between the NGK and the state.

In sum, through the influence of neo-Kuyperian and neo-Fichtean ideas, NGK *volkskerk* leaders promoted a 'theology of apartheid' within Afrikaner society. Although pragmatic evangelicals existed within the NGK, they were not influential enough to halt the purist NGK group's pursuit of stricter segregation. The NGK's purist perspective on race policy from 1934 to 1947 entailed the belief that the extensive segregation of races was not only practical, it was biblically and theologically supported. This perspective clearly clashed with the state's support for accommodationist or tempered segregation.

CONCLUSION

This chapter argues that the situation of coexisting conflict defined NGK–state relations between 1934 to 1947. When analyzing general race policy and education policy, the real and perceived differences between the factions dominating the NGK and the state led to growing conflict. The NGK, dominated by a purist faction, grew increasingly intolerant of the UP-dominated state during the 1934 to 1947 era because the accommodationist form of segregation promoted political and economic goals that did not incorporate the interests of nationalist Afrikaners to the degree that it desired. While dominant factions in both the NGK and the state promoted segregationist legislation aimed at reproducing a cheap labor force, the NGK promoted a stricter view of segregation than the state because its ideological message appealed to Afrikaners who felt threatened by black encroachment and the domination of English-speakers.

This era of church–state relations substantiates an important finding related to state–civil society literature. Civil society institutions operate differently in non-democratic environments, in this case, a racially exclusive parliamentarian democracy. An active, vibrant civil society did exist in South Africa from the 1930s through the 1940s, with the NGK as one such example of a civil society institution, joining other civil society spheres and associations like trade unions, the family, and voluntary associations, but the NGK mobilized and promoted interests for Afrikaners specifically, not whites in general, to the detriment of the black majority and general societal reform. The era of coexisting conflict, however, did not last long. The following chapter will explore the relationship of mutual engagement which existed between the state and the NGK from 1948 to 1961.

4 NGK–State Relations during Apartheid's Early Years (1948–61)

The election of 1948 marked the beginning of National Party rule. From the late 1940s to the 1980s, the NP steadily increased its control over the state and developed and implemented the policy of apartheid.[1] The NGK was an important civil society institution that justified the development and consolidation of apartheid. NGK–state relations during the early years of apartheid were those of mutual engagement.

From 1948 to 1961 leaders dominating the NGK and the state held similar opinions on the majority of policy issues. Most of the time, the NGK leaders gave their unequivocal support to the state; however, situations arose periodically where the groups dominating the state and the NGK arrived at different opinions concerning strategies related to race policy. More specifically, church and state officials interacted closely and even held the same goal of Afrikaner supremacy in political and economic spheres, but they formulated independent policies on *how* to achieve this goal. The reason for discrepancies between NGK–state strategies lies in the factions that existed within Afrikanerdom which developed in relation to the political-economic environment.[2]

POLITICAL-ECONOMIC ENVIRONMENT DURING APARTHEID'S EARLY YEARS (1948–61)

The implementation of apartheid helped define the political-economic environment of South Africa from 1948 to 1961. Earlier chapters have already provided details on the origin and ideology of apartheid. In essence, apartheid was based on the dogmatic notion of cultural separation, and much of its ideology rested on romantic nationalism and Kuyperian Calvinism. Apartheid was supposed to replace the haphazard implementation of segregation policy in the early 1940s with a more coherent race policy. Apartheid policy can be

76

classified into three broad areas: economic or labor regulations, communal apartheid, and political control.[3]

Apartheid policy directed at labor control was concerned with the supply and regulation of labor to agriculture, mining, and industrial sectors.[4] In the first decade of the NP's rule, South Africa experienced considerable economic growth. The introduction of import controls expanded local manufacturing, decreased the trade deficit, and led to increased profits for domestic industry. Dan O'Meara notes that 'Under the governance of this "anti-capitalist" regime, the South African economy grew more quickly than any other capitalist economy except Japan during the 1950s and 1960s ... Between 1948 and 1957, real GDP increased at an annual average of over 5 percent.'[5] The NP government's immediate concern in this time of economic growth was the supply of cheap labor to different economic sectors without relaxing segregation measures, the 'error' of the UP in the 1940s. However, Africans continued to stream into urban areas as the economy grew, threatening white security, challenging white workers, and leaving white farms. The NP responded by tightening pass controls and residential requirements.

In 1952, the state required everybody to carry reference books. Control over migrant and permanent laborers was tightened as the state forced Africans to acquire work permits in urban areas. The enforced pass system appeased some white farmers because it halted the flow of black laborers to the cities. Farmers' interests were also met through the establishment of labor bureaus in 1951 which allocated labor according to the needs of the different economic sectors. Commercial farmers were not the only beneficiaries of tightened labor controls. White workers were also appeased by the prohibitions placed on African strikes (Native Labour Act of 1953) and the extension of job color bars (Industrial Conciliation Act of 1956).

African workers were also controlled through residential requirements. The Native Laws Amendment Act of 1952 placed restrictions on African residence in urban areas. Section 10 of the Native Laws Act, for example, limited residence to Africans born and raised in a town for at least 15 years, who had worked in the city for 15 years, or who had worked with a single employer for ten years. The most serious implication of this law was its creation of a distinction between migrant labor and permanent urban residents. The NP's goal was the gradual flow of 'detribalized' Africans into manufacturing sectors, with migrant labor supplying the labor for mining activities. Over time, the homelands were expected to produce enough jobs so that

Africans could start moving away from the cities back to the reserves. Through the implementation of these labor controls,[6] the state went out of its way to help meet the needs of entrepreneurs, white workers, and commercial farmers.

Although labor laws constituted an important set of apartheid laws, communal apartheid laws also changed the political terrain of South Africa. According to the apartheid state's philosophy, the different races needed to be separated to maintain white and black cultural standards. After 1948, the Nationalist government committed itself to the compartmentalization of races. The Population Registration Act of 1950, for example, classified each South African into a specified race group, namely, 'native', 'Coloured', Asian or white. Racial divisions were also pursued through the Mixed Marriages (1949) and Immorality (1950) Acts which prohibited interracial marriages and sexual intercourse between the races. One of the most far-reaching communal acts of apartheid was the Group Areas Act of 1950 which codified residential segregation. Residential segregation occurred long before 1950, but the Group Areas Act extended residential segregation to 'Coloureds' and Indians, and it also carried with it forced removals.

The final group of apartheid laws dealt with political affairs. The NP was committed to the monopoly of political power by whites. Blacks could not be permitted common citizenship rights because they were 'uncivilized'. Even if they were 'civilized', African concerns were of a distinct nature from white concerns. The different ethnic groups, the NP argued, should experience political rule according to their unique development. Soon after assuming the mantle of power in 1948, the NP abolished the Natives Representative Council. The Natives Representation Act of 1936 was replaced with the Bantu Authorities Act of 1951, based on the idea that African interests would be represented by local authorities in the designated reserves. The monopolization of white power was attained in 1956 after 'Coloureds' were removed from the voters' roll in a lengthy battle that involved the National Party packing the Senate and the Appeals Court so they were disposed to NP sentiments. Political control was also enforced on black civil society through the 1950 Suppression of Communism Act and the 1953 Criminal Law Amendment Act, which prescribed heavy penalties on individuals who 'agitated' against the state.

Despite the harshness of these laws, I argue, based on Posel's work, that the first decade of NP rule was characterized by an *ad hoc* implementation of 'total' apartheid. In some areas, the NP clearly specified the distinct separation of races or cultures, for example, population registration, separate amenities, and residential segregation. In other areas, the NP's efforts at implementing total apartheid were more haphazard, namely, in the regulation of labor and the slowing of African urbanization. Apartheid policy in the first decade of NP rule was more 'practical' than 'total', in part, because economic realities helped determine its implementation. Influx control, color bars, and labor bureaus were relaxed if employers demanded more workers. The implementation of 'full-scale' or total apartheid was *attempted* in the 1960s under H.F. Verwoerd, but not under the rule of the first two NP leaders, D.F. Malan (1948–54) and J.G. Strijdom (1954–8).

Another important aspect of NP rule, which differed from the UP government that preceded it, was the instrumental appeasement of Afrikaner nationalist interests.[7] As mentioned in Chapter 3, the NP was rejuvenated and came to power in the 1940s because of its successful efforts at mobilizing Afrikaners from a variety of classes and regional areas around the ideas embodied within Afrikaner nationalism that were formulated by professional and intellectual leaders associated with organizations such as the Afrikaner Broederbond. Afrikaners, threatened by the loss of ethnic purity and economic competition related to urbanization, were attracted to the NP because it promised to meet their needs through the policy of apartheid.

The NP-dominated state did prioritize Afrikaner economic interests, for example, selecting tariff protections for national firms, awarding government contracts to Afrikaner businesses, and appointing Afrikaners to executive boards (SABC, ISCOR).[8] As a result, Sanlam, *Volkskas*, and *Rembrandt* grew rapidly, reaching a competitive level with English-speaking controlled businesses by the 1960s. Positions were also created for Afrikaners in the judiciary, the civil service, and the military. Finally, Afrikaner farmers and white workers benefited economically because of tighter influx controls and job reservations. By the 1960s Afrikaners had begun to close the economic gap with English-speakers in private income and share of business capital. Throughout the first two decades of NP rule, then, Afrikaner nationalist goals concerning the attainment of an 'Afrikaner capitalism' were achieved.

The dominance of Afrikaner interests and the massive restructuring of South African society took a heavy toll on the majority of South Africans. Immense suffering, grinding poverty, and disrupted family life resulted for blacks as apartheid laws were implemented. Popular protest against apartheid laws increased considerably throughout the 1950s.[9] In 1949 the ANC adopted the 'Programme of Action' in an effort to resist legal discrimination. This program advocated peaceful, persistent tactics, including boycotts, strikes, and stayaways, that went beyond the negotiating tactics of the earlier years. The ANC also demanded that blacks receive the right of self-determination, and it denounced white domination. In 1952 the South African Communist Party and the ANC launched the Defiance Campaign, a program of mass action against the government's discriminatory legislation. Black protest, ranging from boycotts and strikes to non-cooperation with the authorities, was embarked upon enthusiastically. The government responded harshly. It had arrested over 8000 people by the end of 1952, and the Defiance Campaign ceased when the government banned meetings and arrested leaders of the movement. Mass action was suppressed momentarily, but throughout the 1950s, sustained campaigns were organized by the ANC against forced removals, pass laws, Bantu education, and rural policy.

In the 1950s, however, the ANC was challenged by groups that wanted it to adopt an Africanist or materialist approach. Organizations like the Non-European Unity Movement (NEUM) dismissed the ANC because it felt the ANC catered to bourgeois interests.[10] NEUM argued the ANC rejected the working class and glorified racial differences. Other leaders felt the ANC understated racial differences. It tried too hard to be multiracial or even non-racial, and needed to adopt an Africanist approach, rejecting all connections to non-African organizations.[11]

The 1955 Kliptown meeting, which drafted the Freedom Charter, cemented the ANC's adoption of a non-racial approach. Delegates from a variety of African and non-African organizations attended the meeting, and 'Charterism' became the basis of ANC policy from this point forward. Charterism advocated a democratic, non-racial South Africa that was committed to significant economic and social change. The ANC was hardly the most radical organization in the 1950s, but it was the most powerful. After Kliptown, the government arrested many of the leaders who participated in formulating the Freedom Charter. The lengthy treason trial that ensued demonstrated the state's desire to crush any resistance to white dominance and economic security.

Although South Africa was beginning to attract the attention of foreign governments because of its actions against the black majority, international pressure on South Africa to abolish its apartheid policy was moderate in the 1950s. Like the preceding era, South Africa's race policies were not condemned because of the persistence of US segregation and Western colonial practices. Additionally, the Western superpowers maintained profitable business interests in the country. The political climate and economic interests in the West were not conducive to demanding radical reform in South Africa; this allowed the South African state to continue implementing its apartheid policy.[12]

This dynamic and uncertain political-economic environment within South Africa led to a situation of mutual engagement between the NGK and the NP-dominated state. The next section lays the groundwork for understanding the situation of mutual engagement within the first 12 years of apartheid's rule by describing the differences among factions within the NGK and the state over the direction of race policy.

DIVERSITY OF PERSPECTIVES ON RACE POLICY WITHIN THE NGK AND THE STATE

A relationship of mutual engagement between the state and a civil society institution assumes that the leaders or groups dominating each entity hold similar opinions on the majority of policy issues. Most of the time, the civil society institution supports the policies implemented by the state. However, situations arise periodically where the leaders or groups dominating the state and the civil society institution arrive at different opinions concerning policy directions and strategies. One would assume, due to the sociological makeup of the NP and the NGK, that from 1948 to 1961 the NGK would wholeheartedly support, if not collaborate with, the NP-dominated state's policy directives. In reality, while church and political leaders interacted closely and generally held the same goal of Afrikaner supremacy in political and economic spheres, they formulated independent policies on how to achieve this goal in the early years of apartheid. The reason for discrepancies between NGK–state strategies on race policy lies in the presence of different factions that dominated the NGK and the political establishment.

As previously mentioned, one of the common misperceptions regarding apartheid policy is the notion of a linear, systematic, 'grand plan' of apartheid.[13] It is believed that the Sauer Report, commissioned by the NP in the late 1940s to address the issue of race relations, contained the coherent strategy for implementing an 'apartheid blueprint' which led to the NP's electoral success in 1948. It would be more accurate to say that although Afrikaner nationalists believed firmly in the common goal of maintaining Afrikaner interests within

South Africa's political and economic spheres through the more thorough separation of races, they did not follow a cohesive apartheid plan in the first 12 years of apartheid's rule. Instead, various factions arose within the Afrikaner establishment to promote their own version of apartheid policy. Policy implementation was the result of compromises between different factions within Afrikaner nationalist camps, and the master plan of apartheid contained enough ambiguities to appeal to various groups within the Afrikaner nationalist alliance.[14] Briefly, what were the conflicting versions of apartheid policy that emerged within the Afrikaner establishment, but more specifically, the NGK and the state?

The political establishment contained a variety of factions concerning the conception of apartheid policy including accommodationist segregationists (a group defined in Chapter 3), ideological purists, *baasskap* adherents, and purist sympathizers.[15] Ideological or visionary purists promoted the idea of total apartheid or 'vertical' separation in political, economic, and social spheres. Purists, encouraged by the thinking that evolved out of the South African Bureau of Racial Affairs (SABRA), an Afrikaner thinktank established in 1947 to investigate South Africa's race relations, were especially concerned with Afrikaner nationalists who were not convinced of the disadvantages of 'economic integration'. Economic integration was dangerous because (a) it led to the 'detribalization' of Africans, thus, eroding their ethnic or tribal culture; and (b) it caused white dependence on African labor, which endangered economic prosperity in the long run if Africans withdrew from the labor force. The goal for purists was national self-sufficiency in all areas so that white supremacy in political and economic sectors could be achieved. To that end, purists called for the development of 'native' reserves, the establishment of separate political institutions for Africans and whites, and the development of 'Bantu education'. NP leaders who sympathized with the notions of 'vertical apartheid' were M.D.C. (Daan) de Wet Nel, a founding member of SABRA and later appointed as the Minister of Bantu Affairs, and W.W.M. Eiselen, a university professor and also a founding member of SABRA who was appointed Secretary of Native Affairs in 1951. A. van Schalkwyk, a member of the South African Bureau of Racial Affairs, exemplified the ideological purist perspective at a SABRA conference in the following words:

> In conclusion let us say that the only alternative is the policy of eventual total separation, apartheid, or self-sufficient development

of the different race groups … The asserted objections, namely, that it is practically impossible to implement the policy, come down to two insurmountable obstacles which block the path of implementation, viz. the availability of enough land for natives, and the elimination of native labor from the white economy. This will mean from the people dreadful economic losses and it will require great sacrifice …[16]

White *baasskap* (domination) adherents were a dominant group within the NP and state institutions. Like ideological purists, they believed that segregation had to be applied in a more coherent, systematic manner than during the previous Fusion government. Moreover, the Afrikaners' political and economic control had to be consolidated within a racially segregated society, but for *baasskap* adherents this meant privileging Afrikaners in the civil service and the business world, protecting Afrikaner culture, and controlling African labor so that the economic gains of Afrikaners could be maintained without encouraging racial mixing. It did not entail the promotion of economic segregation. *Baasskap* adherents were also concerned with racial ordering and ethnic purity. Whites were superior to or the guardians of blacks, who were not yet civilized. Apartheid policy needed to abolish mixed marriages, segregate entertainment centers, remove the 'Coloured' vote from the common roll in the Cape, and so forth. Adherents of white *baasskap*, or horizontal segregation, included J.G. Strijdom, Prime Minister from 1954 to 1958 and C.R. Swart, Minister of Justice under Malan, Strijdom, and Verwoerd.

The third significant group within the NP-dominated state were the purist sympathizers like H.F. Verwoerd. Verwoerd intended to systematically implement apartheid policy, and while he served as Minister of Native Affairs (1950–8) and Prime Minister of South Africa (1958–66), he committed himself to the construction of 'Grand Apartheid', that is, the state would increase its control over all areas of life concerning racial segregation, including the organization of urban and rural areas, the regulation of labor, and restrictions on social integration. H.F. Verwoerd sympathized with the ideas behind 'vertical' separation because they represented the long-term hope for South Africa; however, when it came to the practical implementation of apartheid in areas like influx control, Verwoerd allowed for economic interdependence to satisfy industrial or manufacturing interests.

The NGK also contained a variety of groups regarding the conception and implementation of race policy in the early years of apartheid, but two stand out – the ideological purists and the moderate pragmatists. NGK leaders inclined toward a purist perspective included E.P. Groenewald, Professor of Theology at the University of Pretoria, W. Nicol, Moderator of the Transvaal Synod, F.J.M. Potgieter, a Dogmatics professor at Stellenbosch, C.B. Brink, Moderator of the NGK Transvaal Synod, G.B.A. Gerdener, Member of the Federal Missionary Council, and W. Landman, Member of the Federal Missionary Council and Secretary of the Cape NGK Synod. Important differences surfaced among the 'purists' with some individuals, including Brink and Gerdener, trained in the missionary-evangelical tradition of the NGK and associated with SABRA, far more sensitive to the possibility of cultural development and the 'equality of peoples through separation' than others. But the majority of purists within the NGK advocated the 'positive' notion of separation in all areas of life based on scriptural norms and theological principles. They sought 'equitable' separation, that is, differences in race and culture had to be respected to the point where development could be pursued to its ultimate end by all cultures. The 'purists' were *volkskerk* or neo-Kuyperian inspired adherents who felt that the diversity of nations and peoples was willed by God and needed to be maintained. These NGK leaders were committed to the cultural purity of the Afrikaner ethnic group, and they continued to respond to the negative impact that urbanization, miscegenation, and/or poverty had on the lives of people, but mainly Arikaners.

Moderate pragmatists in the NGK, on the other hand, resisted the 'vertical' separation espoused by purists because they were not convinced of its biblical and theological foundations. The Bible did not endorse apartheid nor did the Christian church at any time in its history subscribe to the specific principles of apartheid. NGK pragmatists like B.B. Keet, a leader within the Cape Synod, and B.J. Marais, a Professor in Church History at the University of Pretoria, agreed with purists that social and political apartheid needed to be implemented, but they disagreed on the reasons behind such policies. Purists, for examples, felt total apartheid was willed by God and/or it led to the national upliftment of all races. Pragmatists argued that political and social apartheid was the best solution for South Africa *for the time* because of South Africa's multinational status; however, apartheid could be removed in the future if circumstances allowed for it.[17] B.B. Keet, a NGK theologian, expressed the moderate pragmatist perspective at an interdenominational conference in 1953 in the following words:

With us in South Africa the danger is that we forget the unity and emphasize the diversity in such a manner that we cannot see it as anything but apartheid-segregation. Personally, I believe that our brethren who want to maintain apartheid on biblical grounds are labouring under this misunderstanding ... Of course, there are certain practical circumstances which may stand in the way of a full realization of Christian unity such as geographical factors, language, and culture ... Under present circumstances, apartheid cannot be unreservedly condemned ... but this is no proof that it is the ideal or that there is nothing better. What may seem satisfactory in practice today, may be detrimental under changed circumstances tomorrow, and circumstances are changing rapidly.[18]

Pragmatists within the NGK also diverged from *volkskerk* purists in responding to the interests of all South Africans, not just Afrikaners. In B.B. Keet's words,

Surely, the Gospel ... as founded on the compassion of Him who gave His life for all peoples and nations, cannot be inhumane. To love God above all, and your neighbor as yourself – on these two commandments hand all the Law and Prophets. Of a truth there is no way to God that bypasses my neighbor.[19]

These individuals were often drawn to the need for 'healthy' race relations between and among all South Africans rather than the need for maintaining Afrikaner racial domination.

Because of the different factions dominating the NGK and the NP-dominated state concerning the conception of race policy, both entities formulated distinct racial policies. From 1948 to 1958, during the early years of the era of mutual engagement, the NGK's official position entailed an adherence to a more purist position on race policy than the leaders dominating the political establishment. From 1958 to 1961, the NGK's pragmatic faction arose which challenged the state leader's adoption of a more purist race policy.

THE NGK–STATE ERA OF MUTUAL ENGAGEMENT BETWEEN 1948 AND 1961

D.F. Malan and J.G. Strijdom were the two Prime Ministers of South Africa during the early years of apartheid's implementation. The fact that the political establishment did not embrace 'vertical' separation, but instead adopted a form of white *baasskap*, was in part due to their positions on race policy.

D.F. Malan's political career began long before 1948.[20] He was the leader of the Cape NP from 1914 to 1953 and a Cabinet Minister under J.B.M. Hertzog from 1924 to 1934 before taking over the leadership of the GNP/HNP for the remainder of the 1930s and 1940s. His involvement in politics was dominated by issues involving South Africa's relationship with Britain, Afrikaner rights, provincial NP politics, and English-speaking–Afrikaner relations rather than race.

Malan's views on race policy were not as thorough or coherent as other leaders within the NP because he did not see himself as an expert on race issues. He had always believed in segregation as the most correct, just policy for South Africa. Although Malan exploited the UP's divisions over race policy in the 1940s by promoting the policy of apartheid as a more coherent, systematic implementation of segregation, he, in fact, believed that apartheid was not substantively different than traditional segregation. It did not entail the total separation of races into political, economic, and social arenas; instead, Malan 'envisaged local segregation in which inequality would be firmly maintained in all interracial dealings'.[21] Malan believed that if total apartheid were implemented, South Africa's economy would suffer.

Malan's 'underdeveloped' views on race policy allowed him to accommodate more liberally-minded groups and hardline purists within the government. For example, D.F. Malan's first Minister of Native Affairs was E.G. Jansen, an NP leader who had little sympathy for total apartheid and who was supported by UP members. NP hardliners in the parliamentary caucus were not enthusiastic about Jansen. They were incensed when they heard that Jansen 'was seriously considering giving property rights to urban Africans, in total violation of NP policy'.[22] Despite the dissatisfaction of hardliners, Malan took no actions to replace Jansen, nor did he try to remove the moderate Minister of Social Welfare, Dr A.J. Stals. Malan finally replaced Jansen with H.F. Verwoerd, a purist sympathizer, after Jansen moved to the office of Governor-General. Verwoerd's appointment changed the direction of the government's policy implementation as Verwoerd presented policies that implied the arrival of 'Grand Apartheid'.

In many ways, Malan's ideas on race policy reflected the ambiguity of apartheid as presented in the Sauer Report. Malan's ideas on race policy were shaped by the idea that while total apartheid might be the long-term objective, such an end goal had to be implemented gradually to thwart economic disruptions. As discussed in the first section of this chapter, the NP government under Malan (and Strijdom) closed the 'loopholes' of the segregation in the early 1950s regarding societal race-mixing, African political representation, and African urbanization; however, it did not support total apartheid because of economic concerns.

The state leadership's adoption of a form of white *baasskap* contrasted with the NGK's official position on apartheid in the years between 1948 and 1958. However, it should be pointed out that the overriding essence of the relationship between church and state in these years was a high amount of cooperation. Church and state both pursued the interests of economic security and Afrikaner ethnic purity. In 1948, soon after national elections, the NGK's *Kerkbode* editorial of September 22 declared that apartheid was a church policy, pointing to the long NGK tradition of race separation in the church.[23] The NGK also pledged its support for the government in its implementation of apartheid policy.

Many of the laws that the National Party implemented in its first decades were welcomed by the NGK as confirmation that racial separation would be maintained in social and political realms. These laws included the Mixed Marriages and Immorality Acts (1949–50), the Group Areas Act (1950), and separate amenities acts. In fact, the church had lobbied specifically for many of these laws prior to 1948.[24] According to Nico Smith, former NGK minister and currently a professor of theology at UNISA:

> The NGK in the 1930s already said South Africa needed laws against mixed marriages. Why? The church saw that more and more Afrikaner men were marrying black women. And they said this is against the Bible, and you are a chosen people, etc. They also started to say that the Afrikaner is a Christian-National, and so we need certain schools that exclude blacks. Very few of the laws that were implemented in 1948 weren't already asked for by the NGK before that.[25]

Although the NGK supported the NP-dominated state in the early years of apartheid, it also maintained its independence regarding its position on the direction of apartheid policy. Ideological purists dominated the NGK's thinking on race policy, providing the theological and biblical justification of apartheid during the era of mutual engagement. Purist NGK leaders sought sound and rational theological expositions of apartheid theory to 'strengthen' their case against pragmatists like B.B. Keet and Ben Marais who raised serious doubts about the biblical basis for apartheid. Numerous documents and conferences emerged that represent the purists' position regarding the 'native question' within the NGK, but two documents stand out.

In 1948, the Transvaal Synod, after a lengthy and heated discussion, accepted a report entitled *Racial and National Apartheid in the Bible* written by E.P. Groenewald. This report offered an ideological and scriptural justification of apartheid.[26] It argued that the total separation of races or apartheid was the only just policy for South Africa because God had ordained the diversity of humanity (Genesis 10, 11; Deuteronomy 32:8; Matthew 28:19; Acts 2:8ff). God willed that different people groups should live apart and maintain their cultural purity. Apartheid applied to political, social, and religious spheres. Finally, the document implied that the principle of Christian trusteeship had biblical foundations. As Israel cared for other nations, so the Afrikaners, the stronger nation, should devise policies that would improve the lives of non-whites, the weaker nations. The Transvaal Synod did not represent the entire NGK, but it did indicate the presence of a purist perspective on apartheid within an influential NGK synod.

The key NGK statement that represented the purist vision of apartheid was the 1950 Bloemfontein document drawn up by NGK delegates attending an interdenominational church conference organized by the *Federale Sendingraad* (FSR) of the NGK. The Bloemfontein document strove to replace the notion of racial inequality with the equality of nations. Christian trusteeship could be premised on the idea that all people were equal as nations, although not as individuals. It was still imperative for the more developed people-group to help the least developed, but the notion of racial inferiority had to be eradicated. The church's view of total apartheid or 'autogenous development' was clarified in the 1950 Bloemfontein resolutions in the following manner:

> The policy of autogenous development which we advocate ... is no static condition but dynamic in its separate development. It proposes a process of development which seeks to lead each population group to its purest and speediest autonomous destination under the hand of God's gracious providence. The policy is the means to an end, namely an independent status. It envisages the elimination of conflict and friction, of the unhealthy and unequal competition between the more and the less developed.[27]

This report not only laid out the general theory of 'autogenous development' (many church and state leaders interpreted this as separate development), it also addressed a wide range of issues including economics, education, social welfare, and politics. In general, it called for a long-term policy that established national homelands for the 'Bantu' population and promoted political, social, and economic segregation for whites and blacks in their own areas:

> The Conference felt that it was imperative that the reserves should be transformed into true national homes for the Bantu in which a healthy social and family life could be secured for the people ... In order to carry out our policy of separate development of the various race groups it would be necessary gradually to eliminate the Bantu from European industrial life. He should rather be integrated into a new industrial system to be developed in the native areas ... The conference expressly holds that politically the Bantu should gradually be given the opportunity of self-government in his own territory, and of managing his own affairs.[28]

The Bloemfontein document stands alone among NGK documents because it developed, in Johann Kinghorn's words, 'an intricate theological edifice in support of their perception of apartheid. What emerged was: *the theology of humanity as equal because of separation*'.[29] The NGK coined the term 'distinctive or separate development' as the preferred term to apartheid at this congress. Separate or autogenous development meant a more thorough, vertical form of apartheid than previous notions of apartheid.

The Bloemfontein resolutions were not welcomed by the government. Immediately after the conference, a delegation of NGK clergy met Jansen and Eiselen to discuss the ideas within the Bloemfontein document. The NP leaders 'received the deputation warmly, but pointed out that the execution of the policy of apartheid is currently impractical, although it embraces a beautiful ideal'.[30] These state leaders argued, in essence, that apartheid needed to be implemented in a partial way because whites depended on a steady, black labor force. 'There are, however, earnest objections on the part of the Farmers and Industrialists that their Bantu-laborers will be reduced, where there is already a shortage. In the country itself there are not nearly enough whites to do the work.'[31] In addition, Prime Minister D.F. Malan rejected the idea of total apartheid, saying in Parliament that it was impractical, impossible to execute, and definitely not the policy of the National Party.[32]

The second Prime Minister of South Africa, J.G. Strijdom (1954–8), also rejected any possibility of 'total' apartheid being implemented.[33]

> We as a Government can only announce a policy and try to apply what is practicable and what will therefore be accepted by the country and by the majority of the electorate as they come to understand the implications of it and are then prepared to lend support to it. For that reason, as we have repeatedly stated very clearly in the past, we cannot in the present circumstances propagate or apply a policy of territorial apartheid.[34]

Strijdom believed in *baasskap* or horizontal segregation which contrasted the NGK's perspective of separate development. Strijdom felt whites should be the 'masters' over blacks:

> Call it paramountcy, *baasskap* or what you will, it is still domination. I am being as blunt as I can. I am making no excuses. Either the white man dominates or the black man takes over ... The only way the European can maintain supremacy is by domination ... And the only way they can maintain domination is by withholding the vote from non-Europeans. If it were not for that we would not be here in Parliament today.[35]

As mentioned in the first section of this chapter, Strijdom promoted policies that restricted the black vote and forbade socializing among the different races. He was also worried about policies that advanced African interests because they might erode the color line. In his words,

> If we allow the natives in their millions to settle among us and in our towns, and they gradually develop and become civilised, as must and will necessarily happen, I am convinced that the existing color line will slowly disappear and that equality will also slowly be established.[36]

He committed himself to maintaining the political and economic gains of whites by strengthening color bars and labor policies so that the numbers of urban Africans were controlled and 'poor whites' privileged.

One of Strijdom's closest ally's was H.F. Verwoerd, the Minister of Native Affairs. Verwoerd's position on race policy would appear, at first glance, to coincide with the NGK's official position because Verwoerd believed in the ideal of separate development. However, as a leader in the government in the early to mid-1950s, Verwoerd *implemented* a stricter form of 'horizontal' segregation. The details of his ideas and policy implementation will be explained below, but in essence, Verwoerd was a purist sympathizer whose positions on race were influenced by the visionary ideas of individuals within institutions like SABRA *and* the pragmatic needs of an Afrikaner populace that demanded the retention of their economic and political interests.

John Lazar describes the differences on the conception of race policy between SABRA and Verwoerd in the 1950s.[37] Although SABRA contained internal divisions, it continued to champion the idea of 'total' apartheid as the only long-term, moral solution to South Africa's race problems. SABRA members were dismayed at the implementation of apartheid during the first decade of NP rule because it perpetuated economic integration. Africans and whites had to be separated into self-sufficient socio-economic units. If whites continued to rely on cheap black labor, if whites continued to deny Africans a political future, if whites refused to develop African reserves, a semi-slavery among blacks would continue, eventually undermining the status of whites in South Africa as blacks agitated for political equality and change. The eventual separation of Africans and whites in all areas, that is, social, political, and economic, which could be enhanced through the development of African reserves, was at the root of total apartheid, as well as an emphasis on cultural, rather than racial, differences. Although visionary purists disagreed amongst themselves on how long it would take to implement apartheid, they agreed that total apartheid was the only moral solution for South Africa.

While Verwoerd was sympathetic to the ideas espoused by visionaries in SABRA, as Minister of Native Affairs he could not embrace them.[38] Because South Africa's economic situation hung in a tight balance, a short-term commitment to 'practical' policies was necessary until total apartheid could be implemented. Indeed, Department of Native Affairs reports in the 1950s contained no mention of total apartheid. There *was* a concerted effort to establish control over African urbanization through urban housing issues, township planning, and the establishment of effective labor bureaus,[39] but during Verwoerd's tenure as Minister of Native Affairs, minimal effort was made toward 'consolidating' African reserves. This was seen most dramatically in Verwoerd's less than enthusiastic reception of the Tomlinson Commission's Report, which offered a comprehensive plan concerning the development and consolidation of African reserves.

The Commission's conclusions urged the government to adopt the only real solution concerning race relations, that is, 'the separate development of European and Bantu'.[40] The Tomlinson Report recommended, among other things, that the government encourage farming in the homelands through better credit facilities, spend £104,000,000 over a period of ten years to make the reserves economically viable, and allow white industrialists into the reserves to spark industrial development. Verwoerd accepted the report in principle but rejected many of the Tomlinson Commission's specific suggestions. In part this was related to Verwoerd's belief that the commission was 'invading his territory'. The committee was established under the previous Minister of Native Affairs, E.G. Jansen, even though the idea originated with a colleague of Verwoerd's, M.D.C. de Wet Nel. More likely, Verwoerd did not appreciate the Tomlinson Commission's ideas because they clashed with the pragmatic interests represented by Afrikaner industrialists and farmers associated with institutions like AHI and SAAU which relied on African labor.

In sum, the three leaders dominating the South Africa state in the 1950s – Malan, Strijdom, and Verwoerd – dedicated themselves to tightening the segregation measures that had been relaxed in the 1940s. They supported the implementation of white *baasskap*, although they were cognizant of a visionary perspective concerning race policy's direction within their midst. They specifically responded to the interests of Afrikaner farmers and white workers by implementing stricter influx controls which limited the number of urban Africans and kept African laborers on the farms. Africans residing in the cities were viewed as temporary laborers who would eventually move back to the reserves where opportunities would attract them. At the same time, the government gave special preference to 'detribalized' Africans in urban areas who provided industrialists with a stable workforce. Influx controls were also relaxed in these years if industry owners demanded a steady supply of labor.

During the first decade of NP rule, then, NGK–state relations were those of mutual engagement. The leadership in both institutions believed that apartheid represented the most just and effective solution to South Africa's racial problems. However, they did not present identical ideas on race policy because different factions dominated the state and the church. In the state, purist sympathizers existed but *baasskap* adherents determined the actual implementation of apartheid policy. In the NGK, purists and pragmatists interacted and produced reports that combined and accommodated the ideas from within both groups, something that will be explored below, but the official position of the NGK supported 'vertical' apartheid or separate development, as noted in the Bloemfontein document. As a result, the two entities, while more similar than different on their positions concerning race, produced divergent conceptions of race policy. Divergent race policy pronouncements between the NGK and the state occurred from 1958 to 1961 as well, except the factions dominating each institution switched. The NP-dominated state adopted a more thorough, purist position on apartheid while the NGK briefly experimented with a more moderate, pragmatic position on apartheid. How did this 'factional switching' within the state and NGK arise?

By the end of the 1950s, apartheid was thoroughly entrenched into South African life. Influx control, shaped by the 1952 Native Laws Amendment Act and the 1955 Natives (Urban Areas) Amendment Act, controlled the movement and employment of African workers. The adoption of the Bantu Education Act in 1953, something that was promoted by Verwoerd, reproduced a cheap black labor force serving the economic security of whites while instilling in Africans a docile spirit through citizenship training and Christian-National principles. Additionally, the 'so-called Coloured franchise and parliamentary representation of Cape Africans had disappeared ... and the universities had been segregated'.[41] Many other apartheid laws were passed in the 1950s which aimed at furthering the separation of the races, but as much as apartheid policy furthered the political and economic interests of whites, some white South Africans by the late 1950s were expressing their concern that apartheid policy lacked a moral basis. Many Afrikaners, who witnessed the rising demands of African nationalists and the growing movement toward decolonization, realized that apartheid, which could easily be viewed as an openly racist policy, would not ease racial tensions.

Verwoerd responded in part to these concerns by adopting a new approach to apartheid a few months after assuming the position of Prime Minister. In May 1959, he announced the Promotion of Bantu Self-Government Bill which encompassed SABRA's more 'purist' vision of territorial (and economic) racial separation. The bill promised the elimination of African political influence in white areas, whether it was in Parliament or local councils. The bill also created a framework for eight (later enlarged to ten) territorial homelands, which would represent African ethnic groups. These homelands would be self-governing, but eventually they could achieve national independence.[42]

Through this bill, Verwoerd advocated the development of a long-term, comprehensive race policy, often referred to as separate development, to deal with race problems in South Africa. Instead of piecemeal, segregation policy based on the paternalistic idea of guardian–ward relations, separate development was a thorough extension of apartheid that accommodated the different national groups fairly.[43] The South African state could argue that its policy was not based on racial or biological differences, but national, cultural or ethnic differences, like other countries in the world.[44]

Verwoerd could also point to Acts that were devised prior to his premiership, namely, the 1951 Bantu Authorities Act and the 1956 Tomlinson Report, as legislation and reports that laid the foundation or contributed to the political blueprint for separate development. The Bantu Authorities Act sought to replace 'native' representation in Parliament with local authorities in reserves. The 1956 Tomlinson Report investigated the socio-economic condition of the reserves and their possibility for human self-sufficiency and recommended that farming in the homelands be given more opportunity for growth through better credit facilities, valuable crop plantation, and improved market opportunities.[45] Of course, as mentioned above, Verwoerd was not enthusiastic about the Tomlinson Commission's conclusions. Verwoerd did not adopt the Commission's recommendations concerning the development of the reserves or the idea that white living standards had to be lowered to make apartheid viable. However, by the 1960s, the government seemed to echo some of SABRA's concerns about economic integration. The government promised to control economic integration by reducing African urbanization, imposing labor quotas, promoting industrial decentralization to border areas, and developing the reserves.[46]

In sum, Verwoerd could now argue that the bantustan scheme, building on previous legislative Acts, provided a moral basis to apartheid by recognizing the independence and self-determination of 'Bantu' ethnic groups. This new apartheid vision emphasized ethnic identity, not race, and the possibility of each ethnic group realizing their potential through separation. The NP government was able to legitimize this policy, in part, on the ideology of separate development which was theologically justified by the NGK at the Bloemfontein Conference in 1950. The NP-dominated state's emphasis on ethnic identity and a theologically grounded justification in promoting the policy of separate development is evident in the opening remarks by M.D.C. de Wet Nel, Minister of Bantu Administration and

Development, in introducing the Bantu Self-Government Bill to Parliament:

> The first is that God has given a divine task and calling to every People [*volk*] in the world, which dare not be denied or destroyed by anyone. The second is that every People in the world of whatever race or color, just like every individual, has the inherent right to live and develop ... In the third place, it is our deep conviction that the personal and national ideals of every ethnic group can best be developed within its own national community ... This is the philosophical basis of the policy of Apartheid ... To our People this is not a mere abstraction which hangs in the air. It is a divine task which has to be implemented and fulfilled systematically.[47]

Verwoerd's shift from 'horizontal segregation' to 'positive' apartheid was rather dramatic. All throughout the 1950s, Verwoerd's ideas clashed with SABRA and other visionary purists which represented significant differences over the long-term development of 'native' reserves and the practical realization of 'vertical' apartheid.[48] What explains Verwoerd's 'conversion' to a purist formulation of apartheid in 1959?

It is important to point out that Verwoerd's promotion of the bantustan policy did not represent the adoption of a full-scale purist perspective; instead, Verwoerd accelerated the ideological interpretation of *baasskap* apartheid. Verwoerd's promotion of Bantu Self-Government Act continued to fall short of the expectations of supporters of total apartheid. The latter individuals wanted the government to commit itself to the consolidation and development of African reserves which would have involved improving the reserves through supporting agricultural development and establishing border or internal industries. The latter never occurred. Because the reserves were left to languish, supporters of total apartheid lessened their lobbying for separate development and called for consultation with 'Bantu' authorities and investigations into the lifestyles of urban Africans so government policy could alleviate the dissatisfaction and poverty of 'natives'. The new government under Verwoerd's leadership, in the meantime, justified *increased* oppression against urban Africans because they were viewed as 'foreign visitors to South Africa rather than mere "temporary sojourners"'.[49] White domination and control continued through Verwoerd's 'restructured' apartheid vision which assumed a more 'vertical' apartheid but in reality encompassed 'political separation superimposed upon economic and social inequality in an integrated society'.[50]

Despite the disjuncture between apartheid policy and practice, a number of circumstances led to Verwoerd's adoption of a more purist policy perspective on apartheid. First, Verwoerd's vision of apartheid was influenced by the rise of an economically and politically powerful group of Afrikaner intellectuals and professionals who let leaders like Verwoerd know that practical concessions to urban Africans were not necessary for South Africa's economic development.[51] Second, Verwoerd's apartheid shift was a deliberate response to political movements within and outside South Africa. The homelands policy was developed, in part, to contain the rise of African nationalism within South Africa, which was growing in strength because of the anti-colonial movement in Africa. In a 1965 speech to Parliament Verwoerd stated that it would have been preferable for 'old positions' on race policy to be maintained because they were much more comfortable, but changing world circumstances forced South Africa to replace *baasskap*.[52] Finally, Verwoerd could dare to make changes in a more purist direction by the late 1950s and 1960s because of sociological and political changes among Afrikaners. The NP had secured its power position by the early 1960s which alleviated the NP's need to make cautious, short-term policy that appeased Afrikaner capitalists, workers, and farmers.[53]

While Verwoerd was committed to and promoted separate development as a bulwark against internal unrest and international condemnation, the NGK experimented with a more moderate position on race policy between 1958 and 1961. From 1948 to 1958 the NGK's official position on race policy (i.e. separate development) was embodied within the Bloemfontein document. Throughout the first decade of apartheid, however, the NGK's outspoken, minority pragmatic faction sought to influence debates on race policy within the church. This led the NGK purist faction to accommodate the pragmatists on particular issues, for example, racially segregated church structures. The ability of the pragmatic faction to influence NGK debates on race policy peaked at the Cottesloe conference of 1960 where a definitive (but brief) shift toward a more moderate perspective on apartheid policy arose. If this perspective on race policy had been sustained within the NGK after Cottesloe, a situation of mutual disengagement would have arisen between the NGK and the state. Instead, the NGK moderates were quickly stifled by the state which interpreted its positions on race policy as a threat to the nation. Knowing how divergent the 'pragmatic' position on race policy was compared to the *baasskap* adherents or purist sympathizer positions on race policy within the state, how was it even possible for the pragmatic faction within the NGK to set the tone on race policy discussions?

Debates between moderate pragmatists and visionary purists were commonplace within the NGK throughout the 1950s. One could observe them mainly through reading church periodicals, but purists, who dominated NGK policy-making bodies, were also challenged by pragmatists at church conferences. For example, at a 1953 multiracial, interdenominational conference organized by the Federal Council of Dutch Reformed Churches to formulate Christian principles on mission policy, pragmatists questioned the NGK's official perspective on race policy.[54] B.B. Keet and B.J. Marais argued that while some form of racial separation was needed in South Africa and even within the churches for practical reasons, racial separation did not correspond to scriptural norms or theological ideals. In B.B. Keet's words, 'I am chiefly concerned with the Biblical grounds of the theological standpoint of my Church on race relations which I am convinced are wrong.'[55] In response, NGK purists F.J.M. Potgieter, C.B. Brink, and P.S.Z. Coetzee, argued that racial separation in society and in the church could be justified on scriptural principles and theological grounds. They argued that God placed boundaries and differences between nations and peoples, and there remained only one unity, namely, spiritual unity. The policy of integration was detrimental to the spiritual and national development of Africans, but the policy of apartheid meant that each people-group could develop separately and to the best of its ability without interference from other groups. Finally, purists responded to NGK moderates on the creation of separate churches by arguing that 1 Corinthians 12:14 and John 17: 21–2 made racially segregated churches 'not only permissible but essential'.[56]

In 1956, the NGK responded to its inability to present a 'united front' on separate church structures by producing a document that accommodated the different perspectives in the NGK. Although the report did not respond to the issue of general apartheid policy, it admitted that the NGK's policy of church apartheid was based on practical, not principled reasons; it stressed the idea of spiritual and practical unity; and it was more careful in its use of biblical passages justifying apartheid policy in the church. The report was premised on the idea that scriptural principles existed that supported the natural diversity of humanity within the overall understanding of spiritual unity. Thus, separate independent churches can and may exist without being contrary to the Word of God.

It is further necessary to have a clear conception of the institution-ary revelation of the Church. The co-existence of separate Churches resulting from doctrinal differences must be ascribed to our limited knowledge ... This, however, does not mean that the one true Church cannot be embodied in separate independent Churches ... The natural diversity and the different spheres of influence and relationships of authority which God has ordained are in no way broken down by this unity in Christ, but are rather restored and sanctified.[57]

From 1952 to 1958, the NGK's conception of general apartheid policy had not officially changed since the 1950 Bloemfontein confer-ence; however, differing positions among NGK leaders on issues like separate church structures were leading to an accommodation of purist and pragmatist positions. This outcome gave pragmatists an audible voice in the church which led to a noticeable break in NGK–state positions on race policy in the late 1950s when the NP-dominated state adopted a more purist approach.

In the late 1950s South Africa experienced an economic recession that caused rising dissatisfaction among the citizenry and aggravated social conditions in the townships. Even before the recession, blacks were experiencing frustration with the government's tightened apartheid policy.[58] From 1954 to 1956 Africans in Johannesburg organized a campaign against the government's efforts to destroy Sophiatown and relocate its people to Soweto. Pass campaigns and beer hall protests by the ANC's Women's League and the Federation of South African Women were also commonplace in the late 1950s. Finally, the period between 1956 and 1960 saw an increase in the level of rural protest, organized to resist the government's forced removals, pass laws, and the Bantu Authorities Act. One of the most significant developments in the late 1950s was the formation of the Pan African Congress (PAC).

In 1959 the PAC was formed as an alternative liberation movement to the ANC because it objected to the ANC's policy of multiracial alliances. On 31 March 1960, the PAC launched a massive anti-pass campaign. At Sharpeville a large crowd gathered near a police station to surrender their passbooks. The police panicked as the crowd swelled, opened fire on the unarmed protesters and killed 69 people. The Sharpeville massacre led to an international outcry against the South African government and widespread unrest within South Africa itself. General strikes, large-scale marches, stayaways, and boycotts became commonplace. The government responded with a ferocity unparalleled in its earlier years, arresting and detaining over 18 000 people. The government also announced a state of emergency and declared the ANC and the PAC illegal organizations on 8 April 1960.

While the majority of black South Africans criticized the government for its repressive activities after the massacre, nine NGK church leaders, while expressing sorrow about the massacre, condemned the 'agitators' who were stirring up disorder and lawlessness for political gain in the aftermath of the tragedy. These prominent NGK leaders also berated the press for viciously and inaccurately portraying the South African situation. They admitted that the South African government and churches had shortcomings concerning race relations, but they reiterated the NGK's support for separate development:

> The NGK has made it clear by its policy and by synod statements in the past that it can justify and approve of the policy of independent, distinctive development, provided it is carried out in a just and honourable way, without impairing or offending human dignity.[59]

The NGK remained committed to the South African state, but NGK leaders qualified separate development policy by saying it was acceptable, if it was implemented in a just, fair manner. The accommodation between pragmatists and purists in the NGK came to a fore at the December 1960 interdenominational conference convened by the World Council of Churches in Cottesloe.

The Cottesloe conference was aimed at resolving denominational disputes over race policy following the Sharpeville massacre. The NGK delegations from the two provincial synods (Transvaal and Cape) who were members of the WCC presented a report on race relations that became the foundation of the Cottesloe resolutions. The resolutions advocated a more moderate direction for South African society, owing in part to the fact that the document represented a broader ecumenical direction than just the Dutch Reformed perspective.[60] Among the resolutions, the document made no reference to a scriptural or theological justification for apartheid, it stressed the unity (not diversity) of believers, it condemned the government's refusal to grant Africans the right to participate politically or own land in areas where they settled, and it urged the government to take more care at equalizing wages and improving living conditions concerning blacks.[61]

The NGK delegates' general support for the Cottesloe resolutions was astonishing because many of the resolutions dealing with political rights, land rights, and labor controls for Africans were in direct conflict with Verwoerd's policy of separate development, and thus, previous NGK documents. The NGK delegates at Cottesloe had been persuaded by delegates from other churches within South Africa who argued that although in principle the 'policy of differentiation' could be defended on Christian grounds, the daily injustices it perpetrated had to be examined and replaced. The Cape and Transvaal NGK delegates' position at the Cottesloe conference also represented most clearly the rising influence of the moderate, pragmatic faction within the church.[62]

The Cottesloe resolutions and the NGK delegates' involvement with them were roundly denounced by the state and conservative churchmen. In his New Year's address, H.F. Verwoerd said: 'In fact, the churches have not yet spoken. The voice of the church was not heard and it shall be heard at the synods whereupon members as well as preachers shall be present.'[63] Verwoerd's denunciation of the Cottesloe resolutions was followed by similar criticisms made by purist NGK leaders who questioned the integrity and actions of the NGK Cottesloe delegates. Finally, the Afrikaner Broederbond actively resisted the Cottesloe resolutions because they were seen to be a threat to Afrikaner interests. Based on these negative reaction within the Afrikaner establishment, all the NGK synods rejected the Cottesloe resolutions within the next year. The Cape and Transvaal synods also withdrew their membership from the WCC.

The church's rejection of the Cottesloe resolutions returned the NGK to its former position on race policy and economic security. In a 1961 response to NGK members, conservative clergy announced their rejection of the Cottesloe resolutions and their 'wholehearted endorsement of the policy of our church which was formulated in previous synods from 1951–1958 ... a policy of differentiation or autonomous development, which stands upon the principle of Christian guardianship.'[64] This statement did not even offer a qualified position on apartheid's implementation. The church had been silenced effectively by the state not only to support white Afrikaner interests (which it had always done), but to follow its direction on apartheid's implementation.

In hindsight, the Cottesloe resolutions were ahead of their time. The particular makeup of the NGK delegations, the socio-political tensions following Sharpeville, and the independence of the Cottesloe conference explain well the 'moderate' nature of the NGK delegates' resolutions. One of the NGK delegates from the Transvaal synod,

Beyers Naudé, confirmed the fact that the members of the NGK delegation were some of the most progressive in the denomination:

> There were a number of then progressive theologians who were very much aware of what was coming in South Africa compared to the general church people ... We all felt the serious crisis in which South Africa found itself and we couldn't come up with half-baked solutions. We either had to state very clearly what our deepest convictions were in order to save the country from a racial war *or* we had to keep silent.[65]

Whatever the reasons explaining the 'progressive' nature of the Cottesloe resolutions, they were rejected by the Afrikaner establishment because they represented a rejection of the moral foundations of the state's separate development policy which was to achieve the goals of white supremacy and economic security. In fact, the state perceived the Cottesloe resolutions as even more radical, actually a precursor to the complete denunciation of apartheid policy, not just its direction or implementation. Pierre Rossouw, former information director of the NGK, told this story:

> The resolutions were rejected because the rethinking of Scripture had not yet started. And there was also reaction from Prime Minister Verwoerd. I was in his office, and I had a personal interview with him just after Cottesloe and before our synod. He told me, I can still see him sitting there. He told me 'A church–state confrontation is now looming in South Africa. And if it's going to happen, the state will lose.' He had no illusions. He knew if such a crisis emerged, they would lose. He was saying with that if the church had at that point in time stood firm, the whole apartheid policy would have to go and would have gone.[66]

The engagement between church and state could not be broken, according to Afrikaner nationalists like H.F. Verwoerd and conservative clergy, otherwise the goals of white supremacy and economic security would be lost in the long run. With the successful denunciation and rejection of the Cottesloe resolutions, these goals were maintained.

Another reason explaining why the Cottesloe resolutions were rejected by the state and the Afrikaner establishment is the preservation of the *volk*. The unity of Afrikaners in their pursuit of Afrikaner interests was the overriding, unquestioned pinnacle that held Afrikanerdom together. If the NGK synods had voted to support the Cottesloe resolutions, a split would have emerged within the Afrikaner establishment. Afrikaners would have had to choose between following a political direction that emphasized the development and interests of *all* peoples, but mainly whites, or a political direction that emphasized the development and interests of Afrikaners first and foremost. Purist state and NGK leaders knew that Afrikaner identity was central to the support for apartheid policy. In the words of C.B. Brink,

> Therefore, in order to remain faithful to his divine calling and to continue proclaiming the Gospel of God's love in Christ, the Afrikaner had to retain his identity. This obligation rested on him. He had to love himself, that which he had become through the grace of God, in order to able to love his neighbor. He had to separate himself in order to be a blessing to the millions of non-whites. Then he derived his apartheid idea.[67]

Rejecting the Cottesloe resolutions meant that the identity of Afrikaners in their pursuit of Afrikaner interests around apartheid policy could be maintained for a while longer. The NGK would continue to uphold the interests of the Afrikaner people, and it would continue to provide the moral support for the state's apartheid policy.

CONCLUSION

From 1948 to 1961 the NGK and the state exhibited a relationship of mutual engagement in which the two entities held similar opinions on the majority of policy issues. During this era, leaders within the state and the NGK were committed to the goals of the Afrikaners' maintenance of economic and political privilege. However, while the dominant groups within the NGK and the state cooperated with one another, they held slightly different views on the formulation of apartheid policy until 1961. From 1948 to 1958, the 'purist' faction dominated the NGK, leading to the NGK's adoption of separate development which contrasted to the state's *baasskap* position – a form of segregation that involved white domination within a racially segregated society. From 1958 to 1961, the pragmatic perspective on race policy was evident within the NGK which contrasted to the more purist position adopted by the state.

5 NGK–State Relations during Apartheid's Height (1962–78)

The successful attainment of Afrikaner nationalist goals, a relatively stable political-economic environment, and moderate external pressure set the context for a situation of collaboration between the NP-dominated state and the NGK in South Africa from 1962 to 1978. Collaboration assumes individuals, groups, or entities are working together in a combined intellectual, political, or social effort. During the era of collaboration, factions and individuals ruling the NP-dominated state and the NGK were committed to the maintenance of three socio-political goals: (a) white, mainly Afrikaner, dominance in the political and social arena, (b) economic prosperity through the protection of capitalist interests, and (c) the implementation of a racial policy that maintained ethnic purity and overcame the criticisms of 'negative' apartheid. As leaders within the NGK and the state collaborated with one another, the two entites' perspectives on race policy became almost indistinguishable, but it was the official leadership of the NGK which followed the 'state's' perspective on race policy because of the state's dominance and power.[1] The relationship of collaboration between a state and civil society institution is rare because it rests on a high level of official interaction and policy collusion. Before describing the political-economic environment that nurtured the era of collaboration, it is important to discuss the two major groups within the Afrikaner establishment that shaped this particular NGK–state relationship.

THE VERKRAMPTE–VERLIGTE SPLIT

From 1962 through to the early 1970s, and especially under H.F. Verwoerd's leadership, Afrikaner-based organizations appeared to be part of an unbreakable nationalist monolith. However, as in the preceding years, the Afrikaner establishment was composed of ideological, class, and political differences. In general, Afrikaner civil and political society could be characterized by the differences arising out of the *verligte* (enlightened) and *verkrampte* (conservative) groups within Afrikanerdom.[2]

In Dan O'Meara's words, *verligte/verkrampte* struggles within the NP, the AB, the Afrikaner press, and other Afrikaner nationalist institutions, 'essentially pitted those forces which sought to preserve the Afrikaner nationalist class alliance of 1948 – dominated by the interests of farmers and the petty bourgeoisie – against those who realised that in twenty years the social basis of Afrikaner nationalism had shifted profoundly.'[3] *Verkramptes* were traditionalists who wanted to return to a more glorified past concerning the Afrikaner people. They were wary of attempts by Afrikaner leaders in the NP to build a more inclusive white nationalism as a way to thwart the dominance of black South Africans. In terms of race relations, most *verkramptes* desired the return of white *baasskap* (domination) rather than separate development, although all *verkramptes* believed that apartheid policy had to be applied in a thorough, coherent manner. NP leaders who were associated with *verkrampte* positions during this era included M.C. Botha, the Minister of Bantu Administration, Dr Albert Hertzog, Cabinet Minister from 1958 to 1968, Jimmy Kruger, the Minister of Police in the 1970s, and Cornelius (Connie) Mulder, another Vorster Cabinet Minister.

Verligtes were much more comfortable with transforming 'Afrikaner nationalist ideology and politics to suit the changing social composition and material needs of the *volk*.'[4] They were willing to change the Afrikaner nationalist project in ways that recognized the commonalties among English-speaking and Afrikaner classes. *Verligtes* were also characterized by a greater flexibility to change or ease apartheid laws if this meant the improvement of race relations and the achievement of greater economic profits. In other words, *verligtes* believed that the differences between races were substantial and policies needed to be constructed to preserve the security of whites, but they supported a flexible and partial implementation of apartheid because this alone could maintain white privilege and economic growth.[5] Afrikaner leaders with *verligte* or more liberal leanings included Pieter J. Cillie, the editor of *Die Burger* from 1954 to 1977, Piet Gerhardus Jacobus Koornhof, NP parliamentarian from 1964 to 1972 and a Cabinet Minister under Vorster beginning in 1972, and Dr Anton Rupert, the founder of the Rembrandt Tobacco Corporation.

The *verligte/verkrampte* divisions were not the only ones that divided Afrikaners. Provincial differences remained, although they lessened over time; and numerous positions between *verligtes* and *verkramptes* existed. Moreover, some Afrikaner leaders defied such stark labels, among them, individuals like Verwoerd and Vorster. Verwoerd continued to be a purist sympathizer until his assassination in 1966. As mentioned in Chapter 4, H.F. Verwoerd promoted the ideas behind 'vertical' separation because separate development represented the long-term hope for South Africa. However when it came to the practical implementation of apartheid in areas like influx control, Verwoerd maintained the advantages (and disadvantages) of 'horizontal' apartheid to secure white interests. Despite the weaknesses in these labels, the *verligte/verkrampte* split among Afrikaners was the most definitive in this era and along with the political-economic environment of South Africa, they help situate the policies that emanated from the NP-dominated state.

THE STATE'S GENERAL POSITION ON RACE POLICY (1962–78)

From 1962 to 1978, the two Prime Ministers of South Africa – H.F. Verwoerd (1958–66) and B.J. Vorster (1966–78) – promoted distinct racial policies. Verwoerd, a purist sympathizer, continued to be associated with separate development, while Vorster, although committed to the ideals of separate development, ushered in the beginning of reform concerning race policy.

H.F. Verwoerd refused to relax apartheid measures after the Sharpeville massacre. In fact, he was more convinced than ever that the policy of separate development needed to be applied extensively in South Africa. Verwoerd actually opposed the implementation of separate development when he was Minister of Native Affairs through the 1950s on the basis of the policy being detrimental to South Africa's economic growth; however, a variety of circumstances, including rising black nationalism, international condemnation of the apartheid system, and the security of the NP's rein on power, led Verwoerd to advocate separate development. Separate development sounded like a more rational, non-racist policy than *baasskap* apartheid or segregation because it was based on the ultimate 'equality' of nations once they reached the status of full development. In other words, Verwoerd promoted the policy of separate development because it softened some of the moral objections to South Africa's racial policies.

The implementation of separate development became evident with the government's homelands policy – the creation of self-governing or independent 'Bantu territories' out of the existing reserves for the different African ethnic groups. The homelands served two governmental objectives. Economically, the homelands contained surplus black labor from white urban and rural areas. Industrial decentralization was intended to provide jobs for those living in the homelands and to attract Africans back to the homelands. The homelands policy coincided with the stricter enforcement of influx control and the attempt to remove Section 10 rights. It is important to note that although Verwoerd was committed to the political independence of the homelands, he never intended to make the homelands economically viable. There were no additional grants of lands to the homelands, and he discouraged the establishment of industries inside the homelands for fear of a radical African proletariat developing.[6] Only a small proportion of government sources were directed toward the genuine development of the Bantustans.

The homelands policy had a negative impact on South Africa's social and political foundations. First, the government forcibly removed Africans to homelands using the argument that industry and economic growth existed in the homelands. Approximately 3.5 million people were moved out of white areas to the homelands between 1960 and 1980, causing major hardships for families.[7] Second, the government created ethnic divisions along 'tribal' lines in an effort to persuade Africans that political independence was attainable for their ethnic group. By the early 1970s all Africans were designated citizens of 'Bantu' homelands. Political autonomy within the Bantustans occurred in 1963 when the first legislative assembly was set up in the Transkei. Self-government followed for the other homelands in 1971. South Africa granted the Transkei independence in 1976, Bophutatswana in 1977, Venda in 1979, and the Ciskei in 1981.[8]

One of the effects of the NP-dominated state's implementation of separate development was the increased stratification by race and class in occupational structures, income distribution, and population distribution. More pointedly, Verwoerd, who verbally committed himself to the goal of 'fair' separate development, in reality, encouraged governmental policies that imposed a rigidly hierarchical race system which oppressed blacks under white control. Apartheid was thoroughly institutionalized in all areas of South African life, and to enforce it, the state became increasingly authoritarian. The 1960s were the darkest days of apartheid. Fear gripped the country as the state increased the power of its military forces in response to internal threats emerging from underground activities associated with organizations like the ANC and the PAC.[9] The government responded to black resistance with laws that increased police powers including detention without a trial, the deprivation of legal advice while detained, and house arrests. These laws were enforced with the arrest and imprisonment of Nelson Mandela and other national leaders in the early 1960s.

South Africa's extensive security apparatus helped lead to a relatively stable political situation throughout the 1960s and the early 1970s. These years were also accompanied by the regime's new strategy of consolidating white interests which was pursued after South Africa achieved its independent republican status (May 31 1961). Having presided over the period when many of the Afrikaner nationalist movement's long-held political and cultural goals had been achieved, like republican status and Afrikaner political dominance, Verwoerd believed that the NP and the South African state could 'move forward'. The political establishment, he argued, need not concentrate on purely Afrikaner interests anymore; instead, it could help forge 'white nationalism' around the mission of separate development and the homelands scheme.[10]

The effort to build white unity as a bulwark against black nationalism was aided by South Africa's economic boom. From 1963 to 1971, South Africa experienced economic prosperity as a result of state-led development and domestic and foreign investments.[11] The apartheid state channeled cheap labor sources to white economic strongholds, and it protected and encouraged industries by allowing monopolies in all sectors and between international companies. Huge parastatals were protected, Afrikaner control over finance increased, and manufacturing saw a steady increase in profits. Economic growth spurred efforts at white unity because Afrikaners, who especially benefited during these times of economic growth, were now economically 'on par' with English-speaking whites. By the 1960s, for example, Afrikaner males had moved into higher income occupational sectors of the economy, for example, professional and managerial positions, and the income gap between English-speaking and Afrikaans-speaking South Africans was closed considerably.[12] English-speaking whites and Afrikaners could now work together to protect their economic interests.

But these efforts at building white unity had a deleterious impact on the Afrikaner nationalist movement as economic growth caused serious divisions among classes. For example, Afrikaner financiers, industrialists, and commercial capitalists, particularly in the Cape, benefited the most from economic growth and state-led development. Over time, these groups were less reliant on the savings and investments from Afrikaner farmers and workers; their interests had begun to diverge. By the late 1960s, one could no longer speak about the Afrikaner *volk*'s economic interests. Afrikaner industrial and commercial capitalists began to align themselves with English-speaking industrial and commercial capitalists. Afrikaner workers and small farmers, on the other hand, felt ostracized by the policies promoted by these groups and turned to more *verkrampte* causes. In the end, then, economic growth and Afrikaner favoritism benefited Afrikaners economically and they helped forward white unity within similar classes, but they also undermined the ethnic cohesion of Afrikaner nationalism and led to serious ideological differences among Afrikaners. These differences were more or less contained under the leadership of H.F. Verwoerd who dominated the NP, the Cabinet, and the state with his confident, controlling personality. However, when B.J. Vorster became the Prime Minister in 1966, divisions within the NP and among Afrikaners became more noticeable.

B.J. Vorster adopted a more haphazard, pragmatic, and decentralized leadership style than Verwoerd.[13] Vorster, who was involved with the pro-Nazi, *Ossewa Brandwag* during the 1940s, was a latecomer to the NP (1951). He was nominated as party leader in 1966 because he was able to appease important factions within the party. The *verkramptes* were attracted to his tough, even draconian, internal security measures as Minister of Justice under Verwoerd (1961–6), as well as his strong anti-communist stance, while the Cape leadership of the NP was attracted to his weak Transvaal political base and his disinterest in attacking Cape press outlets. When Vorster assumed the position of Prime Minister in 1968, he did not promote a singular vision of Afrikaner nationalism or race policy; one of his primary goals was to keep the *verkrampte/verligte* wings of the party together.[14]

Within a few years of his coming to power; however, the first serious split in the NP occurred. In 1969, four Nationalist MPs, who were expelled from the NP, formed the ultra-*verkrampte*, right-wing *Herstigte Nasionale Party* (Reconstituted Nationalist Party) or HNP.[15] The primary reason for the split was Vorster's decision to allow international sports teams with black players to compete with South African teams, but there was a deeper division that separated the HNP from the NP. The *verkrampte* HNP leaders did not agree with

Vorster's willingness to use the NP as a stepping stone for white reconciliation. The HNP also disagreed with the idea of admitting black diplomats to South Africa, increasing money spent on African education, or any other 'reforms' that were floating around from the *verligte* segment of the NP. HNP members felt such policies threatened Afrikaner supremacy and ethnic cohesion, and they sought an even tighter implementation of apartheid. Although this split within the Afrikaner fold was serious, B.J. Vorster would meet even greater challenges in the 1970s when social, economic, and political problems intensified to the point of further exposing the ideological and class divisions within the NP and the white populace.

By 1973 South Africa's economic boom had ended. The cause of this economic downturn can be linked to the structural limits of the apartheid economy, including the country's shortage of skilled labor, weaknesses related to import-substitution industrialization, its overreliance on exporting strategic minerals, and a domestic market geared toward the demands of a small white minority. South Africa's dependence on international capital meant it was susceptible to an economic downturn when the West experienced a recession in 1973. The government's deficit increased between 1974 and 1976 while mining profits, manufacturing output, and industrial investment decreased. Moreover, inflation and unemployment struck the country as the rand devalued.[16]

Growing internal dissension and external pressure paralleled the economic recession. The English press, the National Union of South African Students (NUSAS), and the Christian Institute (CI) were all involved with protests against the state in the early 1970s. The Black Consciousness movement was also gaining support in the 1970s as other liberation movements were banned. Finally, a wave of strikes by African workers broke out between 1973 and 1975 affecting the economic and political stability of the country.

The rise in internal dissatisfaction coincided with growing external pressure from Western governments and international organizations. In 1969–70 the World Council of Churches (WCC) adopted the Program to Combat Racism which offered financial support to liberation movements in southern Africa. Two years later, the WCC encouraged divestment from companies that did business with South Africa. The international trade movement (especially unions in Britain, Sweden, and West Germany) gave financial and moral support to fledging black unions in South Africa in the early 1970s, and even Western governments by the mid- to late 1970s began to pressure foreign subsidiaries in South Africa 'to promote black job advances, recognize black unions and improve wages and working conditions.'[17]

B.J. Vorster responded to these external and internal demands by relaxing social segregation (for example, sports and recreation), easing separate development initiatives concerning job bars and educational opportunities, and developing relations with African states.[18] The political establishment made the transition away from strict, separate development because the domestic environment had changed and external pressures had developed, as explained above, but also because the regional/international situation was changing. By the 1970s, the majority of African states had received their independence, including Mozambique and Angola – two countries near South Africa's border that were committed to a socialist government. The doctrine of white supremacy and imperialism was beginning to wane, and it could no longer be justified. The South African government responded to these developments in the mid-1970s by promoting international linkages between South Africa and other African countries (e.g., Malawi, Botswana, Zambia) to encourage favorable foreign relations with South Africa in an increasingly isolationist environment.[19]

Moreover, Vorster experienced pressure from industrialists to ease the policy of apartheid. Afrikaans and English-speaking industry owners demanded an efficient, black, skilled, permanent labor force as technological improvements occurred in the mining and manufacturing sectors. However, separate development hindered this because it encouraged industry to rely on a cheap, low-skilled black labor force obtained primarily through migrant labor, and the current system of influx control and restricted residency for Africans made life difficult for workers, hurting productivity. Businesses urged the government to embark upon reforms that included easing influx controls and recognizing the need for regulated trade unions among African workers. The state's effort at relaxing 'petty apartheid', easing job reservations, and establishing commissions that would investigate wider labor reforms (e.g., Wiehahn) was a recognition that the inconsistencies and oppression in apartheid policy concerning labor policy could not go on if profits were to be maintained.

Vorster, in fact, stood at a crossroads in terms of South Africa's race policy. Throughout his term, he defended separate development as a moral and just policy, and he furthered the aims of separate development by increasing forced removals, encouraging homeland independence, and tightening pass controls. Yet Vorster spoke with a divided voice. He was less of an ideologue than Verwoerd. He admitted that separate development was more a method than a dogma, and if it did not work as intended it could be replaced with something else.[20] As class divisions arose among whites, and as managers in all economic sectors demanded an easing of apartheid laws for the purpose of economic growth, Vorster responded with small reforms such as the relaxation of social and sports segregation and permits that allowed Africans to own more than one business in urban areas. Vorster's reforms threatened *verkramptes* who desired a more stringent application of apartheid and the continued dominance of Afrikaners.

More specifically, Vorster presided over a time when *verligtes* like Foreign Affairs Minister Pik Botha, Minister of National Education and of Sport P. Koornhof, and Labour Minister S.P. Botha battled with *verkramptes* like Police Minister Jimmy Kruger, Minister of Information and the Interior Connie Mulder, and Deputy Minister of Bantu Administration and Education A.P. Treurnicht for the direction of the National Party and Afrikanerdom. As mentioned above, *verligte* NP leaders sided with business leaders who urged the government to relax certain apartheid laws, to recognize the permanence of a black, skilled labor force, and to grant some political concessions to urban blacks so that white political and economic arrangements could be maintained. *Verkrampte* NP leaders remained committed to the implementation of separate development. This meant they resisted 'moves to reform labour and industrial policy. While willing to eliminate "petty apartheid" and "discrimination" ... most conservatives refused to acknowledge permanent black urbanisation. They strenuously opposed any idea of black political rights outside of the bantustans.'[21] Vorster straddled both sides, at one time conceding to the *verkrampte* claim for the stricter implementation of apartheid, especially toward the end of the 1970s, at other times, conceding that South Africa had to make some concessions to its 'multiracial' elements.

Although Vorster's changes affected Afrikanerdom considerably, black South Africans were not convinced that Vorster was committed to the eventual abolition of apartheid. Instead, blacks realized that Vorster's 'reforms' were merely cosmetic, intended to preserve white supremacy. This became clear when the state relied on repressive brutality vis-à-vis black opponents during the Soweto uprising (June 1976). The initial protest by students revolved around the involuntary imposition of Afrikaans as a medium of instruction, but it developed into a broad-based protest against the oppressive apartheid state and the institutions which sustained economics profits. The unrest lasted longer and included more people than any of the previous protests. The government responded by supporting a military and police clamp-down that led to the killing and detaining of thousands of protesters (many students).

The international, economic, and internal response to Soweto was significant. International organizations like the UN and EC condemned the South African state.[22] In 1977, the EC adopted a code of conduct concerning South African subsidiaries of EC companies, and the UN imposed a mandatory arms embargo on South Africa. In addition, the late 1970s saw increased anti-apartheid activity from individuals in countries like the Netherlands, Sweden, and Denmark. But the resistance of Western activists was powerless against intransigent Western administrations. Many Western administrations desired to maintain contact with *verligtes* in power in order to maintain business and commercial ties.

The political leadership's immediate reaction to the growing international, internal, and economic pressure was support for increased repression and a massive military build-up to stifle unrest. The apartheid regime banned 17 liberation organizations in 1977, suppressed leading anti-apartheid newspapers, and escalated its military activity. The regime also adopted an isolationist mentality to combat international pressure. During the 1977 election campaign, Vorster attacked foreign pressure on South Africa as biased toward blacks. Whites rallied to his cause giving the NP a huge victory. However, Vorster's term in office ended soon after the NP's election victory when he was ousted from power by the 1977–8 Muldergate scandal, an incident consisting of the misappropriation of funds to finance an elaborate, secretive propaganda war involving BOSS and the Information Department that was linked to Connie Mulder's claim on the Premiership after Vorster's supposed retirement.[23]

THE NGK'S GENERAL POSITION ON RACE POLICY (1962–78)

The NGK was one of the prominent white civil society institutions in South Africa that supported the apartheid regime from 1962 to 1978. The church's position on apartheid rarely deviated from the state's policy directives. The NGK exhibited a strong dependence on, or a domination by, the state whose leaders had effectively silenced the limited autonomy or independence the NGK displayed regarding policy matters in the early 1960s.

All throughout the NGK–state era of collaboration, a high amount of official interaction occurred. The frequency and quality of meetings between leaders within the NGK and the state demonstrated an 'open door' policy. For example, the records of the NGK's Mission Council and General Synod from the early 1960s (even throughout the 1950s) to 1978 show frequent meetings with high-level government officials, like the Minister of Native Affairs or the Prime Minister, over issues like education policy, labor control, mixed marriages, and so forth. The details of these meetings were not available to the public. In fact, the NGK was criticized by English-speaking churches for the lack of transparency when it met with the government because English-speaking churches often notified the press concerning issues discussed when delegations were sent to the government. NGK meetings with the government, in contrast, were held behind closed doors, and at most, the skeleton of the minutes were published in General Synod documents. In the 1970s the NGK responded to the criticisms lodged against it by saying that its method of governmental interaction was more productive because it did not embarrass the state.[24] The NGK preferred to 'approach the authorities directly and in a responsible manner' rather than take 'alleged grievances to the public press'[25] as the former method aligned itself with scriptural norms like respecting political authorities (Romans 13).[26]

State leaders, in turn, felt comfortable with delegations from the NGK in large part because there was continuity between state and NGK leaders in terms of social-political background and conformity regarding political opinions. As such, leaders within the political establishment listened to the church leaders' concerns, allowed the NGK to operate freely in South Africa's society, and did everything they could to satisfy the church's needs (which coalesced with the needs of its Afrikaner constituents). The NGK was one of the apartheid regime's most important 'legitimating' instruments in the 1960s and 1970s. The church supported the government in its policies and actions, it continued to offer a moral basis for apartheid policy, and it went out of its way to avoid confrontations with the NP. For these reasons, the church was dubbed the 'National Party in prayer'.

Because there was a great amount of overlap between the NGK and the NP in terms of membership, informal negotiations between the two institutions played an equal if not more important role in church–state collaboration than formal meetings. Johan Heyns, former clergyman and moderator of the NGK, said the following:

> Well, it's been said that the 'NGK is the NP in prayer'. That is not so completely wrong, numerically and ideologically speaking anyway. Numerically, remember that, as in its present (1993), about 95 percent of the cabinet members belong to our church. And 70 percent of the members of parliament belong to our church. So there is a very, very close link between the two. My second congregation in Rondebosch – I had the access to the ministers, the Prime Minister and the President. They were all members of my congregation. And I visited them regularly, and I prayed with them, and I had discussions with them on current affairs. You see there was a very, very close link and overlap between church and state.[27]

The connection between NGK and state leaders through private or more personal interactions, whether this was at a Broederbond meeting or in a NGK consistory room, was influential in cementing cozy church–state relations. For example, B.J. Vorster's brother, J.D. 'Koot' Vorster, was the moderator of the NGK in 1970. A close friend of H.F. Verwoerd was J.S. Gericke, a prominent Cape and General Synod NGK leader in the 1960s. These close personal relationships meant that leaders within the NGK and the state could be fully informed of key issues being decided within each entity, even if leaders within the state or church disagreed with each other, and this helped foster the collusion that developed in support for apartheid policies.

High policy collusion actually cemented the era of collaboration during the Verwoerd and Vorster years. The NGK, in these years, did not deviate from its support for separate development. NGK clergymen were committed to preserving the Afrikaners' cultural uniqueness and privileges during the era of collaboration, and they were concerned with applying Christian principles and biblical norms to the racial situation in South Africa. The concept of separate development, formulated at the Bloemfontein conference, allowed for the merging of these two goals. It stipulated that the total separation of ethnic groups could honor God-willed diversity thereby preserving Afrikanerdom and it allowed for the autonomous development of all peoples in a way that would not oppress non-whites.

After Verwoerd promoted the ideal of separate development, and after he had effectively silenced the minority pragmatic faction of the

NGK at Cottesloe, the NGK's 'purist' faction was able to support in an unhindered way separate development and the specific legislation underpinning it (e.g., the creation of independent homelands, security legislation). One could argue that the NGK was decidedly 'trapped' into its collaborative role with the state.[28] The church in the early 1950s provided the ideological and theological foundation for apartheid which said that separate development was the only just and moral racial solution for South Africa. It had also propagated the notion that the National Party was the only legitimate political organ that could meet the Afrikaners' interests.[29] When some NGK clergymen realized in the late 1950s and early 1960s that there were serious flaws in apartheid's ideological and theological foundation, the NP-dominated state stifled this independent thinking because it would have meant the disintegration of the separate development project and the cohesion of the Afrikaner people.

By the 1960s, then, the National Party had become the dominant institution formulating the goals and values of the Afrikaners. The NGK still remained a prominent civil society institution that identified itself with the interests of the Afrikaner people, but unlike the 1930s and 1940s when NGK leaders helped formulate Afrikaner values within an Afrikaner nationalist alliance (*volkskerk*) in contrast to state leaders who represented general white interests, and unlike the 1950s when NGK leaders crafted the ideal of separate development that coincided with the interests of a particular segment of Afrikaner thought within Afrikanerdom; in the 1960s and 1970s, the NGK carefully followed the NP-dominated state's lead on race policy. The NGK had been so successful at providing the moral basis for apartheid, at promoting Afrikaner cultural unity, and supporting the NP, that its independence was stifled. The NP-dominated state 'needed' the NGK to help provide its legitimacy and to hold the Afrikaner people together through the dramatic political-economic changes occurring within society. And the NGK 'obeyed' the NP. In the era of collaboration, the NGK's positions on apartheid mirrored the positions of state leaders. During the 1960s and 1970s, NGK leaders published two major reports that confirmed the church's support for a 'fair and just' apartheid policy that maintained white, but mainly Afrikaner, dominance in the political, economic, and social arena as well as ethnic purity.

The first publication was the Landman Report of 1968, a response by W.A. Landman to the Reformed Church of America's (RCA) criticism of the NGK's 'theology of apartheid'. Landman, the Information

Director of the NGK, replied in depth to the Reformed Church of America's accusations that apartheid was an oppressive, racist policy. He spent a considerable amount of time pointing to the 'facts' of separate development, that is, the policy's attempt to bring development to all nations in South Africa. In addition to quoting Verwoerd and Vorster's justifications of the policy, Landman stated, 'the policy of the SA government is the very opposite to that contained in the accusations in your statement. The objectives of this policy are the uplifting of the peoples concerned, their emancipation from the guardianship of the governing White people, their attainment of self determination ...'[30]

Subsequent NGK documents continued to provide support for apartheid policy by arguing that although the Bible did not contain a specific political blueprint, policies like apartheid did conform to scriptural norms. At the General Synod meeting of 1970, the NGK rejected unreservedly the notions of equality and unity. The church stressed the God-willed evidence of diversity and concluded the meeting by saying, 'Above all, this indicates clearly that the NGK's policy of autonomous development is in fact thoroughly in accordance with the demands of Scripture and practice.'[31] It is important to point out that although the NGK remained a steadfast ally of the state, in truth, NGK leaders ended up supporting a more idealist (purist) notion of separate development than was being implemented by state leaders, particularly under Vorster, for theological and historical reasons. Nevertheless, the NGK continued to produce documents during this era that supported the policy of apartheid as implemented by the South African government.

The General Synod's 1974 report entitled *Human Relations and the South African Scene in the Light of Scripture* (HR) offered the clearest idea of where the NGK stood on prominent social issues facing South African society in this era of collaboration. Commissioned in 1962, it took over ten years for the NGK to devise HR in a form acceptable to its membership.[32] It contained many conservative features like a critique of ecumenical horizontalism; the continuation of an exegetical interpretation that justified apartheid policy; and the emphasis on diversity as the principle that should guide social and political life.[33] The justification of apartheid along neo-Calvinist lines continued, and in some ways, it reached its height in terms of sophistication. The report used concepts like 'creation ordinance', 'God-willed diversity', and 'spheres' to interpret biblical passages and norms. Through its reliance on Kuyperian logic and its interpretation of certain texts, the diversity of humanity was argued to be the guiding principle of life. This allowed the conservative leadership of the NGK to justify separate development in the following way:

> In specific circumstances and under specific conditions, the New Testament makes provision for the regulation on the basis of separate development of the co-existence of various peoples in one country ... A political system based on the autogenous or separate development of various population groups can be justified from the Bible.[34]

The information in the HR report suggested that separate development was the only Christian solution for South Africa. Apartheid as a 'just, fair' policy, judged according to Christian norms, was the starting point concerning South Africa's social situation. One of the report's glaring omissions was the lack of attention given to the injustices associated with apartheid or the opposition to apartheid by the majority of South African citizens.

One could also argue that this report ended up affirming the government as it tried to reform apartheid to accommodate the demands of managers in the industrial, farming, and mining sectors. For example, on the issue of labor control, the NGK's position, already expressed in earlier decades, was that migrant labor and influx controls were necessary for South Africa's economy. If migrant labor and influx controls were to be removed suddenly, South Africa's economy would falter and Africans would experience tremendous hardship.[35] Such controls benefited both blacks and whites. However, the NGK recognized that migrant labor created hardships for African families: it caused the disintegration of family life, led to divorces, and did not allow for steady incomes. Because of the negative impacts associated with migrant labor, the NGK called on the government to limit the harmful effects that arose out of the functioning of the migrant labor system. It thanked the state for the efforts already taken, like allowing for more family visits to the reserves and developing border industries.[36] The NGK's hope was that homelands would becomes self-sufficient and migrant labor would be eliminated:

> The migrant labour system reinforces the tendency among the Bantu not to make a contribution to the development of their own homelands ... Moreover, the labourers tend to move about doing mostly unskilled labour on a temporary, contractual basis – which inevitably retards the development of a conservative middle class, so essential

for a sound national life ... Although the migrant labor system cannot be said to be contrary to the teachings of the Bible, as such it should be eliminated as far as possible to avoid its disruptive effects.

The church welcomes all efforts on the part of the authorities and other bodies to promote the viability of the Bantu homelands. The church is convinced that the rapid economic and industrial development of the Bantu homelands should be given top priority so that these regions can become happy homes to the largest possible proportion of the various Bantu peoples.[37]

The NGK leadership supported the development of homelands because if homelands became self-sufficient, the white 'nation' would no longer have to depend on the multitude of blacks living in urban areas. The NGK leadership's position on homeland development was probably more demanding than the NP government's, but it was cognizant of the importance of the issue and did not oppose the state's support for the political autonomy of homelands which was occurring throughout the 1960s and 1970s. Overall, HR signified that the NGK's positions on specific social policies and general policy coalesced with the state's. The church offered no recommendations for change that went beyond what the state was considering at the time. Through an analysis of church documents and through a careful study of particular issues like influx control, mixed marriages, security legislation, and education policy, the latter of which I could not deal with in this book, it becomes apparent that NGK–state relations during the 1960s and 1970s exhibited a collaborative tendency related to the natural overlap in the socio-economic background of Afrikaner leaders and the ideological cohesion of the Afrikaners' political project.

CONCLUSION

In the 1960s and 1970s, the NP-dominated state and the NGK collaborated with each other to forward the idea of separate development as a morally just racial solution for South Africa. The relationship of collaboration between a state and civil society institution rests on a high amount of official interaction and policy collusion. This era of collaboration between the state and Afrikaner civil society ushered in strong authoritarian rule by an Afrikaner-dominated state that engaged heavily with civil society institutions which voluntarily gave their loyalty to the state and Afrikaner interests.

The relationship of collaboration achieved its economic and political goals for Afrikaners in South Africa. Afrikaners, or whites more broadly, remained dominant in the social and political realms and economic security was maintained. Indeed, the power of Afrikaners in economic and political realms seemed insurmountable. Although external pressure on the country increased and black protest gained in strength in these years, it was not enough to challenge white minority rule. Only toward the mid-1970s did serious cracks appear in the Afrikaner nationalist edifice; ironically, due to the success of Afrikaner nationalism's economic movement.

6 NGK–State Relations during Apartheid's Demise (1979–94)

The world eagerly anticipated South Africa's dramatic political changes in the 1990s. In May 1994 Nelson Mandela became the country's first black president, a long-awaited moment for many South Africans. Significant events in the 1980s preceded the end of white minority rule in South Africa, including the effective protest of apartheid laws by the masses, the intensification of international pressure, and the initiation of political change by P.W. Botha.

Although the main participants in South Africa's democratic transition were political institutions like the African National Congress (ANC) and the National Party (NP), civil society organizations like the NGK also played an important role in the change. This chapter focuses on the relationship of mutual engagement between the factions dominating the South African state and the NGK from 1979 to 1994. Most of the time, the NGK continued to give its unequivocal support to the state, as it had during the first three decades of apartheid rule; however, situations arose periodically where groups dominating the state and the NGK arrived at different opinions concerning policy directions and strategies. During these years, state leaders took the lead in promoting the attainment of white survival and economic prosperity through political reform while leaders within the NGK seemed to lag behind, supporting the goals of white, but more specifically Afrikaner, survival and economic prosperity through a slower implementation of reform.

Sociological upheaval among Afrikaners explains the differences between the NGK and the state in this era of mutual engagement, or differences between the groups dominating the NGK and the state's position on reform can be attributed to the class and ideological interests they identified with in the 1980s. After 1979 the dominant faction within the NP-dominated state represented more pragmatic political directives and middle-class economic interests while the NGK's leadership identified with the spiritual and cultural needs of Afrikaner moderates and conservatives.

This period of NGK–state relations reveals an interesting finding regarding state–civil society relations in times of transition. A civil society institution like the NGK presented a greater obstacle to the realization of widespread democracy than the state. Mainstream accounts of state–civil society relations often assume that while over-centralized, authoritarian states hinder democratic transitions, civil society institutions will successfully help usher in the establishment of democracy. This era shows that one sector of white civil society, the NGK, because of its identification with narrow, ethnic interests, resisted the establishment of democracy to a greater extent than the South African state.

THE NP-DOMINATED STATE'S GENERAL POSITION ON RACE POLICY (1979–89)

P.W. Botha became the Prime Minister of South Africa in 1978. His leadership represented a significant shift within the National Party and the government because he promoted *verligte* political change within a military-dominated state that contained strong, centralized rule.[1] Although Botha's domineering personality and his support for the military made him an unlikely reformer, his proclivities toward pragmatism and flexibility led to the unraveling of Verwoerdian apartheid and laid the foundation for further reform under F.W. de Klerk in 1989. More specifically, under Botha, the goals of an Afrikaner 'people's' economy and ethnic purity through separate development were replaced with the goals of white economic prosperity and survival through neo-apartheid. Neo-apartheid accepted black urbanization and economic integration in the attempt to maintain economic interests and ensure white survival.

It was the Muldergate scandal of 1978–9, the details and importance of which have been recounted elsewhere, that directly led the political turnover within the NP. Essentially, the *verligte* or more 'enlightened' wing of the NP gained the stronger hand over the NP *verkramptes* or 'conservatives' in the late 1970s, and in the aftermath of this event, P.W. Botha stood at the center and identified with the shared interests of two important groups in South African society: the military and the capitalists.

Botha, Defence Minister of South Africa since 1966, sympathized with the SADF's desire for a strategic, long-term, military plan that addressed South Africa's deteriorating regional situation and internal unrest. South African leaders, military and civilian, by the late 1970s believed that instability within South Africa could in part be alleviated if blacks received benefits within the capitalist system that would improve their social situation and make them more supportive of the capitalist system.[2] To garner black support and thwart social unrest, military and civilian leaders supported the easing of apartheid measures (for example, pass laws, access to housing) that would encourage black economic improvement. The ideological connection between capitalism and the security establishment was forwarded by economic ties. Since the arms embargo was imposed on South Africa in 1964, the production of local arms, coordinated by ARMSCOR (Armaments Development and Production Corporation) had emerged into an important industrial group.[3] Many private industries' fortunes were linked with the state's growing arms industry. The arms industry demanded highly skilled labor, but due to the structural problems in South Africa's economy, such laborers were in short supply. In the end, the military establishment, along with industrialists, called for political reform to rectify economic structural problems and to alleviate the social oppression of black South Africans.

For the first four years of Botha's premiership, *verkramptes* and *verligtes* coexisted in the Cabinet and the National Party and debated the future direction of South Africa.[4] *Verligte* leaders like Labour Minister S.P. (Fanie) Botha, the Minister of Cooperation and Development Piet Koornhof, and Foreign Minister R.F. (Pik) Botha were open to easing apartheid laws if this meant the improvement of race relations and the achievement of greater economic profits. They were also willing to change the Afrikaner nationalist project in ways that recognized the commonalties among English-speaking and Afrikaner classes. *Verkramptes* actually made up the majority of the NP caucus in the late 1970s. Leaders like A.P. Treurnicht, Transvaal NP leader and Minister of Public Works and Tourism from 1978 to 1982 and NP MPs like Tom Langley, Willie Snyman, and Jan van Zyl were considered traditionalists who emphasized group rights, ethnic separation, and the maintenance of both 'petty' and 'grand' apartheid. Over time, the differences between the *verligte* and *verkrampte* wings of the NP over Botha's reform strategy, to be explained below, reached a point where right-wing, *verkrampte* elements of the NP formed an alternative party, the Conservative Party.

One of the main reasons Botha initiated neo-apartheid reforms in the 1980s was the economic recession affecting the country. From 1980 to 1985, South Africa's economic growth rate was 1.1 per cent and inflation ran at 10 per cent. The slight increase in the gross domestic product could not equal the population growth rate of 2.3 per cent, so real incomes for all South Africans lowered.[5] South Africa's economic recession can be explained by the detrimental effects that apartheid had on the economy.

As mentioned in Chapter 5, capital-intensive, manufacturing industries dominated South Africa's economy by the 1970s and 1980s and 'demanded' a semi-skilled or highly skilled workforce that could manage the technological and structural change needed for capitalist accumulation. However, a decreasing white labor force and apartheid policies that restricted blacks to unskilled labor led to a labor skills shortage. Second, South Africa's economy suffered from poor investment choices as the state diverted funds that could have been invested in education or social areas into defense and security, homeland administration, and/or parastatals. Finally, the international anti-apartheid movement led to economic sanctions and disinvestment that deprived South Africa of foreign money and technology.[6] All of these events led NP leaders to realize that apartheid needed to change if the demands of a capital-intensive economy were to be met.

South Africa's anemic economy corresponded with the second major factor leading to change, namely, Afrikaner socio-economic upheaval. Afrikaner solidarity across class lines from the 1940s to the 1960s declined by the 1970s because of the achievement of economic prosperity by Afrikaners.[7] By the late 1970s, Afrikaners placed class above ethnic interests. For example, many Afrikaner businesspeople, wealthy professionals, and large-scale commercial farmers aligned themselves with English-speaking capitalists who encouraged reform for purposes of economic profit and the softening of international criticism.

Finally, political reasons, in addition to the economic slowdown and class cleavage, explain why Botha embarked on a new strategy of implementing apartheid. Beginning in the mid-1970s, membership in trade unions grew and anti-apartheid politicization on a mass level increased. Additionally, international pressure intensified in the 1980s in the form of sanctions and boycotts. South Africa became a pariah state after countries witnessed the repressive tactics the regime used against its citizens. The government also faced a changing order in southern Africa. By the 1980s, many of its neighbors had won their independence, something that presented a challenge to South African leaders accustomed to European colonialism and white control.

In response to the external pressure and internal change, P.W. Botha implemented a set of policies from 1979 to 1985 known as 'total strategy'. 'Total strategy' was a comprehensive political plan put into effect by the South African state through key institutions like the SADF and the State Security Council that coordinated South Africa's white power bases against internal and external threats.[8] The regime argued that a 'total strategy' of political reform and military might was needed to face the 'total onslaught' from (communist) revolutionaries inside and outside the country. Total strategy sought support from businesspeople and the black middle class through domestic reforms that included the relaxation of petty apartheid, the initiation of labor reform and the implementation of constitutional change, while it simultaneously suppressed domestic dissidents and destabilized 'radical' frontline states.

Regarding apartheid reversals, the government announced in 1979 that it would remove 'unnecessary race discrimination'. Over the next ten years, the state allowed sports competition between multiracial teams; it desegregated public amenities, at least regarding certain hotels, beaches, and parks; it abolished laws prohibiting interracial marriage; and it turned away from the strict enforcement of the Group Areas Act, allowing black occupants to move into 'white' residential areas.[9]

The removal of some significant segregation laws coincided with the state's effort to replace its traditional racial ideology.[10] Moreover P.W. Botha believed that for white survival to occur, apartheid needed to be moderated, and he even suggested that 'healthy power-sharing' might arise with non-whites. He actively pursued engagement with the Inkatha Freedom Party (IFP) because Mangosuthu Buthelezi represented a moderate, 'pro-capitalist' black leader in contrast to the radical, 'communist-inspired' leaders associated with underground organizations like the ANC and SACP.[11]

Total strategy's domestic reforms also included significant changes concerning labor reform and African urbanization. Following the release of the Wiehahn Report (1979), 'Statutory job reservation in manufacturing industries was abolished and restrictions on the mobility and training of African labour eased.'[12] Such actions were intended to stabilize the workforce by providing outlets for discontented black workers.[13] The Riekert Commission's proposals (1979) responded to the issue of African urbanization. The report suggested the relaxation of strict influx controls on Africans who could prove their urban residence while tightening controls on migrants or temporary laborers. The legislation that grew out of these proposals tried to create a privileged strata of urban laborers as those who could prove their residency were placed above others regarding economic opportunities, home ownership, and educational advantages. Through the creation of a privileged strata of urban laborers and/or a middle class, the NP-dominated state sought to divide blacks, making it easier to control the masses, and provided businesses with a permanent, reliable African labor force. In 1986, the state continued its urbanization reforms by abolishing pass laws and granting South African citizenship to those residing in urban areas with permanent residential rights.

In order for these domestic reforms to be accepted on a widespread basis, however, the state needed to offer blacks some type of political representation. One measure enacted by the state to co-opt certain sectors of the population was the tricameral legislature of 1983. The new legislative arrangement provided for three uniracial parliamentary chambers, one for white, 'Coloured', and Indian members. The white chamber had the majority of members, and it also had a virtual veto over any matter of 'general affairs'. The head of state was the President (P.W. Botha) who had political powers including the ability to appoint cabinet members, dissolve Parliament, and decide which issues were 'general' affairs.

One of the major problems with the new constitution was that it excluded Africans from any national role. Africans were supposed to seek their political rights in designated homelands or township councils, both of which were regarded as illegitimate by the vast majority of blacks.[14] In addition, the constitutional restructuring divided black opposition by separating 'Coloureds' and Indians from Africans regarding national power. The vast majority of Indian and 'Coloured' voters boycotted elections to the tricameral parliament as a measure of protest against the government's divisive reform.

Botha's political reforms, unacceptable to the black majority, also caused a serious rift within the Afrikaner nationalist alliance and the NP in the early 1980s. Botha's reforms appeased middle-class Afrikaner and English-speaking whites, but they contradicted the social and economic interests of small Afrikaner farmers and Afrikaner workers based in areas like the Transvaal. These differences among Afrikaners (and whites) led to serious schisms. In 1982 Andries Treurnicht and a significant number of *verkrampte* members were expelled from the NP because they did not agree with the government's limited power-sharing arrangements in the tricameral Parliament. Treurnicht formed the Conservative Party (CP) which gained strength throughout the 1980s, replacing the more liberal Progressive Federal Party as the official opposition party in the 'white' House of Assembly in 1987.[15] The sociological upheaval among

Afrikaners, to be explored further below, not only divided the National Party, but the Afrikaner Broederbond, the NGK, the Afrikaner press, and just about every institution associated with the Afrikaner nationalist alliance.

Total strategy involved more than domestic reform. Its other component was increased militarization and the destabilization of surrounding states. The militaristic side of total strategy was based on the idea that South Africa faced internal and external pressure from revolutionaries. Internally, South African liberation movements increased the scope and effectiveness of their activities in the 1980s, providing a direct threat to the apartheid regime. Regionally, the state felt threatened by 'communist sympathizers' in Zimbabwe's new government (1980) and the Marxist leanings of the Front for the Liberation of Mozambique (FRELIMO) in Mozambique and the Popular Movement for the Liberation of Angola (MPLA) in Angola.

The South African state used the South African Defense Force (SADF) and various security structures to combat the unrest that was a threat to free enterprise and western civilization.[16] Under P.W. Botha's approval, structures of decision-making were reorganized to implement 'total strategy'. Under what was called the 'national security management system' (NSMS), the state was heavily militarized. At the top of the NSMS was the State Security Council (SSC), the main policy-making body under Botha's administration. The SSC was composed of the Prime Minister, the Minister of Law and Order, the Minister of Defence, and the Minister of Foreign Affairs, as well as the heads or chiefs of the main security apparatuses. At the base of the new system was the Joint Management Centers, smaller networks of security and civil administrators. Over time, only those ministers and leaders who had access to the State Security Council influenced the debates that led to policy-making in the 1980s.[17]

The South African state combated internal insurrection by granting enhanced power to police and security forces. The visibility of police and SADF forces increased in the townships as mass resistance grew. Detentions, arrests, and bannings became commonplace. Increased military expenditures and the extension of compulsory military service for whites also indicated the importance of the security apparatus for 'total strategy's' policy-making, and the military's prominence solidified white control over many areas of life: economic, political, and social. The state combated regional unrest mainly through the destabilization of frontline states.[18] The South African regime used their military superiority to stop pro-liberation guerrilla activity in frontline states and it organized counter-revolutionary groups that wrecked the economies and destroyed the social lives of Africans. In some cases, the counter-revolutionary groups (e.g., RENAMO in Mozambique and UNITA in Angola) decimated whole villages as well as railroads, factories, and bridges. Destabilization campaigns cost frontline states approximately US$45–60 million in lost production and economic damage.[19]

From 1979 to 1985, then, Botha's regime adopted a new strategy of indirect rule aimed at ensuring white hegemony in economic and political realms. The strategy of indirect rule demanded cooperation between moderate blacks and whites rather than the stark separation of races as envisioned by separate development. Botha's total strategy campaign, in essence, acknowledged the serious flaws in the 'moral legitimacy' of separate development which upheld white supremacy. Botha's political strategy was supposed to legitimize the white government by stabilizing the business environment, controlling internal and external dissent, appeasing a black middle class, and placating international opinion. It achieved none of these goals.

Increased militarization and partial reform, successful for a short while, were incapable of reaching their goals in the long run. First, resistance to apartheid continued to mount in South Africa throughout the 1980s.[20] The masses refused to believe that the government was engaged in sincere reform. Actions which strengthened the resolve of liberation movements included *Umkhonto we Sizwe's* attacks on a number of military and power stations in the early 1980s and the boycott of tricameral parliamentary elections by Indian and 'Coloured' voters in 1984. The liberation movement grew larger and more organized as the 1980s continued. The United Democratic Front (UDF), formed in 1983, consolidated over 400 national, regional, and local organizations which resisted apartheid. It effectively organized election boycotts and supported student activity that resisted the racist system of education.[21] Indeed, as the political crisis worsened, trade unions, students, and community-based organizations organized to protest apartheid through effective rent boycotts and political protests.[22] These protests posed a tremendous challenge to the state. In July 1985 the government declared a limited State of Emergency covering certain areas of the country. The restrictions were lifted briefly in early 1986, but a nationwide State of Emergency was announced in June 1986, during which thousands of activists were detained and tortured, meetings and organizations were banned, and the media were regulated heavily.[23]

By the mid- to late 1980s, South Africa had reached a political stale-mate. Botha's efforts at political reform had been rejected by the masses, whether it was the tricameral Parliament or African urban councils, and unrest continued. Moreover, Botha was unwilling to ini-tiate any further reform. In 1985 Botha dismissed any notion of significant reform or majority rule in a speech (Rubicon) that received international attention. The apartheid regime's intransigence caused even conservative governments in the United States or Great Britain, which had been supportive of South Africa through the early 1980s with their policies of 'constructive engagement', to call for further reform on the part of the apartheid regime.[24] Western governments could not stifle the growing swell of anti-apartheid activity from the British Anti-Apartheid Movement, Transafrica, and the Washington Office on Africa. From the mid-1980s economic sanctions against South Africa escalated, private companies began to withdraw their investments in South Africa, and many more were reluctant to invest new capital in the country because of anti-apartheid pressures.[25] Finally, UN resolutions condemning apartheid and urging widespread sanctions became frequent in the 1980s.[26] The international tide against South Africa could not be ignored.

The loss of international capital because of sanctions and the growing unrest in South Africa led to serious economic weakness from 1981 to 1987. As interest rates rose, foreign debt grew, average incomes decreased, and poverty deepened. Business leaders contin-ued to press Botha for further political reform, economic deregula-tion, and privatization, but they grew increasingly disillusioned with a leader that appeared to rely on force rather than a 'strategic plan' to stabilize South Africa.

NGK–STATE RELATIONS DURING THE 1979–89 ERA OF MUTUAL ENGAGEMENT

As the South African state faced increasing pressure from external and internal sources, institutions like the NGK continued to legiti-mate the state and lent it consistent support. However, the NGK's relationship with the state, identified primarily with Botha's confidants in the Cabinet and the State Security Council because of the latter's control over state policies and institutions like the military, the bureaucracy and so forth, can be described as mutual engagement instead of collaboration. The two entities continued to hold similar opinions on the majority of policy issues (e.g., internal unrest), but situations arose where the leaders dominating each entity maintained varying preferences on official policy (e.g. domestic reform) with NGK leaders appearing to support a more conservative opinion then state or NP leaders.

The predicament of the NGK 'lagging behind the state' is an outcome that has been mentioned in previous studies.[27] It has been suggested that NP leaders dominating the state promoted reform in the 1980s because of an altered political environment which forced the party to moderate its policy directives in contrast to the NGK which could not easily distance itself from the moral and biblical underpinning of apartheid that it helped to construct. Although political circumstances and ideological differences explain part of the divergence on political reform, this reasoning by itself is incomplete.

The differences between NGK and state leaders can be more fully explained by the sociological upheaval that was also occurring among Afrikaners.[28] By the mid-1970s many Afrikaners had achieved a large measure of wealth and power. For example, the majority of Afrikaners (approximately 70 per cent) had reached a middle-class status. This dramatic rise in the status of Afrikaners can be attributed to the NP's use of state resources to aid Afrikaner businesspeople, workers, and farmers ever since the National Party came into power. Not surprisingly, Afrikaners experienced economic advancement concerning their control of private industry, from 10 per cent to 21 per cent, and industrial output, rising to 45 per cent between 1948 and 1975.[29] More and more Afrikaners moved into professional and managerial fields, while the number of farmers and blue-collar workers declined.

Botha's domestic policies, particularly labor reform, responded to the needs of Afrikaner, middle-class industrialists who wanted a skilled, manageable labor force. The NP sided with bourgeois interests, and in doing so, it contributed to the break down of ethnic unity that previous regimes, particularly H.F. Verwoerd's, created among the different classes. For example, the state's incorporation of organized, African laborers angered white workers who feared for their job security. The cracks in Verwoerdian separate development, namely, the removal of petty apartheid and the power-sharing arrangements with blacks, also indicated political integration and the loss of political control for many lower-class whites.[30]

The growing class and ideological differences within Afrikanerdom affected the composition of every Afrikaner nationalist institution, including the National Party, the Broederbond, and the NGK. The divisions within the NP, discussed above, were comprised of *verkrampte–verligte* differences. Different factions, with interests and positions sometimes distinct from those found within the state, also dominated the NGK with three main groups emerging – hardline conservatives, *verligte* moderates, and liberals.

The first group in the NGK, composed of conservatives hardliners, resisted any form of socio-political change away from vertical apartheid. These individuals were committed to the goals of Afrikaner ethnic preservation and a 'people's economy' which could be achieved through separate development. Many of the conservatives were the 'purist' advocates in the first era of mutual engagement and in the era of collaboration. Conservatives represented a significant portion (between 15 and 30 per cent) of the NGK laity who believed that 'apartheid' could still be justified on various grounds, seen in their support for right-wing parties like the CP.[31] NGK *'verkramptes'* included ministers and theologians like Reverend S.J. Eloff and F.J.M. Potgieter who had been inspired by Abraham Kuyper's ideas or who held onto the *volkskerk* ideal. These leaders no longer occupied the top echelon of the NGK's administrative structure by the 1980s but they still wielded considerable influence.

The second faction found in the NGK were the *verligte* moderates who were committed to serving the spiritual and cultural needs of their Afrikaner membership by respecting past decisions of the church concerning the biblical and theological foundations of separate development, but also prodded the church laity to consider micro-change that maintained group rights for the benefit of all South Africans. NGK *verligtes* had been trained in the Reformed tradition and reflected a Calvinist commitment to doctrinal purity and scriptural authority, but they did not embrace the neo-Kuyperian Calvinism of the 'purists of old'. Some moderates had been considerably influenced by the changing socio-political environment and the external and internal pressures placed on the church to lessen its biblical and/or theological justifications of apartheid. Outspoken moderates included individuals like Willie Jonker, Professor of Theology at the University of Stellenbosch, and P.A. Verhoef and D.J. Hattingh to a lesser extent. Interestingly, by the late 1980s, *verligtes* also comprised the top echelon of NGK leadership, for example, Dr P. Rossouw, Scribe and Information Director of the NGK in the 1980s, J.A. Heyns, Moderator of the NGK (1986–90) and Professor of Theology at the

University of Pretoria, and P.C. Potgieter, Moderator of the NGK (1990–4), but these NGK leaders could not be as outspoken concerning socio-political issues because of their responsibility toward the full composition of NGK membership.

The third faction found in the NGK were the liberals who ministered to certain Afrikaners by promoting significant reform away from apartheid policy because this would alleviate oppression against black South Africans and lead to the spiritual and cultural upliftment of all South Africans. Some NGK liberals, like Nico Smith, Department of Theology at UNISA, Herbie Brand, NGSK clergyman in Cape Town, and Willem Saayman, Department of Theology at UNISA, broke their ties with the NGK by the mid- to late 1980s because they believed the NGK had not gone far enough in rejecting its 'theology of apartheid'. NGK liberals who remained within the NGK included people like Willem Nicol and B.J. Kotze. During the 1980s, outspoken moderates and liberals often worked together for change within the NGK.

The different political and class alliances dominating the NGK and the state in the 1980s explain the situation of mutual engagement. With the Conservative Party's breakaway in 1982, the political establishment no longer needed to appease the *verkrampte* faction to the extent that it had done so previously. Under P.W. Botha, the *verligte*, pro-reform faction dominated the state. Botha made his position clear. He was reaching out to middle-class, capitalist interests through partial reforms that would achieve the goals of white survival and economic prosperity. He also expanded his support base as he drew in English-speakers and minority groups through the political establishment's 'power-sharing' arrangements and its campaign against communism.

The NGK's membership lacked the cohesiveness of the NP's. Its top echelon of leadership contained moderates, but its laity included conservatives, moderates, and even some liberals. A prominent church leader who asked to remain anonymous, and Adrio König, a theology professor at UNISA, indicated the divided nature of the NGK in the following words:

> I think that in their top structure (synodical) and among their thinking theologians, there is definitely a leaving behind of their apartheid theology. But the Afrikaner people are split between the CP people and the more pragmatic NP people. And this means within the NGK there is a large body within it that is still conservative and stuck with the old ideology of apartheid.[32]

I am aware that Heyns and Potgieter are ready to join with the sister churches. But they don't represent the rank and file of the church. They don't represent the majority of the church that has been exposed to apartheid for forty years and still believe in it.[33]

The NGK found itself in a difficult situation because of the diversity of its membership regarding ideological, political, and class backgrounds. Although the NP was officially separated from the *verkrampte* faction, the NGK continued to be influenced by laity and leaders who were influenced by this worldview. B. Geldenhuys, an NP member of parliament in 1993 and a former NGK clergyman, explains the existence of the different political factions in the NGK and how this related to the NP:

When the CP split from the NP (1982), there was a gradual split between the NP and NGK. The NGK members supported different parties, so there was divided loyalty within the NGK. The NGK couldn't be so closely allied to the NP because NGK members split their loyalty between the NP and CP.[34]

The NGK's divided nature meant that if the church took a firm stance on Botha's reform efforts, it could face a schism as large or larger than the NP. In an effort to avert a split, the NGK took a more moderate stance on the issue of reform than state leaders were promoting. Its conservative, even ambiguous, position on the reform initiative appeased hardline members and generally maintained church unity. This is not to say that the NGK opposed the political establishment's policies. The NGK's actions meant that it took an apolitical position or a more conservative position on certain issues (e.g., educational reform, structural unity) in an effort to avoid a split in the church. On the great majority of issues (e.g., security concerns, sanctions), the NGK agreed wholeheartedly with NP-dominated state policies.

For example, the NGK's official position on violence and the 'communist threat' paralleled the NP's. In 1982 the NGK presented a document on conscientious objection that demonstrated its support for the state's military policy. The document's premise was that South Africa was involved in a state of war against external forces. The state had a right to defend itself by means applicable to the circumstances, and in order for this to occur, the state needed to rely on its citizens. Citizens were bound to obey the state and no difference of opinion with the government could deliver an individual from their duty to defend the state. According to the NGK, conscientious objection directly countered the orderly function of the state. In fact, the document attacked proponents of conscientious objection as being enemies of the state and disguised militants.[35] The NGK's position mirrored the state leadership's perspective that South Africa faced security threats that needed to be met through increased military action.

The NGK's support for state security efforts revealed its fears concerning communism. General Synod documents between 1982 and 1986 contained letters from ecumenical organizations like the South African Council of Churches and the World Council of Churches that supported peaceful protest against the South African state. The NGK dismissed such appeals because the organizations were viewed as communist fronts.[36] Willem Nicol, an NGK clergymen in Pretoria, expressed the NGK's alliance with the government in its efforts to combat communism in the following words:

> In the 1980s, the ideology of state security was the main thing. The church was very close to the government because it supplied the ideology of 'our sacred calling to defend the southern African continent against communism'. You had religion being directed toward the needs of the people. And by means of the chaplain service in the army of which the DRC was the main supplier – that whole thing was very devious I might add ... In the 1980s, the strongest thing was anti-communism and state security.[37]

The NGK mirrored the government's view on the 'communist threat' and the need for militarization, but the similarity on these issues was not entirely unexpected. *Verligtes* dominated the leadership of both state and NGK institutions, and militarization was accepted by such individuals as a vital part of the 'total strategy' package. Strong security measures meant that South African society could be controlled for political and economic purposes. Conservatives in the NGK and the state also supported strong security measures because they stifled black encroachment, and upheld Afrikaner security. It was not difficult for the NGK to support the state's militarization efforts, then, because the majority of its laity and leaders desired increased security. In other areas, however, differences emerged. The NGK's commitment to a more conservative direction was evident in its response to internal dissent, which was connected to the issue of political change and reform.

Beginning in the 1980s, the NGK faced increased pressure from liberal and moderate theologians. In the early 1980s, a number of challenging pronouncements emerged including *Stormkompas* (1981) and the Open Letter (1982).[38] *Stormkompas* was a book that consisted of 12 essays and responses by NGK theologians and ministers. The articles dealt with weighty issues like reconciliation, race relations, and structural church unity. The Open Letter was a short memorandum published in the *Kerkbode* and signed by 123 ministers, many of them liberals, who felt the NGK and the government were ignoring the injustices of apartheid.[39] Forty-one of the signers were NGK ministers. Both *Stormkompas* and the Open Letter called on the NGK to be a true initiator of change, a force for reconciliation, and a prophetic voice in South African society. The Open Letter, initiated by people like David Bosch, Willem Nicol, and Nico Smith, rejected the scriptural defense of apartheid laws like the Mixed Marriages and Group Areas Acts, denounced apartheid in its application, and called on the NGK to seek structural church unity with black Reformed churches.

The NGK's official response essentially dismissed or downplayed these initiatives.[40] First, the NGK argued the publication of these reports was in conflict with the standard practice of dealing with grievances in a private manner. Second, the NGK's official leadership announced that the timing of publication was wrong since the documents could only be debated by the next general synod in 1986. Finally, the NGK argued that *Stormkompas* and the Open Letter spread falsities about the NGK (e.g., the NGK was reluctant to embrace change) and they hurtfully exposed Afrikaner disunity. Although the leadership promised to discuss the matters at a later time, the discussions never took place because by the time the general synod met in 1986 other issues competed with *Stormkompas* and the Open Letter for attention.[41]

The NGK's response to liberal and *verligte* dissenters within their midst demonstrated the church's apprehension of the policy perspectives promoted by this group. The NGK, led by moderate leaders who had to appease conservatives within their midst, was not willing to adopt these reports because this would have meant the church stood behind efforts of partial reform which could have caused a schism in the church and the *volk*. It was easier for the church to downplay the ideas these individuals raised, and maintain church and Afrikaner unity, than to engage with this group.[42] It is interesting to note that even though the NGK went out of its way to downplay liberal dissent, a group of conservatives broke away from the NGK in 1987 because of the adoption of the synodical church publication *Church and Society*.[43] The NGK's official response was that it 'lamented' the action and was 'sorrowed' by the breakaway. This church schism did not involve the same amount of numbers as the parallel political breakaway of the Conservative Party, but it did frighten the NGK, causing it to become even more conscious of this group concerning its policy statements. W.A. Saayman, theology professor at UNISA, commented on the significance of the conservative breakaway in the NGK in the following words:

> The church experienced the split on a much more emotional level than the NP. The breakaway of the CP in 1982 was traumatic for all people, but it was hard politics and you make choices that you live with. But within the church when the APK split, it was much more traumatic. And the church at the moment is trying very, very hard to keep those members that are still together. It doesn't want a further split.[44]

The NGK's handling of internal dissent demonstrated its desire to maintain the unity of the church. Other examples can be posited that point to the NGK falling behind the state regarding reform efforts in the 1980s to retain the cohesion of the church and Afrikaner people. In essence, when the political establishment enacted political reform in the 1980s, the NGK, like other societal organizations, had the option of taking a clear position on specific reforms, but the NGK remained remarkably silent or opposed reform efforts in its official newspapers and synodical meetings in order to promote the symbolic unity of the Afrikaner peoples.

A specific policy issue on which the NGK avoided taking a stance was the Group Areas Act. In a *Kerkbode* editorial dealing with revoking the Group Areas Act, the editor pointed out that the law caused great harm to those who were forcibly removed, but it also brought calm to the country.[45] It warned people against romanticizing the communities that existed before the Group Areas Act was implemented. It insinuated that the people who had been removed had been living in squalor and high-crime areas; thus, the laws brought stability in the end. The editor ended by saying the issue of revoking the Group Areas was a complex one that needed to be viewed from all angles. On this issue, the NGK's position was an ambiguous one, a position that worked for all groups within the NGK. The NGK's position contrasted with the government's which was considering revoking the act because it fit within the domestic side of 'total strategy'.

The debates surrounding the repeal of the Mixed Marriages and Immorality Acts in the 1980s also indicate the differences between the NP-dominated state and the official NGK position in this era of mutual engagement. The historical background and ideological context to the construction and implementation of these laws are complex and not the focus of this book,[46] but it is important to note that by the 1980s the NP government's desire to reconsider (and repeal) the laws differed from the NGK's official stance that the laws should be retained.

Numerous NGK meetings and reports between 1979 and 1985 clarified the NGK's conservative position on the mixed marriages issue which can be summarized in the opinions of NGK leaders like G.S.J. Möller, D.C.G. Fourie, and P. Rossouw who spoke at a 1983 commission investigating the 'desirability' of the miscegenation laws. The NGK delegates admitted that no scriptural passages existed to prohibit mixed marriages, but a large number of sociological reasons existed.[47] They expressed their belief that diversity was a fact of South African life, and it was something that needed to be maintained. Racially mixed marriages were undesirable because they destroyed cultural, historical, and linguistic differences that obliterated the biblical essence of marriage, that is, unity. The NGK's position on mixed marriages appealed to Afrikaners who feared the social integration of races and the lessening of Afrikaner purity would occur if the mixed marriages law were repealed.

On the other hand, political leaders dominating the state held positions on mixed marriages that urged the repeal of petty apartheid laws as long as they did not affect white hegemony. In 1985 a debate occurred in the House of Assembly over the repeal of the Mixed Marriages and Immorality (Section 16) Acts. The NP faction generally argued the laws needed to be repealed for four main reasons: (1) there was no scriptural justification for the laws; (2) the laws were discriminatory; (3) the laws negatively affected particular families; and (4) if the laws were repealed, they would not erase white privileges. NP leaders argued that these particular laws could be revoked because many other laws and practices remained that kept white privilege and group rights intact:

> It is clear from the report that the continued ordering of own communities in the social, educational and constitutional spheres will

not be affected by the repeal of the legislation concerned ... With regard to the road ahead prophets of doom may appear, and there will be many of them to predict the ruin of the White man in this country and more specifically also the ruin of the Afrikaner in this country ... We shall only become stronger if we utilize what we have at our disposal, namely our talents, skills and abilities, because then the White man in SA will be what he has been over the years.[48]

The Assembly voted to repeal the legislation in 1985. Revoking the laws was an important component in the Botha's 'total strategy' policy. It appeased moderates in business areas and international leaders looking for change in apartheid's implementation. Leaders dominating the NGK, in contrast, did not enthusiastically support the repeal of the miscegenation laws because of the 'multinational' situation in South Africa. Such laws maintained the identity of the separate nations, and they also upheld Afrikaner ethnic purity, a goal that the NGK continued to endorse in the 1980s.

Finally, the publication of *Church and Society* (CS) reflected the official NGK response to South Africa's socio-political environment in this era of mutual engagement. In some ways, CS was a dramatic break from previous church statements on social and racial policy. CS rejected biblical justifications for apartheid, it declared racism a sin, it allowed for multiracial church services, it admitted that strong church–nation ties hindered the confessional nature of the church, and it downplayed the emphases on race and nation embodied in earlier church reports. But in the end, CS was a very ambiguous document that reflected the NGK's need to accommodate a variety of ideological and class interests within the church. For example, on the issue of apartheid, the NGK rejected the practice of apartheid, not the theory.[49] It believed that social and political systems which protected minority or ethnic groups could be justified and upheld *if* they were applied justly and according to biblical norms. The 'good intentions' of past governments were acknowledged by the NGK, even though concrete application, unseen at the time of implementation, led to some negative side-effects. This position resonated with moderates and even liberals within the church who felt the NGK's past positions on race policy had not clarified the distinction between policy and practice; but it also helped appease conservatives (and moderates) because the NGK did not denounce apartheid as an idea. The NGK continued to uphold past positions that gave moral and biblically normative legitimation to the apartheid ideal so its members could rest assured that the denomination did not necessarily produce heretical statements in the past.

In sum, CS was crafted ambiguously in an attempt to meet the majority of its members who were not ready to embrace drastic political change. The church did not take a lead anywhere in the document supporting specific government reforms nor did it push for socio-political change (for example, revoking specific apartheid laws). Instead, it safely commented on issues that had already been enacted upon by the government. For example, the church supported but it did not go any further than the state regarding mixed marriages, labor reform, and African urbanization. Beyers Naudé, former director of the Christian Institute, commented on the vague or ambiguous positions on socio-political matters in the CS in the following words:

> CS 1986 was an attempt to formulate the theology of apartheid in such a way that it was acceptable to the majority of the DRC; so it would not lead to too severe a split in the DRC. Because I think they know there is a possibility of a split in the DRC, and that's why the formulations in the documents are very, very guarded. They were a result of compromise. They were deliberately vague so as not to create a crisis situation in the DRC.[50]

The NGK's apprehension regarding political reform was related to its commitment to the needs of the Afrikaner people. NGK leaders throughout the 1980s attempted to maintain Afrikaner interests and cohesion despite the multitude of political and economic changes affecting the country. It was the NP-dominated state, not a civil society institution like the NGK, which took the lead in implementing change that helped bring about the greater democratization in South African society, and this was related in part to the NP's constituency which was more inclusive and open to reform than the laity associated with the NGK.

THE NP-DOMINATED STATE'S GENERAL POSITION ON RACE POLICY (1989–94)

Beginning in 1990, South Africa entered a transition from authoritarian rule to an inclusive democracy.[51] The 1980s and 1990s saw a flurry of political transitions from authoritarianism to democratic rule, primarily in Latin American and Eastern European countries. In the attempt to understand South Africa's transition, works have emerged that apply the broader theories and concepts of democratization literature to the South African case study.[52]

In many ways, South Africa's political transition mirrored the assumptions found in the 'process' approach, namely, the South African regime entered the transitional process because of a widespread popular perception of crisis and its inability to resolve it. Moreover, the democratization process was characterized by successful pact-building between the ANC and the NP wherein compromises occurred that allowed for the establishment of a new political arrangement. Finally, the process was accompanied by a gradual phase of negotiation that fostered stability and moderation.

But South Africa's transition away from authoritarian rule differed in many ways from the Latin American and Eastern European transitions. First, the apartheid state left an indelible legacy on South Africa's negotiating process by leaving behind an extremely divided society. Second, apartheid left deep socio-economic cleavages and scars among its populace; effects that had to be addressed as the country was moving toward liberalization and democratization. Third, South Africa's authoritarian nature was unique. The regime was an oligarchical democracy, or a democracy for whites only. This meant the state could extend the existing democratic institutions to population groups that had been excluded *if* the negotiating partners agreed on this pattern.[53]

Finally, South Africa's transition differed from others in its unique civil society arrangement. Under apartheid, state leaders encouraged civil society institutions in Afrikaner and English-speaking circles, like the NGK, FAK, and so forth, because these organizations offered the state legitimacy. In non-white or mixed sectors, however, civil society associations were severely constrained or challenged, for example, the SACC. As noted in other chapters, the significance of this distinction is that some of the most active, above-ground civil society institutions, like the NGK, were greater obstacles to the achievement of inclusive democracy than the state because they catered to exclusive, nationalist interests. When the time was ripe for democratic liberalization, it was the state, rather than these visible civil society institutions, that led the effort toward negotiation and political reform. Before exploring NGK–state relations in the 1990s, it is important to understand more fully the details of the events leading to South Africa's democratic transition.

By the late 1980s, the South African government faced unremitting problems: the National Party was a spent political force; the liberation movement continued to gain strength; and the economy experienced slow growth.[54] Leaders in the National Party and the business community realized that repression and micro-reform offered inadequate solutions to the long-term health of South Africa.[55] These leaders considered the possibility of negotiating with leaders of major liberation movements – the end goal being a formula that would retain white control and economic privilege. Further reform and negotiations, however, could not occur while P.W. Botha was in office. Botha sided with the securocrats in his later years, and he gave no intention of engaging in further reform after 1985. When P.W. Botha suffered health problems in 1989, the opportunity to initiate reform became a possibility. F.W. de Klerk, Minister of National Education and the Transvaal NP leader, replaced Botha as the head of the NP in February 1989. He became the President of South Africa after general elections were held on 6 September 1989.

With the succession of De Klerk to power, the political landscape in South Africa changed dramatically. First, the Mass Democratic Movement, an alliance of United Democratic Front and COSATU supporters, organized a mass campaign to challenge apartheid policy. Second, meaningful change began to occur under De Klerk. In September 1989 large demonstrations displaying prominent ANC and SACP banners were allowed for the first time. In October 1989 eight political prisoners, cohorts of Nelson Mandela, were released from prison, and in November, De Klerk stated that the National Security Management System would be restructured in a way that lessened the influence of the security forces in political affairs.

De Klerk announced unprecedented reforms in his historic parliamentary speech of February 1990. He legalized 61 organizations, including the African National Congress (ANC), the South African Communist Party and the Pan African Congress, eased the State of Emergency's regulations, and lifted press restrictions. Nine days later, on February 11, Nelson Mandela was released from prison.

Within a few months of Mandela's release, Mandela and De Klerk signed the *Groote Schuur* accord (May 2–4) which called for negotiations that would bring about a peaceful settlement in South Africa. The phase of negotiations defined the years between 1990 and 1993, even though many other important events occurred including the revoking of key apartheid laws, the lifting of the State of Emergency, and the suspension of armed struggle by the ANC.

Formal negotiations took place in the early years of transition through the Convention for a Democratic South Africa (CODESA I), a forum of 19 political groups that arranged to meet on 20–21 December 1991 to devise working groups which would propose a mutually acceptable form of government for the 'New South Africa'.[56] After considerable progress on several issues through CODESA I 'working groups' and a successful white referendum in March 1992,[57] CODESA II (May 15–16) stalled amidst renewed hostility between the government and the ANC. ANC members on the local level expressed dissatisfaction with the compromises that the ANC leadership was making concerning the cessation of armed struggle, the postponement of a constituent assembly, the influence of minorities in the new political structures, and other issues. In late May, ANC leaders called for a return to protest action and general strikes as a public show of strength, similar to the government's March 1992 referendum. In early June (1992) the Goldstone Commission issued its interim report revealing the government's financial and military backing of Inkatha Freedom Party (IFP) vigilantes as a contributing factor regarding the ongoing political violence. This judgment seemed to vindicate the ANC's belief that the government was forwarding 'third force' activity for purposes of stifling political progress. Finally, the Boipatong massacre, in which the IFP, in collaboration with the SADF, was suspected of killing over 40 blacks on 17 June 1992, the day after the ANC had kicked off its mass action campaign, sullied relations between the two major negotiating partners, confirming the ANC's argument that the NP was not a neutral or gracious negotiating partner. The ANC, at this point, withdrew from the negotiating process.

After a four-month breakdown of formal negotiations, the ANC and the NP re-entered the negotiating process. It was the Bisho massacre, in which the Ciskei military force killed 28 ANC supporters and injured about 200 others during an opposition march in early September, that stirred Mandela and De Klerk to sign a 'Record of Understanding' on 26 September 1992 pledging the ANC and the NP to restart political discussions that would lead to a democratically elected constitution-making body. The government promised the ANC that it would release the remaining political prisoners, control police and security activity, and investigate violence.[58]

Multi-party negotiations continued, reaching their greatest success in 1993. Twenty-six parties convened in April 1993 to form the first fully representative forum (the Multiparty Negotiating Process) to negotiate South Africa's future. Great pressure was on the leaders to achieve plans for a transitional authority and nonracial elections because of increased tension over the tragic assassination of SACP leader Chris Hani and rising political violence. The negotiation phase involved many triumphs and setbacks as the partners, particularly the NP and the ANC, expressed divergent interests on significant issues.

Throughout the negotiation phase, the NP's intentions for political change were clear. The NP desired an evolutionary transformation of society that retained white minority privileges and lessened the dominance of black majority rule. The NP supported consensus, not majority, rule, veto mechanisms for whites, proportional voting, and rotating executive presidents. NP proposals were based on notions of consociational arrangements, or political models promoted by scholars like Hermann Giliomee, Lawrence Schlemmer, and Arend Lijphart.[59] Consociationalism refers to the model of governance in 'divided societies' where conflict among the social 'segments' (usually referring to race or ethnic groups) is resolved not by simple majority rule but by other arrangements (like power-sharing, mutual vetoes, and/or proportional representation) that foster peace and stability. The NP argued that ethnic and racial differences within South Africa limited the possibility of South Africans being able to respect the individualism and majoritarianism that were at the base of liberal democracy and one-person, one-vote models – consociationalism was the better governance model.

Leaders of the ANC and other liberation movements rejected the notions underlying the NP's power-sharing proposals. They rejected the view that ethnicity was at the root of South African society, arguing instead that the apartheid state created the ethnic and race divisions that destroyed the common humanity in South African society. Besides, the NP's demands for mutual vetoes and power-sharing could easily turn into the continuation of minority rule and massive inequalities. In contrast to the NP, the ANC desired a unitary, non-racial, one-person, one-vote political system that would permit all South Africans equal rights of political participation and responsibility. The ANC also promoted an interim government and a constituent assembly. An interim government would replace the discredited apartheid state, and a constituent assembly would be elected democratically to write the constitution of the future South African state. These measures ensured the voices of the masses in the construction of the future South African state.

The differences between the ANC's and the NP's views regarding South Africa's future led to heated negotiations. An eventual agreement on the form of government – a non-racial liberal democracy protecting group rights within a capitalist economy – involved substantial shifts in the views of the major political organizations as well as shifts within the factions of the ANC and the NP. The three years of negotiations also led to the first non-racial election in South Africa from Tuesday, April 26 to Friday, April 29 1994. Euphoria spread throughout the land, dispelling for the moment the hardships that would inevitably follow.

NGK–STATE RELATIONS DURING THE ERA OF MUTUAL ENGAGEMENT (1989–94)

During the transitional phase, the NGK's relationship to the NP-dominated state continued to be one of mutual engagement, or the two entities supported one another for the most part, but situations arose periodically where leaders within the church and state arrived at different opinions about policy directions.[60] One area where the NGK, led by moderate leaders, *maintained* its support for state leaders associated with the National Party was its position on apartheid. The NGK, like the NP, offered a qualified rejection of apartheid in the 1990s. Throughout the 1990s state leaders and the National Party suggested that apartheid's application was flawed, not the idea as such. In a parliamentary address, F.W. de Klerk explained that reform had to occur because of the impracticality and poor application of apartheid:

> The policy of separate development was visibly and tangibly failing. The realities of our society compelled us to the realization that absolute self-determination in a heterogeneous country such as ours was not attainable. The fact that we were demographically and geographically intertwined as well as socio-economic realities, made this impossible. The best efforts of outstanding leaders over a period of almost four decades proved irrefutably that policies of ethnic and territorial separation could not offer our country a viable solution.[61]

Moreover, F.W. de Klerk had difficulty apologizing for apartheid, saying:

> Some of our people continue to be obsessed with past grievances. Some insist on apologies to everything that has occurred in the past. Many mistakes were made by all sides and parties. If we dwell on

the real or imagined sins of the past, we shall never be able to find one another in the present.[62]

De Klerk eventually expressed regret about apartheid, but it was a qualified statement. In October 1992 he recognized that Afrikaners had held on to the apartheid dream for too long, even when it was obvious the dream could not be realized. For this, he apologized. But he went on to point out that apartheid was never intended to be evil or malevolent. Instead, it was supposed to bring justice to all.[63]

The moderate leadership of the NGK followed state leaders in offering a qualified rejection of apartheid in the 1990s. The NGK's inability to sign the resolutions at the Vereeniging Consultation and the Rustenburg Conference, which in the latter case condemned 'apartheid in its intention, its implementation, and its consequences as an evil policy', signified its similarity with state leaders associated with the NP on this matter.[64] In *Church and Society* (1990), the NGK rejected racism, but it also stated that apartheid had good intentions – it was only its implementation that led to unfortunate consequences:

> There were also honest and noble intentions by those concerned to achieve the optimal development of all population groups ... Gradually it became clear to the DRC that the policy of apartheid as a political system in practice went much further than the acknowledgment of the right and freedom of peoples and cultural groups to stay true to their own values ... Any system which in practice functions in this way, is unacceptable in the light of Scripture and the Christian conscious and must be rejected as sinful.[65]

The 1990 *Church and Society's* statement on apartheid was an attempt to explain to its laity why a system that caused so much evil and/or oppression could be accepted by a church for so many decades. Institutional support for apartheid takes years and decades to 'undo' and shame accompanies such actions. In the end, the NGK's qualified rejection of apartheid mirrored state leaders' opinions.

Not surprisingly, outspoken *verligte* leaders within the NGK were much more willing to push the NGK on 'apologizing' for apartheid than the official NGK leadership who felt that they needed to retain the church's ideological, class, and cultural cohesiveness. At the Rustenburg Conference (November 1990), an ecumenical gathering of 230 church leaders from over 800 denominations, delegates were invited to formulate a strategy for a united Christian witness in a changing South Africa. During the course of the proceedings, W.D. Jonker, Theology Professor at the University of Stellenbosch, declared that 'I not only confess my own sin and guilt, and my personal responsibility for the political, social, economical and structural wrongs that have been done to many of you ... but vicariously I dare also to do that in the name of the NGK ... and for the Afrikaner people as a whole.'[66] The NGK delegation later declared that Jonker's confession could not be accepted as a confession for the church as a whole. The official leadership of the NGK had to be very sensitive in supporting the more liberal wing within the NGK for fear of schism within the church *and* for fear of making political statements that would push the government toward political reforms that it could not accept. P.C. Potgieter, former moderator of the NGK, explained why the NGK could not accept the liberal reforms suggested in documents like Vereeniging:

> If you look at the declaration of Vereeniging, you will find that it refers to particular laws they wanted rescinded. At that stage, we knew that the people fighting for the repeal of these laws were political bodies that were still banned, the ANC and so on. By supporting those, we could in a certain sense be accused of making revolutionary political statements ... . What we also detected in the speeches of the people taking part were certain phrases that very much reminded us of things like the Harare Declaration and the Freedom Charter. So these things were present, and this was rather political language.[67]

The NGK's position on apartheid and its reluctance to embrace 'radical reform' demonstrated its support for state leaders associated with the NP in this transitional phase. But while the NGK continued to support the NP during the era of mutual engagement, it also had to distance itself from the pace and types of reform the NP state leaders were embracing.

For example, leaders dominating each entity held divergent positions on the March 1992 referendum. In February 1992, De Klerk declared an all-white referendum after suffering a parliamentary defeat by the Conservative Party in a Potchefstroom by-election. The referendum tested whether white voters supported the 'continuation of the reform process which the State President began on 2 February 1990, and which is aimed at a new constitution through negotiation.'[68] Regarding the referendum, the NGK told its members that it could not tell them how to vote. A February 1992 *Kerkbode* editorial summarized the NGK's official position in these words:

> The church has a task: ... to ask that all those involved with the referendum campaign shall execute it in a Christian attitude and style and carry it out in a responsible way ... However, what the church cannot do – not in its various meetings or with its official leaders – is to recommend to its members to vote 'yes' or 'no'.[69]

The NGK explained that it supported the norm of political justice and it rejected political systems that hurt people, but it could not take a stance on the referendum because this was engaging in party politics. An account by Piet Meiring, a liberal NGK theologian, suggests another reason for why the NGK was unable to concur with the NP-dominated state's position on reform:

> Johan Heyns talked with F.W. de Klerk the day De Klerk needed to devise the wording of the referendum document. Heyns told De Klerk not to formulate it in the way he did because the NGK would not be able to tell its members to vote for it since the referendum's wording was indicative of the removal specifically of apartheid by the National Party, which the church, because of its past, couldn't accept. De Klerk didn't listen because he didn't want churches to back it. He simply wanted people to vote.[70]

This account indicates the imprisoned nature of the NGK in the 1990s. It was unable to take a stand on reform because of the 'shackles' its past placed on its policy. The NGK could not denounce apartheid or support far-reaching reforms because it had given moral and biblical justifications to apartheid in previous decades. Elia Tema, a progressive clergyman in the NGKA, attested to the NGK's dilemma in the following words:

> The current leadership of the DRC is cornered. We must understand their problem. They have been badgering the country, members, community to be loyal to God, by fighting for the upholding of apartheid as a protection of the survival of the white race in this country ... The question is now, 'Mr. Pastor, please tell us, for all these years were you not telling us a lie? What is the truth?' They are in a plight today. And this is why it is very difficult for them.[71]

The NGK's past made it reluctant to embrace substantive reform but the NGK, unlike the NP, also had to recognize the fears of conservative and moderate members who felt negotiation with 'the enemy' on the removal of apartheid would mean the demise of white control and security. The NGK had also historically stood for the survival and cohesion of the Afrikaner people which were at stake in things like the March referendum; as such, the church could not tell its laity to vote 'yes'.

The story above also points to the high amount of informal interaction that continued into the 1990s between church and state leaders. Church leaders like Johan Heyns called F.W. de Klerk about weighty issues like the referendum. Although the distance between the church and the NP widened in the era of mutual engagement, informal discussions among leaders continued because both 'ministered' to Afrikaners and both entities relied on the other to meet the 'people's' socio-economic needs.

Above all, the incident shows that moderate leaders in the NGK were much more open to the reforms that state leaders embraced than the NGK's official position suggested. Heyns, a close confidant of P.W. Botha, was a skilled *verligte*. He tried to push the NGK to accept partial reform, but was unable to do so because of the weight of the NGK's past, the existence of conservative interests, and the need to preserve Afrikaner cohesion. He recognized conservative fears and followed up on them. Like so many of the NGK leaders, Heyns put aside his own preferences for the sake of the church's unity. Ironically and sadly, Heyns was the victim of a fatal, right-wing assassination on 6 November 1994.

The issue of structural unity also raised significant differences in terms of policy goals between the NGK and the state. While state leaders recognized that structural reforms needed to take place that would alter apartheid indefinitely, including the unbanning of political parties that met the needs of black South Africans, the establishment of democratic decision-making, and the opening of the NP to other races, the NGK rejected the opportunity to instigate structural reforms affecting the church.

The NGK's history involved separate church structures for 'separate nations'. Starting in the 1930s, NGK theologians argued that the diversity of humanity embodied a creational norm. Because diversity was normative, it, not unity, was the leading principle for organizing societal life, including church structures. The church's position on the need for separate church structures was demonstrated as late as 1974 in *Human Relations*: 'In its visible structure the church should not exist divorced from the people to whom it must preach the Word of God ... Therefore a diversity of peoples can lead to a diversity of indigenous churches.'[72] Conservative NGK ministers argued that spiritual unity could be recognized in the present age in terms of confession and service, but not in one non-racial Reformed church.[73]

The unity–diversity debate was reopened at the 1982 Pretoria Theological Conference. Theologians like Adrio König, Jaap Durand, and David Bosch questioned the NGK's justification for separate church structures for separate nations because they argued the NGK misinterpreted Biblical passages and elevated the diversity principle, overlooking the fact that unity should be the normative principle. A unified church structure was the avenue for reconciliation among South Africans. These arguments, although not new, greatly challenged the NGK because never before had they received such a receptive audience. In addition, reforms in the South African society made it more difficult for the NGK to maintain its structural feature without appearing racist. However, as late as 1986, the NGK's position on church structures remained unchanged. It did not elevate the diversity principle as much as it had in previous years and it allowed for open church services, but it still justified separate churches structures for separate peoples.[74]

In the late 1980s, beginning with Vereeniging, efforts toward structural unity began among the NGK 'family'.[75] The Vereeniging Consultation tried to develop proposals for structural church unity among the Reformed churches in South Africa, but the NGK was unable to embrace structural church unity at Vereeniging. The NGK could not identify with the pledge of a united, non-racial Reformed Church 'because their church, while recognizing the need for spiritual and visible unity, is not yet ready to say what the structural model of the one-church-to-be will be.'[76]

Throughout the 1990s, the *Nederduitse Gereformeerde Sendingkerk* (NGSK) and the *Nederduitse Gereformeerde Kerk in Afrika* (NGKA) called for unification into one church structure, but the NGK delayed progress on the affair. It argued that changed attitudes among the church family had to occur before structural unity could happen. It also proposed models suggesting unity on the synodical, not local, level. The NGSK and NGKA rejected the NGK's positions. They felt structural unity was more imperative than changed attitudes (because the latter could take decades), and the NGK's insistence on local options meant another form of separate development among the churches.

The NGK, on the other hand, could not move beyond the position it stated in its 1990 CS document:

> ... that with a view to the effective ministry of the Word and in order to minister to the needs of various linguistic and cultural group, allowance may be made for the church to be indigenous ... The concept of the fundamental unity of the human race is of immense importance to the biblical perspective regarding the dignity ... of every person. In the Bible, this unity is always referred to in its religious context, namely man's God-given status, ... and the universal presentation of the Gospel message.[77]

The NGK continued to delay structural church unity by promoting the argument that unity was essential but it could be achieved in a spiritual way rather than an earthly context. Diversity needed to be accommodated in church structures in a manner that embodied diversity within unity: 'In the structuring of the church, provision may be made for linguistic and cultural differences related to the diversity of peoples, but then in such a way that the church's unity is not jeopardized, but served.'[78]

The issue of structural church unity represents more than the NGK's ability to theologically reconsider its views on race and society; it is an issue that pointedly tests whether the NGK can distance itself from apartheid's racism. Separate churches for the different 'nations' is separate development for the church. While the NP was able to distance itself from apartheid in a structural manner after 1990, for example, by helping to dismantle some of the laws undergirding separate development, the NGK refused to budge on the issue of structural church unity. The NGK's continuation of separate church structures was an indication that it promoted a form of separate development. State leaders, on the other hand, had withdrawn their support for the vision of separate development by promoting a form of substantive democracy. W.A. Saayman described the NGK's unwillingness to follow the NP on structural change in these words:

> The politicians can do that [make change] ... because they are forced into it. But it's very difficult for the church to follow them. And so it's interesting that the church is lagging behind. They are

consistently 3–4 years behind the NP at the moment. The NP has opened its membership, for example, and indeed have taken in black members. The DRC still can't bring itself to fully accept that. It can't bring itself to unity with the black churches.[79]

From 1993 to 1994, various meetings were held throughout South Africa where the NGK met delegates of the NGKA and NGSK to discuss the issue of church unity. In March 1993, at a World Alliance of Reformed Churches Conference (WARC) on church unity, the NGK agreed that the acid test about whether the NGK was distancing itself from apartheid's racism was the unity of the NGK family. It committed itself to the process of church unity. The NGKA and NGSK assumed that this meant the NGK was willing to join its efforts toward church unity which were already in progress, meaning movement toward one, united Reformed church. However, the NGK had something else in mind. In the words of Frits Gaum, one of the leading participants from the NGK in the WARC conference on church unity, 'We are saying we don't want to start all over with the unity process. We want to be part of the unity process ... But at the meeting, our ideas and models will be on the table, and our models will be one with all the other models.'[80] The NGK did not embrace structural unity wholeheartedly as the NGKA and NGSK had hoped. Jaap Durand, a member of the NGSK and delegate of the WARC conference, tells why the NGK was reluctant to embrace structural unity:

> I suspect that DRC leadership consciously or unconsciously fears that a determined drive toward church unity within clearly stated parameters could cause a mass exodus from the church, dwarfing the members lost when the *Afrikaanse Protestantse Kerk* was established in the wake of the acceptance of *Church and Society* at the DRC's 1986 General Synod.[81]

Adrio König makes a similar point in suggesting that the NGK was unable to move toward structural unity for fear that its conservative laity would leave the NGK or cause an even larger secession than the APK:

> You might remember that there is a certain difference in mentality between two different groups of DRC people and ministers. There has always been the group which opposed apartheid. We

all rejected apartheid, but we never threatened to withdraw, to split and create a new church ... But you have the second group who was always the 'in' group in terms of apartheid. And when the DRC started moving toward unity in 1986 and 1990, this group simply broke away ... The mentality behind it: you do as we ask and we do what we want. Now if the DRC wants to move into structural unity with the other churches, you'll see a split 3, 4, 5 times bigger ... It will not be able to negotiate with these people.[82]

The NGK, historically a powerful civil society institution offering an element of cohesion among Afrikaners, had lost its ability to give its laity firm political guidance in the 1980s and 1990s because it continued to cling to policy goals and directions that appeased conservatives in an effort to avoid a schism. The 'weakness of some' guided NGK policy on issues like scriptural unity, rather than the Word of God. In the end, the church's position differed from positions held by state leaders who were willing to revise the directives of separate development for the purposes of white survival and economic prosperity. This situation revealed the NP-dominated state moving ahead of a societal institution like the NGK on reform and democratization.

CONCLUSION

From 1979 to 1994 leaders dominating the NGK and the state exhibited a relationship of mutual engagement in which they held similar opinions on the majority of policy issues. Most of the time, NGK leaders continued to give their unequivocal support to the state, as it had during the first three decades of apartheid rule; however, situations arose periodically where state and NGK leaders arrived at different opinions concerning policy directions and strategies. During these years, state leaders took the lead in promoting the attainment of white survival and economic prosperity through political reform while the NGK lagged behind, supporting the goals of white, but more specifically Afrikaner, survival and economic prosperity through a slower implementation of reform.

The NGK, representing an avenue of Afrikaner civil society, was unable to foster the realization of full-scale democracy. Contrary to the expectations of mainstream literature, civil society institutions can be a hindrance to the realization of political reform and demo-cratization. Although the South African state led by the NP did not willingly embrace democratic change, it opened itself to such initia-tives long before institutions like the NGK. NGK leaders, on the other hand, were unable to embrace political reform efforts whole-heartedly because they sought to appease the more exclusivistic needs of conservative and moderate laity in an effort to keep the church body together.

7 Conclusion

The focus on NGK–state interactions over a 60-year period reveals important changes in NGK–state relations related to the various factions dominating both entities. It also points to the possibility of civil society posing a greater obstacle to the realization of widespread democracy than the state in situations where civil society institutions are associated with exclusive, ethnic interests. In this final chapter, I summarize the various strands of conflict and cooperation in NGK–state relations from 1934 to 1994, anticipate what the NGK's position as a civil society institution will be in a democratic South Africa, and relate current state–civil society debates in South Africa to the broader theoretical conclusions of this study.

COOPERATION AND CONFLICT BETWEEN THE STATE AND THE NGK

This project examined how the NGK's relationship to the South African state changed vis-à-vis the development of race policy from 1934 to 1994. The focus on the NGK to the exclusion of civil society institutions like the South African Council of Churches or the South African Students' Organization was an attempt to demonstrate the significant influence that the NGK wielded as an Afrikaner civil society institution within South Africa during most of the twentieth century. Three distinct types of NGK–state relations were discovered over a 60-year period.

From 1934 to 1947, state–NGK relations were described as coexisting conflict, a situation characterized by moderate policy collusion and moderate to low official interaction. The factions dominating the NGK and the state were relatively autonomous from one another regarding the development of race policy in this phase. Although cooperation between the two entities occurred, they held differing opinions on the implementation of race policy. The dominant factions in both the NGK and the state promoted segregationist legislation aimed at reproducing a cheap labor force; however, the 'purist' faction dominating the NGK supported a stricter implementation of segregation than the UP-dominated state based on particular class interests and socio-political concerns. Over time, Afrikaner civil society institutions like the NGK grew increasingly dissatisfied with the UP-dominated state's commitment to partial segregation, supporting political change through organs like the National Party in an effort to achieve the objectives of Afrikaner nationalism broadly conceived.

From 1948 to 1961 the NGK and the NP-dominated state exhibited a relationship of mutual engagement in which the groups dominating each entity held similar opinions on the majority of policy issues. However, situations arose periodically where NP leaders dominating the state and NGK leaders arrived at different opinions concerning strategies related to race policy. More specifically, church and state officials interacted closely and even held the same goal of Afrikaner supremacy in political and economic spheres, but they formulated independent policies on how to achieve this goal. The reason for discrepancies between NGK–state strategies on race policy lies in the diversity of positions that existed within Afrikaner nationalist circles. Within the NGK, purist and pragmatist factions disagreed over the implementation of apartheid, or purists and pragmatists forwarded vertical apartheid or partial apartheid respectively. From 1948 to 1958, the 'purist' faction dominated the NGK, leading to the NGK's adoption of separate development which contrasted to the NP-dominated state's *baasskap* position – a form of segregation that involved white domination within a racially segregated society. From 1958 to 1961, a 'switch' in factions occurred. As NGK leaders suggested the relaxation of race policy, state leaders implemented the more comprehensive policy of separate development.

Collaboration described NGK–state relations from 1962 to 1978. During the era of collaboration, leaders dominating the NP-dominated state and the NGK were committed to the maintenance of three goals: (a) white, mainly Afrikaner, supremacy in the political and social arena, (b) economic prosperity through white or Afrikaner-based capitalism, and (c) the implementation of a racial policy that maintained ethnic purity and overcame the criticisms of 'negative' apartheid. While leaders within the NGK and the state collaborated with one another, the two entities became almost indistinguishable with the NGK paralleling the NP-dominated state's perspectives on race policy. South Africa's era of collaboration was characterized by strong authoritarian rule in an Afrikaner-dominated state that engaged heavily with white civil society institutions which were forced or voluntarily gave their loyalty to the state and Afrikaner interests.

From 1979 to 1994 the NGK and the state again exhibited a relationship of mutual engagement. Most of the time, the NGK continued to give its unequivocal support to the state, as it had during the first three decades of apartheid rule; however, situations arose periodically where leaders within the NP-dominated state and the NGK arrived at different opinions concerning policy directions and strategies. During these years, NP leaders ruling the state responded to pragmatic political directives and middle-class interests by promoting the attainment of white survival and economic prosperity through political reform while the NGK lagged behind, supporting the goals of white, but more specifically Afrikaner, survival and economic prosperity through a slower implementation of reform. This is because NGK leaders tried to accommodate the needs of its conservative and moderate members who were not willing or ready to embrace political reform that repudiated the ideal of apartheid and weakened the cohesion of the Afrikaner *volk*.

The examination of this church–state case study shows varied and dynamic state–civil society relations. Some of the interactions, for example, the first era of mutual engagement between the NGK and the NP-dominated state, defy expected outcomes, but all of them help to unravel the complexities of state–civil society relations. The analysis of other state–civil society relations in South Africa or any other country, within an authoritarian or democratic context, can only further enrich our understanding of state–civil society interactions, a point that will be elaborated in the final section.

THE NGK'S POSITION IN A NON-RACIAL, DEMOCRATIC SOUTH AFRICA

Some broad directions can be discerned regarding the NGK's position in a non-racial, democratic South Africa. In general, the NGK will not be as politically prominent as it was during most of the twentieth century. Church leaders will concentrate on the 'spiritual' dimension of their ministry, in part, because they want to avoid the detrimental effects that collaboration and engagement brought to the NGK during the apartheid years (e.g., loss of autonomy, loss of respect). Moreover, the ANC leaders who dominate the state do not have a natural affinity with the NGK because of the church's strong identification with Afrikaners.

Nevertheless, the state's new leaders cannot ignore the importance of religion and the church. The great majority of South Africans identify themselves as Christians. In the 1980s religious organizations like the South African Council of Churches and the Institute for Contextual Theology, and the churches associated with them, generally supported the liberation struggle and promoted widespread democratic reform.[1] They gave hope to those Christians who felt churches like the NGK were opposing the spirit of Christianity because of their positions on apartheid. Nelson Mandela, the State President, has indicated that religious leaders can give the current government guidance in setting moral standards:

> What I'm stressing is that the church is a very powerful organization, which has played an important role in our struggle for democratic changes and it is necessary for us to recognize that role. And the church is committed to high moral values ... the involvement of the church in government will help us to raise moral standards in government ...[2]

The new government has also recognized the importance of establishing warm relations with the NGK because of its 'moral force' among Afrikaners who hold prominent positions in all areas of society. The NGK leadership has the ability to persuade its membership to support the government's programs and to help the country build national unity. Nelson Mandela commented on the need to work with the NGK and other Afrikaner civil society institutions in the following way:

> Let me indicate to you that there is not a single opinion-maker, as an organization among the Afrikaners, that I have not seen. I have seen a wide range of such organizations – the generals ... I have seen twice the full leadership of the Dutch Reformed Church. I have seen the leadership of the Broederbond, the *Vryheidstigting* ... I have done so because it is absolutely necessary for us to speak with one voice on all the major national questions in this country ...[3]

Churches and religion will continue to have a great influence in South Africa, and the NGK can prove to be an important institution forwarding national unity; however, the NGK's political influence will certainly be diminished in South Africa's current political dispensation compared to earlier eras. This is because it will not have the open door it once had with governmental leaders. In interviews conducted in 1993 with three of the top leaders of the NGK (i.e., J. Heyns,

P.C. Potgieter, F. Gaum), I was told this situation would actually be a healthy one for the NGK. Frits Gaum, the editor of *Die Kerkbode* and Johan Heyns, former moderator of the NGK (1986–90), expressed the benefits of a church 'delinked' from the state and the government in the following way:

> Everything can't be the same as it was in the past. Many NGK members were members of parliament, but it won't be so in the future. In the past, we agreed so much with the government, but I think that in the future, we won't have this arrangement, and we'll be more willing to look at the Bible rather than members of parliament. In a sense, the DRC will be more free. We will be free to say what we think.[4]

> Our church will have a tremendous role in the new South Africa. Perhaps circumstances will force the church to be a real church, and not to play a sort of semi-political party role. Not to be so closely linked with a particular party or with the culture of one group of the population – the white Afrikaners. The church was much too closely tied to the state and the Afrikaner *volk* in the past, and this hurt the church ... Obviously, this won't be the case in the future – to the betterment of the church.[5]

From interviews with these leaders, there was almost a sense of relief that the NGK would no longer have an 'inner connection' to the government nor would it have to represent only the needs and interests of the Afrikaner people. Responses from such leaders also indicated the church could be a force for change in the future. With a new political dispensation, the NGK could take the lead in promoting change, reconciliation, and unity in a new South Africa. Johan Heyns expressed this hope in the following way:

> In a future South Africa, church and state will be far away from each other in comparison to the past. I think the role of the church will be that of an agent of reconciliation. Reconciliation between the different churches and the different political parties and the different sectors of our population.[6]

Despite the hope that NGK leaders have expressed concerning the church's desire and ability to forward reconciliation and national unity, it is unlikely that the NGK will do so in the near future. For generations, Afrikaner institutions promoted the message that 'blacks' could not be trusted because of their liberal or undisciplined nature, that 'blacks' were of a different nature and culture than whites and so forth. The NGK's top leadership, which dismisses these caricatures of black South Africans, cannot convince its members overnight to rid itself of these ideas. A new generation exposed to more accurate ideas is necessary. As Herbie Brand, a minister of a NGSK congregation in Cape Town, said, 'It will take a whole new generation of people, maybe even two, before they can accept the situation that has been created. It will take a long time.'[7]

Moreover, the NGK will have a very difficult time divorcing itself from the needs of the Afrikaner people and pursuing efforts at national unity among all South Africans. In an October 1996 meeting with Nelson Mandela, Ministers S. Bengu and G. Fraser-Moleketi, and W. Sisulu of the South African Broadcasting Corporation (SABC), NGK delegates, led by Reverend Freek Swanepoel, Moderator of the General Synod, stressed the need to maintain Christian values and principles in South Africa, but they seemed more concerned about preserving Afrikaner values and principles.[8] The delegation noted that English was rapidly becoming the language of communication within the government and within the SABC – a cause of great concern for Afrikaans-speaking peoples since Afrikaans is their mother-tongue and a source of great pride and cultural cohesiveness. The NGK's lobbying efforts regarding the problems associated with the dominance of English is not unusual considering its constituency, but a more inclusive understanding of the situation might have recognized that English can help build national unity because of its lack of 'political baggage' and the sheer number of South Africans who can speak English. The latter issues may have been explored at this particular meeting, but overall, the NGK's support for things like the maintenance of Christian-National education, the Afrikaans language, and power-sharing arrangements tends to expose the church's desire for the upkeep of Afrikaner group interests and/or privileges first and foremost.

Some would argue that, as a way to 'cleanse' its past, the NGK should officially support the notion of 'collective guilt' being expressed for all Afrikaners due to the past grievances of apartheid. Although the NGK has acknowledged that apartheid became a political ideology protecting white minority interests to the exclusion of others, and while it has admitted that it sided with Afrikaner interests for too long, it has not supported the expression of 'collective guilt' because it views the confession of guilt as a personal matter.[9] These NGK positions bind

Afrikaners together but they do not necessarily find common ground with the ANC-led government. Moreover, the NGK's reluctance to embrace the new government because it does not adopt a 'Christian viewpoint' creates an automatic distance between the two entities.[10] It is likely that the NGK's relationship with the state will be one of co-existing conflict as the church respectfully disagrees with and distances itself from many of the ANC-promoted policies dominating the state.

For all its weaknesses, the NGK is a Christian church which has genuinely struggled to reform itself. It has made great strides in the last 15 years to distance itself from the 'theology of apartheid', to apologize for the pain and oppression it has caused, and to seek more inclusive arrangements of worship within Reformed institutions. In 1997, the NGK produced an 82-page document entitled 'Journey with Apartheid' that traced the NGK's cultural and racial positions since 1962. The NGK continues to argue that it did not have any evil intent in promoting apartheid, but it admits that it had 'not always heard the word of God correctly' in devising its positions. It also admitted to adhering too closely to the government of the time and for siding with Afrikaners to the exclusion of others:

> Due to the fact that in many instances members of one were also members of the other, an interplay between church and party/ruling body came into being which, although understandable, brought about the fact that the church did not always maintain the required critical distance from the powers that be ... Due to a deep and justified association with the plight of the people to whom the DRC ministered in the first instance – the Afrikaners – the church frequently tended to set the interests of its own people above that of others.[11]

The statements in 'Journey with Apartheid' affirm the NGK's commitment to greater unity in the church and South African society. These efforts should be recognized as sincere and encouraged so that bolder statements can be made in the future. The NGK also gave its general support to the Truth and Reconciliation Commission which many argue had at its root the hope of reconciliation and justice among races. Some would argue the NGK continued to look after its own people's interests when it reminded the government that the TRC must search out all the truths concerning apartheid, not just the atrocities committed under the white minority regime,[12] but it has also made statements like the following which indicated the church's earnest commitment to the TRC goals:

As people who have been saved by Christ, we are called to promote reconciliation among people. This means, inter alia, that we want to listen to other peoples' stories, that we seriously want to become aware of their pain and need, and to work together towards the healing of society and the solution of problems. We are called in this to acknowledge our own weaknesses unconditionally and to forgive other people theirs. In order to have a truly meaningful and visible share in reconciliation, we as a church would want to start on our own doorstep.[13]

In the end, outsiders can be reminded that the Afrikaners' commitment to a sovereign God, their connection with South Africa's land, and their personal talents could be powerful instruments in an effort to build a democratic South Africa *if* institutions like the NGK can help guide the Afrikaners away from the powerful pull of exclusive interests that have weighed them down in the past.

THEORETICAL CONCLUSIONS

Since the 1980s, the concept 'civil society' has been resurrected in academic circles. In large part, this is due to the wave of global democratization and the belief that civil society organizations play a pivotal role in democratic transitions. Contemporary scholarship examines many issues, but it especially concentrates on the proper interaction between state and civil society and the role of civil society regarding the emergence of a democratic transition.

The results of my research contribute to these contemporary debates. As indicated throughout this book, South Africa's white-settler colonial heritage and its unique type of authoritarianism inarguably shaped the nature and role of civil society during the twentieth century. South Africa's oligarchic, racist government disenfranchised and limited the civic activities of millions of South Africans. The majority, then, were excluded from engaging in autonomous, independent civic activities and joined the liberation movement instead. South Africa did contain active, above-ground civil society institutions, like the SACC, NGK, and the FAK, which mobilized, aggregated, and defined opinions vis-à-vis public policy, even representing the interests of their constituents to broader arenas. However, many of these civic institutions were limited in their racial, ethnic, and class make-up and they did not necessarily forward widespread democratic interests.

In fact, the NGK represented an civil society institution that was reluctant to embrace political reforms when the state was willing to promote it.

Despite the limitations of South Africa's civil society arrangements under apartheid, it can be argued that the associational activity within white and black civil society helped foster the relatively robust and pluralist civil society in South Africa today. A variety of trade unions, civic associations, women's groups, voluntary associations, and non-profits, with their origins in the apartheid era, exist and serve to strengthen South Africa's fledgling democracy today. It would be presumptuous, however, and altogether too optimistic to argue that South Africa's civil society has matured to the point of containing governmental abuses, generating a democratic political culture, and structuring a multitude of political channels that represents societal interests. In fact, some observers argue that South Africa's civil society arrangement today is too divided, exclusive, or co-opted to be considered healthy and autonomous. What lessons can South African learn from its past that will nurture a healthy, autonomous, and pluralistic civil society arrangement, one that can hold the state accountable and strengthen democracy?

First, the South African citizenry must engage in an extended debate about the proper role of state and civil society. For now, the debate is centered within academic institutions and among national leaders. Mark Swilling, an academic who contributed to the civil society debate in its early years, argued that the ANC and the South African government must embrace true democratic socialism and reject the anti-democratic elements of socialist democracy.[14] With this in mind, state leaders must encourage a vibrant civil society where groups can engage in voluntary, even autonomous, activity constrained by the law and oriented toward grassroots, local self-government. 'Associational socialism' allows for the possibility of voluntary organizations negotiating with state leaders, business leaders and other power players on behalf of their constituency. Swilling also argued that civil society institutions needed to be supported by the state through a strong legal framework and fiscal measures.

Other individuals, including Blade Nzimande and Mpumelelo Sikhosana, criticize these views because they ignore the reality of the South African situation and civil society. Nzimande and Sikhosana argue that state and civil society cannot be viewed independently; they are interdependent entities. Second, civil society does not ensure democracy; in fact, it usually represents bourgeoisie or elite interests that conflict with true democracy. Finally, civil society may not be necessary for the democratic process of consolidation because it diminishes the state's role in constructing socialism. These individuals display a marked suspicion of romantic views of state–civil society relations and go so far as to place hope in 'organs of people's power' or social movements rather than civil society in an effort to establish a more socialist democracy.[15]

On the other side of Marxist approaches (Nzimande and Sikhosana) and revisionist perspectives (Swilling) are more liberal perspectives. Steve Friedman and Maxine Reitzes fear that the concept 'civil society' can easily become a shroud for the hegemonic aspirations of the left, or even the elite in power (i.e., ANC), who will capture civil society and stifle its pluralism and autonomy. Radical national leaders have assumed that 'civil society' institutions oriented toward liberation epitomize the essence of participatory, grassroots democracy that can bring about development, societal change, accountability, and transparency in the economic sector. Thus, civil society institutions need to be incorporated or co-opted into the state. But this, Friedman and Reitzes argue, neglects the fact that liberation-oriented civil society institutions are not homogenous in their interests nor do they represent the interests of all South Africans. A strong, limited, and autonomous state is needed in South Africa that includes leaders who will guarantee the rights of all peoples against a domineering civil society, allow for the autonomy of civil society, and encourage a truly representative democracy.[16]

While the Marxist perspective is overly suspicious of the beneficial role that civil society can play in consolidating democracy, the neo-liberal perspective is often criticized for holding too closely to a Western notion of state–civil society relations. Its emphasis on the functional separation of societal spheres does not address the issues of inequality that would hinder the consolidation of democracy. A model of state–civil society relations is needed for South Africa where a strong, transparent, autonomous state, that is, one able to deliver public goods equitably and openly in the interests of all its citizens, coexists with a pluralistic, inclusive, autonomous civil society that holds the government accountable through critical engagement – a model the merges the strengths of the various South African visions on state–civil society relations.

This ideal arrangement can at least be encouraged through the establishment of fundamental freedoms that encourage and protect the activity of civil society. Those rights important for an independent, vigorous civil society would include the right to free speech and the right to assemble – basic civil and political rights enshrined in a constitution (the Bill of Rights) which would create a discrete, non-threatening environment for civil society. But it is not enough to ensure political and civil liberties, or individually based rights, as these do not guarantee equality. It is also necessary to assure a minimum level of socio-economic rights (right to education, right to employment) which would create a broader agenda for civil society institutions in an effort to democratize and empower society. Appropriate human rights organs should also be established to guarantee governmental compliance with human rights and to uphold civil society institutions.[17] South Africa's constitution contains a detailed Bill of Rights that includes political, civil, and socio-economic rights and it contains a Human Rights Commission that complies with these basic fundamental norms for encouraging a vibrant, plural civil society.

Related to a 'rights-based' culture would be the creation of just acts. South Africa must avoid the adoption of legislative acts beneficial to the majority party. The ANC, as the governing party in South Africa, has shown tendencies toward 'in-bred authoritarian rule', for example, readily dismissing members who are outspoken (e.g., Bantu Holomisa), a consolidation of central authority, and a clampdown on internal dissent – trends that are worrisome.[18] It must embrace laws that lead to a healthy political environment and full participation within its organization.

Third, South Africa must achieve or encourage an economic climate conducive to the needs of South African citizens. The South African government must be involved in redistributive efforts to close the massive social deficits hurting the lives of black South Africans. Approximately 40 per cent of Africans are unemployed, over half of all African families live in grinding poverty, and an estimated 7.5 million Africans live in shanties without electricity or running water.[19] South Africa must tackle these disparities at the same time that IMF structural adjustment programs will begin making austerity demands. The absence of a healthy economy absolves the masses from responsibility in the welfare of their country because they are engaged with their own survival and material well-being.

Finally, a culture of tolerance, civility, and appreciation of diverse ethnic groups needs to be established in South Africa. The examination of NGK–state relations shows that a civil society constructed along ethnic, particularistic lines damages a country's political future and democratic prospects. South African civil society, in many ways, has to make up lost ground because it has lacked the nurturing soil of a society and culture committed to accommodation, moderation, and civility. But a pluralistic, inclusive, and autonomous civil society can be established in South Africa if the overt prejudice and distrust of other 'people-groups' is attenuated and if respect for and appreciation of other cultures is encouraged. These attitudes can be fostered through the work and outcome of civic education campaigns, educational and church programs committed to cultural awareness and reconciliation efforts, and even special commissions like the Truth and Reconciliation Commission.

Of course, it is easy to prescribe the conditions and/or preconditions needed for a healthy civil society, that is, an inclusive legal framework, a culture of rights and duties, a tradition of political tolerance, and a legitimate government, and it is easy to suggest how the South African governmental and political apparatus should respond, but the actual attainment of a pluralistic, inclusive civil society and a strong, autonomous state is an enormously difficult and tiresome task.

In conclusion, the typology I present offers a continuum of state–civil society relations that can be used to describe other state-civil society interactions besides the NGK and the South African state. For example, how would other civil society institutions like the South African Council of Churches, the Anglo-American Corporation, or the Congress of South African Trade Unions have interacted with the South African state during the apartheid years? How did these state-civil society relations affect South Africa's democratic transition?

Also, how do state–civil society relations in southern African countries like Mozambique and Zimbabwe compare to South Africa's? Questions about how similar or different South Africa's state–civil society relations are to other countries beg further study.[20] Finally, how do African state–civil society relations in democratic transitions differ from those in Eastern Europe or Latin America? These are much broader questions that aim at the incorporation of state–civil society frameworks into bodies of literature that explore democratic transitions, political development, and the political economy. Although the typology is applied to one case study (the South African state and the NGK), it has the possibility of application across other case studies which can lead to comparative insights across regions and countries.

The findings in this work, in essence, build on the foundations of mainstream scholarship concerning state–civil society relations. Civil society is a necessary, but not sufficient, condition for the establishment of democracy. An active civil society does not guarantee that a country will be protected against autocracy. The NGK, for example, and many other hegemonic institutions during the apartheid years, suppressed the realization of widespread democracy more than the NP-dominated state because the church identified itself with an exclusive nationalism. However, a civil society which is nurtured and encouraged to develop tolerant, inclusive civic attitudes independent of the state and other societal institutions can and will hold the state accountable and contribute to healthy state–civil society relations.

Appendix A   Christian Church Membership in South Africa

RELIGIOUS AFFILIATION TO CHRISTIAN CHURCHES

Religion	Total	White	Coloured	Indian	African
Gereformeerde Nederduitse	198 776	127 235	7 349	258	63 934
Gereformeerde Nederduitsch Hervormde	3 493 552	1 695 875	674 781	2 435	1 120 461
Church of the Province of SA	288 958	258 769	2 528	1 099	26 562
Church of Eng. in SA	478 363	111 742	181 244	2 342	183 035
Church of England	72 814	20 411	11 312	288	40 863
Anglican	289 647	121 869	19 910	317	147 551
Methodist	805 793	207 521	149 460	4 915	443 897
Presbyterian	2 231 981	420 957	149 181	4 056	1 657 787
Unit. Congregationalist	531 876	129 771	9 183	1 607	391 315
Lutheran	492 918	25 231	185 949	1 469	280 269
Catholic	888 664	43 187	102 293	763	742 421
Apostolic Faith Mission of SA	2 406 699	388 336	266 150	20 590	1 731 623
Baptist	284 168	125 501	39 074	2 849	116 744
Pentecostal Protestant	257 583	72 500	17 165	4 090	163 828
Faith Mission Healers	68 364	37 302	16 859	2 617	11 586
Full Gospel	3 167	495	326	22	2 324
Greek	185 582	64 802	23 178	24 980	72 892
Mormon	31 005	29 518	289	51	1 147
Pentecostal	9 573	6 132	343	27	3 071
Salvation Army	50 231	10 229	15 963	2 744	21 295
Seventh Day Adventist	45 614	5 105	1 239	105	39 165
SA General Mission	81 307	17 331	12 140	1 507	50 329
Swiss	7 211	179	797	2 018	4 217
Assemblies of God	83 878	359	342	124	83 043
Zion CC	144 878	19 638	12 510	1 817	110 697
Other Black Independent Church	531 183	0	3 481	0	527 702
Other Christian	4 674 704	0	77 840	0	4 596 864
	411 539	123 271	122 343	16 433	149 492

Source: The following figures on church membership are based on the 1985 census. They are provided by Scott Hazelhurst from the soc.culture.african newsgroup on December 30 1993, 21:11:44-0500.

Appendix B Interviews

From January to May 1993, I conducted interviews with 40 clergymen, parliamentarians, and academics. The titles given are those that were held by the individuals at the time of the interview.

Badenhorst, Piet. Retired National Party Parliamentarian. Somerset West, South Africa, 26 April 1993.

Bingle, P. GK Minister and Confidant of F.W. de Klerk. Cape Town, South Africa, 26 April 1993.

Boshoff, Carel. Founder of the *Afrikaner Volksunie*; Former Professor of Theology, University of Pretoria. Pretoria, South Africa, 31 March 1993.

Botha, A.J. Scribe of the NGSK (1990–4). Bellville, South Africa, 23 February 1993.

Botman, H.R. Assessor of the NGSK (1990–4). Cape Town, South Africa, 10 March 1993.

Brand, H.J.D. NGSK Minister. Cape Town, South Africa, 2 February 1993.

Buti, S. Moderator of the NGKA (1990–4). Alexandra, South Africa, 5 April 1993.

De Beer, S.J. National Party Parliamentarian; Minister of Education under F.W. de Klerk. Cape Town, South Africa, 7 May 1993.

Durand, J.J.F. UWC Vice Rector; Member of the National Peace Secretariat. Bellville, South Africa, 9 March 1993.

Du Toit, D.A. Department of Theology, University of Stellenbosch. Stellenbosch, South Africa, 24 February 1993.

Eloff, S.J. Retired NGK Minister. Parys, South Africa, 31 March 1993.

Esterhuyse, W.P. Department of Philosophy, University of Stellenbosch. Stellenbosch, South Africa, 24 March 1993.

Gaum, F.M. Editor of *Die Kerkbode*; Scribe of the NGK (1990–4). Cape Town, South Africa, 18 March 1993.

Geldenhuys, Boy. National Party Parliamentarian; Retired NGK Minister. Cape Town, South Africa, 26 April 1993.

Hattingh, D.J. NGK Minister. Stellenbosch, South Africa, 24 February 1993.

Heyns, J.A. NGK Minister; Department of Theology, University of Pretoria; Moderator of the NGK (1986–90). Pretoria, South Africa, 30 March 1993.

Jonker, W.D. Department of Theology, University of Stellenbosch. Stellenbosch, South Africa, 5 February 1993.

Kinghorn, Johann. Department of Religious Education, University of Stellenbosch. Stellenbosch, South Africa, 15 February 1993.

Kleynhans, W.A. Department of Political Studies, UNISA. Pretoria, South Africa, 12 May 1993.

König, Adrio. Department of Theology, UNISA. Pretoria, South Africa, 1 April 1993.

Kotze, B.J. NGK Minister. Cape Town, South Africa, 2 February 1993.

Kritzinger, J.J. Department of Theology, University of Pretoria. Pretoria, South Africa, 30 March 1993.

Lategan, B.C. Department of Religious Education, University of Stellenbosch. Stellenbosch, South Africa, 5 February 1993.

Lubbe, Gerrie. Department of Theology, UNISA. Pretoria, South Africa, 7 April 1993.

Malan, Wynand. PFP/DP Parliamentarian. Johannesburg, South Africa, 5 April 1993.

Marais, B.J. Retired NGK Minister. Pretoria, South Africa, 29 March 1993.

Meiring, P.G.J. Department of Theology, University of Pretoria. Pretoria, South Africa, 30 March 1993.

Möller, G.S.J. Editor of *Die Kerkbode* (1970–86). Bloubergstrand, South Africa, 22 February 1993.

Naudé, C.F.B. Former NGK Minister; NGKA Minister. Johannesburg, South Africa, 8 April 1993.

Nicol, W. NGK Minister. Pretoria, South Africa, 29 March 1993.

Potgieter, P.C. Moderator of the NGK (1990–4); Department of Theology, University of Bloemfontein. Bloemfontein, South Africa, 14 April 1993.

Rossouw, P. Former Scribe and Information Director of the NGK. Pretoria, South Africa, 1 April 1993.

Saayman, W.A. Department of Theology, UNISA. Pretoria, South Africa, 31 March 1993.

Serfontein, J.H.P. Journalist. Johannesburg, South Africa, 31 May 1993.

Smith, N.J. Department of Theology, UNISA. Pretoria, South Africa, 29 March 1993.

Strydom, A. Information Director of the NGK. Cape Town, South Africa, 8 February 1993.

Tema, E.M. Assessor of the NGKA (1990–4). Orlando, South Africa, 7 April 1993.

Verhoef, P.A. Retired Professor of Theology, University of Stellenbosch. Stellenbosch, South Africa, 3 March 1993.

Viljoen, G. Retired National Party Parliamentarian; Minister of Constitutional Development under F.W. de Klerk. Pretoria, South Africa, 1 June 1993.

Van Zyl, Koos. Retired Chaplain-General of the SADF. Pretoria, South Africa, 2 April 1993.

Notes

CHAPTER 1 STATE–CIVIL SOCIETY RELATIONS

Portions of this chapter are reprinted, with changes, from the *Journal of Church and State* 38 (1996): 841–72.

1. The *Nederduitse Gereformeerde Kerk* is the largest and most influential of the three main Afrikaner-based churches in South Africa. The other two denominations – the *Nederduitsch Hervormde Kerk* (NHK) and the *Gereformeerde Kerk* (GK) – and the black Reformed churches will not be the focus of this work. Since the late 1800s, the 'NGK family' has been divided into the *Nederduitse Gereformeerde Kerk* (or NGK for the white population), the *Nederduitse Gereformeerde Sendingkerk* (or NGSK for the 'Coloured' population), the *Nederduitse Gereformeerde Kerk in Afrika* (or NGKA for the African population), and the Reformed Church in Africa (or RCA for the Asian population). Although a detailed examination of how the policies of these churches merged or diverged over time with the NGK's would be beneficial, I have chosen to concentrate on relations between the race-based state and the NGK.
2. Gustav Thiel, 'The Church is Sorry, But Not too Sorry', *Electronic Mail & Guardian*, www.mg.co.za/mg/ news/97 sept 1/17 sep-ngh.html. See Appendix A for a list of church membership in South Africa. The structural composition of the NGK includes local congregations, presbyteries, 11 regional synods, and one general synod. The General Synod (*Algemene Sinode*), established only in 1962, meets every four years. It is composed of pastors and elders/deacons from the white NGK who make decisions concerning church policy. The top leaders of the NGK, elected by the General Synod, include the moderator, the assessor, the scribe, and the actuarius. The Federal Council, a body that was comprised of representatives from the four churches of the Dutch Reformed 'family' and the 'black' churches associated with the Dutch Reformed mission work in southern and central Africa, disbanded in 1990. It was far less influential than the General Synod concerning policy and doctrinal matters. For more information on the structure of the NGK, see Pierre Rossouw, comp., *The Dutch Reformed Church Information Booklet* (Bloemfontein: NG Sendingpers, 1990).
3. Until the late 1700s, the NGK was the only church allowed to hold official services in the Cape. From its inception, the NGK was closely connected to the white settlers and the governing authorities. See J.A. Loubser, *The Apartheid Bible: A Critical Review of Racial Theology in South Africa* (Cape Town: Maskew Miller Longman, 1987): 3–5.
4. The NGK's history includes important discoveries, like the Cape NGK's autonomy from the Dutch church in 1824, the church's ambivalence on proselytizing, and the unique congregational make-up of the churches

in the Boer Republics. References to the earlier years of the NGK's history are found in the following sources: David Bosch, 'The Fragmentation of Afrikanerdom and the Afrikaner Churches', in *Resistance and Hope: South African Essays in Honor of Beyers Naude*, ed. Charles Villa-Vicencio and John W. de Gruchy (Grand Rapids: William B. Eerdmans, 1985), 61–73; and John W. de Gruchy, *The Church Struggle in South Africa* (Grand Rapids: William B. Eerdmans, 1986).

5. Jonathan Gerstner, *The Thousand Generation Covenant: Dutch Reformed Covenant Theology and Group Identity in Colonial South Africa, 1652–1814* (Leiden: E.J. Brill, 1991); and J. Alton Templin, *Ideology on a Frontier: The Theological Foundation of Afrikaner Nationalism, 1652–1910* (Westport: Greenwood Press, 1984).

6. The 'primitive Calvinist' paradigm coalesces with liberal historiography's emphasis on the 'frontier thesis'. See E. Walker, *The Frontier Tradition in South Africa* (Oxford: Oxford University Press, 1930).

7. Du Toit's work was not the first that challenged the 'frontier' hypothesis. The seminal work criticizing the frontier thesis was Martin Legassick's article entitled 'The Frontier Tradition in South African Historiography', in *Economy and Society in Pre-Industrial South Africa*, ed. Shula Marks and Anthony Atmore (London: Longman, 1980), 44–79. Yet Du Toit's work was one of the first to criticize the 'primitive Calvinist' paradigm regarding religion's (and the NGK's) formative role in Afrikaner nationalism's development. See André du Toit, 'No Chosen People: The Myth of the Calvinist Origins of Afrikaner Nationalism and Racial Ideology', *American Historical Review* 88 (1983): 920–52.

8. South African society was comprised of a number of classes in the Cape Colony. Settler colonialists included DEIC officials, *trekboers*, and free burghers. 'Non-whites' included the San and the Khoikhoi, free blacks, and slaves.

9. Irving Hexham, *The Irony of Apartheid: The Struggle for National Independence of Afrikaner Calvinism Against British Imperialism* (New York: Edwin Mellen Press, 1981).

10. A.J. Botha, *Die Evolusie van 'n Volksteologie* (Bellville: UWK Drukkery, 1984); Johann Kinghorn, ed., *Die NG Kerk en Apartheid* (Johannesburg: Macmillan Suid-Afrika, 1986); and Susan Rennie Ritner, 'Salvation through Separation: The Role of the Dutch Reformed Church in South Africa in the Formulation of Afrikaner Race Ideology' (PhD diss., Columbia University, 1971).

11. T. Dunbar Moodie published one of the best works examining how neo-Kuyperian Calvinism was wedded with romantic nationalist notions in the early 1900s in an effort to legitimize race policy. See *The Rise of Afrikanerdom: Power, Apartheid, and the Afrikaner Civil Religion* (Berkeley and Los Angeles: University of California Press, 1975).

12. Quoted in Chris Loff, 'The History of a Heresy', in *Apartheid is a Heresy*, ed. John W. de Gruchy and Charles Villa-Vicencio (Cape Town: David Philip, 1983), 19.

13. See Johann Kinghorn, 'The Theology of Separate Equality: A Critical Outline of the DRC's Position on Apartheid', in *Christianity amidst Apartheid*, ed. Martin Prozesky (London: Macmillan, 1990), 59–60.

14. Dan O'Meara, *Volkskapitalisme: Class, Capital and Ideology in the Development of Afrikaner Nationalism, 1934–1948* (Cambridge: Cambridge University Press, 1983).

15. Although it is sorely needed, a 'gendered' perspective is not developed concerning the NGK.

16. One area that is not focused on in this book is the regional differences within the NGK. In a relatively short book that covers a long period of time, I decided to forgo this emphasis, although it remains fertile ground for future studies.

17. Samuel P. Huntington, *The Third Wave: Democratization in the Late Twentieth Century* (Norman, OK: University of Oklahoma Press, 1991). Space does not permit a detailed examination of democratization debates, but further analysis of the democratization literature would include the following works: Larry Diamond, Juan J. Linz, and Seymour Martin Lipset, eds., *Democracy in Developing Countries*, 3 vols. (Boulder: Lynne Rienner, 1988–9); Barrington Moore, *Social Origins of Dictatorship and Democracy: Lord and Peasant in the Making of the Modern World* (Boston: Beacon Press, 1966); Guillermo O'Donnell and Philippe C. Schmitter, *Transitions from Authoritarian Rule: Tentative Conclusions about Uncertain Democracies* (Baltimore: Johns Hopkins University Press, 1986); and Dietrich Rueschemeyer, Evelyne Huber Stephens, and John D. Stephens, *Capitalist Development and Democracy* (Chicago: University of Chicago Press, 1992).

18. Michael W. Foley and Bob Edwards, 'The Paradox of Civil Society', *Journal of Democracy* 7 (1996): 38–52.

19. Eboe Hutchful, 'The Civil Society Debate in Africa', *International Journal* 51 (1995–6): 54.

20. The original work of philosophers like John Locke, Thomas Paine, and Karl Marx need to be consulted for further insights, but excellent secondary sources on the philosophical foundation of civil society include John Keane, ed., *Civil Society and the State: New European Perspectives* (London: Verso, 1988); John Keane, *Democracy and Civil Society: On the Predicaments of European Socialism, the Prospects for Democracy, and the Problem of Controlling Social and Political Power* (London: Verso, 1988); and Steven M. DeLue, *Political Thinking, Political Theory, and Civil Society* (Boston: Allyn & Bacon, 1997).

21. To explore the ongoing debates about civil society, see Hutchful, 'Civil Society Debate', 54–77.

22. Larry Diamond, 'Civil Society and Democratic Consolidation: Building a Culture of Democracy in a New South Africa', in *The Bold Experiment: South Africa's New Democracy*, ed. Hermann Giliomee and Lawrence Schlemmer with Sarita Hauptfleisch (n.p., Southern Book Publishers, 1994), 48.

23. Daryl Glaser, 'South Africa and the Limits of Civil Society', *Journal of Southern African Studies* 23 (1997): 5.

24. Larry Diamond, 'Toward Democratic Consolidation', *Journal of Democracy* 5 (1994): 4–17; John W. Harbeson, Donald Rothchild and Naomi Chazan, eds., *Civil Society and the State in Africa* (Boulder:

Lynne Rienner, 1994); and O'Donnell and Schmitter, *Transitions from Authoritarian Rule*, 1986.

25. Diamond, 'Toward Democratic Consolidation', 5.

26. Michael Bratton, 'Beyond the State: Civil Society and Associational Life in Africa', *World Politics* 41 (1989): 407–30.

27. Pierre du Toit, *State Building and Democracy in Southern Africa: A Comparative Study of Botswana, South Africa, and Zimbabwe* (Pretoria: HSRC Publishers, 1995), 34–5.

28. Michael Bratton, 'Micro-Democracy? The Merger of Farmer Unions in Zimbabwe', *African Studies Review* 37, no. 1 (1994): 13. At times, scholars use associational life and civil society interchangeably. Others define civil society more precisely as that part of associational life which is engaged in rule-setting activities related to the political order.

29. Bratton, 'Micro-Democracy?', 32.

30. E. Gyimah-Boadi, 'Civil Society in Africa', *Journal of Democracy* 7 (1996): 118.

31. Peter M. Lewis, 'Political Transitions and the Dilemma of Civil Society in Africa', *Journal of International Affairs* 46 (1992): 31–54. Sheri Berman's research concerning the Weimar Republic also points to the limitations of a robust associational life, absent strong national institutions, in maintaining democracy. See 'Civil Society and the Collapse of the Weimar Republic', Paper presented at the 1996 Annual Meeting of the American Political Science Association, San Francisco, California, August 29–September 1, 1996.

32. Neo-Marxist scholars counter the claims of liberal scholarship – pointing to its ideological and substantive flaws. They argue that mainstream scholars uphold an undifferentiated, bourgeois notion of civil society, an ethnocentric understanding of liberal democracy, and a limited, non-interventionist idea of the state. Because the concept 'civil society' has significant analytical and conceptual flaws, it would be better to use the concepts of gender or class to understand political change. See Chris Allen, 'Who Needs Civil Society?', *Review of African Political Economy* no. 73 (1997): 329–37; or Lloyd Sachikonye, ed., *Democracy, Civil Society and the State: Social Movements in Southern Africa* (Harare: SAPES, 1995).

33. Richard Humphries and Maxine Reitzes, eds., *Civil Society after Apartheid* (Doornfontein: Centre for Policy Studies, 1995); and Hennie Kotzé, ed., *Consolidating Democracy: What Role for Civil Society in South Africa?* Papers presented at a conference organized by the Centre for International and Comparative Politics, Stellenbosch, South Africa, August 1996.

34. Joel Migdal, *Strong Societies and Weak States: State-Society Relations and State Capabilities in the Third World* (Princeton: Princeton University Press, 1988), 19.

35. See Dan O'Meara, *Forty Lost Years: The Apartheid State and the Politics of the National Party, 1948–1994* (Johannesburg: Ravan Press, 1996), 419–20.

36. A government refers to the leadership and party in power at a given moment, or the personnel who occupy decision-making positions in the polity. A regime determines the relationship that national authorities

and institutions have to society. Regime change, then, refers to changes in regime type, from authoritarianism to democracy, from democracy to one-party rule, and so forth.

37. O'Meara, *Forty Lost Years*, 420.
38. See F.A. Johnstone, 'White Prosperity and White Supremacy in South Africa Today', *African Affairs* 69, no. 275 (1970): 124–40; and Harold Wolpe, 'Capitalism and Cheap Labour-Power in South Africa: From Segregation to Apartheid', *Economy and Society* 1 (1972): 425–56.
39. Colin Stoneman and Lionel Cliffe, *Zimbabwe: Politics, Economics, and Society* (London: Pinter Publications, 1989), 17.
40. O'Meara, *Forty Lost Years*, 420–1.
41. Ian Shapiro, 'Democratic Innovation: South Africa in Comparative Context', *World Politics* 46 (1993): 125.
42. Karen Barkey and Sunita Parikh, 'Comparative Perspectives on the State', *Annual Review of Sociology* 17 (1991): 525. The issue of state autonomy arose within the state debates of the 1970s and 1980s. Neo-statist literature is characterized by the view that states are more than a reflection of societal preferences – they have an independent nature of their own. To explore further the nature and autonomy of the state, see works by Stephen Krasner, Joel Migdal, Eric Nordlinger, and Theda Skocpol.
43. Du Toit, *State-Building and Democracy*, 317–18.
44. Society is understood to encompass every major institution and entity that affects the social relationships of human life. It is an all-embracing term that represents the environment of humanity's social existence including the state, civil society, the economy, the polity, and so forth.
45. Despite its limitations, I will primarily be defining civil society in an empirically-analytic fashion.
46. Diamond, 'Civil Society and Democratic Consolidation', 55.
47. Ibid., 56.
48. Steven Friedman, 'An Unlikely Utopia: State and Civil Society in South Africa', *Politikon* 19 (1991): 8.
49. Patrick Fitzgerald, 'Democracy and Civil Society in South Africa', *Review of African Political Economy*, no. 49 (1990): 94–110; and Mark Swilling, 'Political Transition, Development and the Role of Civil Society', *Africa Insight* 20 (1990): 151–60.
50. Khehla Shubane, 'Civil Society in Apartheid and Post-Apartheid South Africa', *Theoria* 79 (1992): 33–41.
51. It should be noted that civil society as a whole or civil society segments can respond to the state. In the definitions that follow, I assume that certain segments of civil society respond to the state in the manner described.

CHAPTER 2 NGK'S DEVELOPMENT (1910–33)

1. This section relies on the work of Christopher Saunders. See 'Historians and Apartheid', in *South Africa in Question*, ed. John Lonsdale (London: James Currey, 1988), 13–32; or *The Making of the South African Past: Major Historians on Race and Class* (Totowa, New Jersey:

Barnes & Noble, 1988). See also Nicoli Nattrass, 'Controversies about Capitalism and Apartheid in South Africa: An Economic Perspective', *Journal of Southern African Studies* 17 (1991): 654–77.

2. Works with a liberal perspective have different emphases, for example, a 'settler colonial' bias, the reliance on the 'frontier myth', or a focus on political-constitutional matters. See C.W. de Kiewiet, *A History of South Africa: Social and Economic* (Oxford: Oxford University Press, 1941); I.D. MacCrone, *Race Attitudes in South Africa: Historical, Experimental and Psychological Studies* (Oxford: Oxford University Press, 1937); W.M. Macmillan, *The Cape Colour Question* (London: Faber and Gwyer, 1927); E. Walker, *The Frontier Tradition in South Africa* (Oxford: Oxford University Press, 1930); and Monica Wilson and Leonard Thompson, eds., *The Oxford History of South Africa*, 2 vols. (Oxford: Clarendon and Oxford University Press, 1969, 1971).

3. The terms Boer and Afrikaner are difficult to define. Boer is often used in a derogatory fashion referring to the backward white settlers of the 1700s and early 1800s. Afrikaner refers to the people identified as a distinct ethnic group within the white population of South Africa after the late 1800s. They are primarily of Dutch, German or French descent, speak Afrikaans, and share a common history.

4. Some of the earliest 'revisionist' work included D.D.T. Jabavu, *The Black Problem* (Lovedale: Lovedale Press, 1920) and Edward Roux, *Time Longer than Rope* (Madison: University of Wisconsin Press, 1964). The revisionist scholarship produced in the 1970s included F.R. Johnstone, *Class, Race and Gold: A Study of Class Relations and Racial Discrimination in South Africa* (London: Routledge & Kegan Paul, 1976); Martin Legassick, 'The Frontier Tradition in South African Historiography', in *Economy and Society in Pre-Industrial South Africa*, ed. Shula Marks and Anthony Atmore (London: Longman, 1980), 44–79; and Harold Wolpe, 'Capitalism and Cheap Labour-Power in South Africa: From Segregation to Apartheid', *Economy and Society* 1 (1972): 425–56.

5. This section relies on Nigel Worden, *The Making of Modern South Africa: Conquest, Segregation, and Apartheid* (Oxford: Blackwell, 1994): 18–25.

6. Worden, *The Making of Modern South Africa*, 25–33.

7. Ibid., 37–50.

8. See P. Harries, 'Capital, State and Labour on the 19th Century Witwatersrand: A Reassessment', *South African Historical Journal* 18 (1986): 25–45; and A. Jeeves, 'The Control of Migratory Labour in the South African Gold Mines in the era of Kruger and Milner', *Journal of Southern African Studies* 2 (1975): 3–29. The revisionist perspective is countered by those who argue that political factors explain the war's outbreak. Some of the political causes of the war include Britain's distaste of Afrikaner nationalism, the ambitions of particular individuals, and Britain's rivalry with other imperial powers. See A. Porter, 'The South African War (1899–1902): Context and Motive Reconsidered', *Journal of African History* 31 (1990): 43–57; and I. Smith, 'The Origins of the South African War (1899–1902): A Reappraisal', *South African Historical Journal* 22 (1990): 24–60.

9. Worden, *The Making of Modern South Africa*, 25–8.
10. John Pampallis, *Foundations of the New South Africa* (Cape Town: Maskew Miller Longman, 1991), 47.
11. T.R.H. Davenport, *South Africa: A Modern History*, 4th edn (Toronto: University of Toronto Press, 1991), 213–14.
12. Dan O'Meara, *Forty Lost Years* (Johannesburg: Ravan Press, 1996), 419.
13. T.R.H. Davenport, *South Africa: A Modern History*, 3rd edn (Toronto: University of Toronto Press, 1987), 243–9.
14. For the ideas in this paragraph, see Pampallis, *Foundations*, 50
15. T. Dunbar Moodie, *The Rise of Afrikanerdom: Power, Apartheid, and the Afrikaner Civil Religion* (Berkeley and Los Angeles: University of California Press, 1975), 75.
16. Davenport, *South Africa*, 4th edn, 232.
17. Moodie, *The Rise of Afrikanerdom*, 75.
18. The SANNC reorganized itself into the African National Congress (ANC) in 1923.
19. For further exploration of nationalist movements in the early 1900s, see Paul B. Rich, *State Power and Black Politics in South Africa, 1912–51* (New York: St. Martin's Press, 1996); Shula Marks and Stanley Trapido, *The Politics of Race, Class and Nationalism in Twentieth-Century South Africa* (London: Longman, 1987); and Peter Walshe, *The Rise of African Nationalism in South Africa: The African National Congress, 1912–1952* (Berkeley and Los Angeles: University of California Press, 1971).
20. J.W. Hofmeyr, J.A. Millard, and C.J.J Froneman, *History of the Church in South Africa* (Pretoria: Promedia Publishers, 1991), 179.
21. Ibid., 180.
22. Ibid.
23. One of the most successful political organizations in the 1920s was the Industrial and Commercial Workers' Union (ICU) formed in 1919. See Peter Wickens, *The Industrial and Commercial Workers Union of South Africa* (Cape Town: Oxford University Press, 1978). See also Worden, 51.
24. For more information on the political economy during the interwar years, see Robert Davies et al., 'Class Struggle and the Periodisation of the State in South Africa', *Review of African Political Economy* no. 7 (1976): 4–30; D.E. Kaplan, 'Relations of Production, Class Struggle and the State in South Africa in the Inter-War Period', *Review of African Political Economy* nos 15/16 (1979): 135–45; and David Yudelman, *The Emergence of Modern South Africa: State, Capital and the Organized Labour on the South African Gold Fields, 1902–1939* (London: Greenwood Press, 1983).
25. Ben Fine and Zavareh Rustomjee, 'The Political Economy of South Africa in the Interwar Period', *Social Dynamics* 18 (1992): 26–54.
26. Donald Denoon and Balem Nyeko, *Southern Africa Since 1800*, 2nd edn (London: Longman, 1984), 155–60.
27. A considerable amount of scholarship addresses the phenomenon of Afrikaner nationalism. Scholars that emphasize its ideological, socio-cultural, economic and structural roots include Heribert Adam,

Hermann Giliomee, T. Dunbar Moodie, and Leonard Thompson. For a work that points to the materialist base of Afrikaner nationalism, see Dan O'Meara, *Volkskapitalisme: Class, Capital and Ideology in the Development of Afrikaner Nationalism, 1934–1948* (Cambridge: Cambridge University Press, 1983). For work highlighting the 'gendered' nature of Afrikaner nationalism, see Lou-Marie Kruger, 'Gender, Community and Identity: Women and Afrikaner Nationalism in the Volksmoeder Discourse of Die Boerevrou' (MA, University of Cape Town, 1991).

28. Hermann Giliomee, 'Western Cape Farmers and the Beginnings of Afrikaner Nationalism, 1870–1915', *Journal of Southern African Studies* 14 (1987): 38–63.

29. Hermann Giliomee, 'The Beginnings of Afrikaner Ethnic Consciousness, 1850–1915', in *The Creation of Tribalism in Southern Africa*, ed. Leroy Vail (London: James Currey, 1989), 30.

30. Ibid., 28.

31. Worden, *Modern South Africa*, 88.

32. René de Villiers, 'Afrikaner Nationalism', in *The Oxford History of South Africa*, ed. Monica Wilson and Leonard Thompson, vol. 2 (Oxford: Oxford University Press, 1971). Afrikaner nationalists refer to Afrikaners involved with causes committed to the maintenance of Afrikaner culture and identity because of the perceived economic, political, and social threats posed on them through contact with blacks and English-speaking South Africans.

33. Davenport, *South Africa*, 4th edn, 290.

34. For more information on the Broederbond, see Ivor Wilkins and Hans Strydom, *The Broederbond* (New York: Paddington Press, 1979); J.H.P. Serfontein, *Brotherhood of Power: An Exposé of the Secret Afrikaner Broederbond* (Bloomington: Indiana University Press, 1978); and Charles Bloomberg, *Christian-Nationalism and the Rise of the Afrikaner Broederbond in South Africa, 1918–48*, ed. Saul Dubow (London: Macmillan, 1990).

35. The AB's promotion of Afrikaners as a special people was aided by the presentation of Afrikaner history in mythological terms. Scholars constructed an ethnic/nationalistic form of history that promoted the theme of the Afrikaners' special calling in an isolated, forsaken South Africa because of their overcoming events like the Great Trek, British annexations of the Boer Republics, and the Anglo-Boer War. The myth of Afrikaner group cohesion incorporated a veneration of past heroes, the use of symbolic events, and the belief in divine intervention. See F.A. van Jaarsveld, *The Afrikaner's Interpretation of South African History* (Cape Town: Simondium Publishers, 1964) and Leonard Thompson, *The Political Mythology of Apartheid* (New Haven: Yale University Press, 1985).

36. The AB's membership was only open to men; however, J.H.P. Serfontein recently uncovered the existence of a parallel female-led nationalist society, the *Dameskring*. J.H.P Serfontein, 'Broeders – en susters…', *Vrye Weekblad* 22 Januarie 1993, 16.

37. This argument is suggested by Wilkins, Strydom, and Serfontein.

38. This argument is used by Broederbonders or other Afrikaner nationalists. See the NP's commissioned report on the Broederbond, *The Report of the Commission of Enquiry into Secret Organizations* (Pretoria: Government Printer, 1964) or the Broederbond-sponsored book by A.N. Pelzer, *Die Afrikaner-Broederbond: Eerste 50 Jaar* (Cape Town: Tafelberg, 1979).

39. Susan Rennie Ritner, 'Salvation Through Separation' (PhD diss., Columbia University, 1971), 38.

40. Moodie, *The Rise of Afrikanerdom*, 97, 296.

41. De Gruchy, *The Church Struggle*, 31.

42. See J.A. Loubser, *The Apartheid Bible: A Critical Review of Racial Theology in South Africa* (Cape Town: Maskew Miller Longman, 1987).

43. The paragraphs that follow rely on Chapter 4 of Moodie's *The Rise of Afrikanerdom*.

44. Moodie, *The Rise of Afrikanerdom*, 68.

45. Jaap Durand, 'Afrikaner Piety and Dissent', in *Resistance and Hope*, ed. Charles Villa-Vicencio and John W. de Gruchy (Grand Rapids: William B. Eerdmans, 1985), 42–5.

46. Moodie, *The Rise of Afrikanerdom*, 61.

47. Davenport, *South Africa*, 4th edn, 288.

48. Moodie, *The Rise of Afrikanerdom*, 72.

49. See Davenport, *South Africa*, 3rd edn, 319.

50. *Het Armen Blanken Vraagstuk*, Verslag van het Kerklike Kongres, Gehouden te Cradock op 22 en 23 November 1916 (Cape Town, 1917); Verslag van die Gesamentlike Kongres oor die Arme Blanke Vraagstuk (Bloemfontein, 1923)

51. Ritner, 'Salvation Through Separation,' 101–2.

52. Ibid., 132–3.

53. Quoted in J.H.P. *Serfontein, Apartheid, Change, and the NG Kerk* (Emmarentia: Taurus, 1982), 61.

54. Saul Dubow, *Racial Segregation and the Origins of Apartheid in South Africa, 1919–36* (New York: St. Martin's Press, 1989), 1. For an excellent discussion of the origin and development of segregation policy in the early 1900s, see Paul Rich's 'Race, Science, and the Legitimization of White Supremacy in South Africa, 1902–1940', *International Journal of African Historical Studies* 23 (1990): 665–86.

55. To review the evidence that shows discriminatory race policy existed in the pre-industrial period, see John Cell, *The Highest Stage of White Supremacy: The Origins of Segregation in South Africa and the American South* (Cambridge: Cambridge University Press, 1982); Richard Elphick and Hermann Giliomee, eds., *The Shaping of South African Society, 1652–1840* (Cape Town: Maskew Miller Longman, 1989); and David Welsh, *The Roots of Segregation: Native Policy in Colonial Natal, 1845–1910* (Cape Town: Oxford University Press, 1971).

56. See Dubow, *Racial Segregation*, 177–8, for the ideas represented in these paragraphs.

57. Some revisionists argued there was little difference between segregation and apartheid because apartheid reproduced the capitalist

economic structure. See Martin Legassick, 'Legislation, Ideology and Economy in Post-1948 South Africa', *Journal of Southern African Studies* 1 (1974): 5–35.

58.   Dubow, *Racial Segregation*, 178.
59.   Robert Davies, 'Mining Capital, the State and Unskilled White Workers in South Africa, 1901–1913', *Journal of Southern African Studies* 3 (1976): 41–69.
60.   The original amount of land set aside for purchase was 7 per cent; it increased to about 14 per cent in 1936.
61.   J.D. Omer-Cooper, *History of Southern Africa* (London: James Currey, 1987), 169. A more detailed analysis of the Natives Act with regard to the Stallard Commission is found in Alf Stadler, *The Political Economy of Modern South Africa* (New York: St. Martin's Press, 1987), 86–101.
62.   For more details, see Davenport, *South Africa*, 3rd edn, 292–7.
63.   For a description of the bills, their political packaging, and their ultimate passage, see Dubow, *Racial Segregation*, 131–76.
64.   English-speaking intellectuals contributed greatly to the ideological development of segregation. See Paul B. Rich, *Hope and Despair: English-Speaking Intellectuals and South African Politics, 1896–1976* (London: British Academic Press, 1993).
65.   Dubow, *Racial Segregation*, 39, 52.
66.   William Beinart and Saul Dubow, 'Introduction: The Historiography of Segregation and Apartheid', in *Segregation and Apartheid in Twentieth-Century South Africa*, ed. William Beinart and Saul Dubow (New York: Routledge, 1995), 10–11.
67.   Dubow, *Racial Segregation*, 15.
68.   Despite the significant differences between Smuts' and Hertzog's segregation theory, it is difficult to distinguish between the *practice* of their segregation policies. Hertzog's ideas sounded more strident, but when he came to power, he implemented policies that followed Smuts'. While Smuts sounded more accommodationist, he ruled South Africa during the height of segregation policy.
69.   Dubow, *Racial Segregation*, 44.
70.   J. du Plessis (convener), *The Dutch Reformed Church and the Native Problem* (Stellenbosch, 1921), 11–12.
71.   Ibid., 20.
72.   *European and Bantu*. Papers and addresses read at the Conference on Native Affairs. Held under the Auspices of the Federal Council of the DR Churches in Johannesburg, South Africa, September 27–29 1923, 44.
73.   Quoted from Johann Kinghorn, 'The Theology of Separate Equality', in *Christianity Amidst Apartheid*, ed. Martin Prozesky (London: Macmillan, 1990), 60.
74.   Quoted from Ritner, 'Salvation Through Separation', 125.
75.   Saul Dubow, 'Afrikaner Nationalism, Apartheid and the Conceptualization of "Race"', *Journal of African History* 33 (1992): 214.
76.   Ritner, 'Salvation Through Separation', 129.
77.   Ibid., 130.

CHAPTER 3   UP GOVERNANCE (1934–47)

1. See John Pampallis, *Foundations of the New South Africa* (Cape Town: Maskew Miller Longman, 1991), 139–40 for the ideas in this paragraph.

2. See T.R.H. Davenport, *South Africa: A Modern History*, 3rd edn (Toronto: University of Toronto Press, 1987), 302–14.

3. Newell M. Stultz, *Afrikaner Politics in South Africa, 1934–1948* (Berkeley and Los Angeles: University of California Press, 1974), 24.

4. Ibid., 37.

5. The name of the National Party changed over the years – from the National Party (1914) to the Purified National Party (*Gesuiwerde Nasionale Party* or PNP) in 1934 to the Reunited National Party (*Herenigde Nasionale Volksparty* or HNP) in 1940 to the National Party (1951–2) again.

6. T. Dunbar Moodie, *The Rise of Afrikanerdom: Power, Apartheid, and the Afrikaner Civil Religion* (Berkeley and Los Angeles: University of California Press, 1975), 116–45.

7. The petit bourgeoisie included teachers, professors, clergyman, lawyers, and lower-level civil servants who developed the goals of Afrikaner nationalism and provided ideological justifications for nationalist policies.

8. The unique class basis of the PNP and the differences among the four provincial parties is elaborated in Dan O'Meara's *Volkskapitalisme: Class, Capital and Ideology in the Development of Afrikaner Nationalism, 1934–1948* (Cambridge: Cambridge University Press, 1983), 49–56.

9. Ibid., 59–77.

10. Nigel Worden, *The Making of Modern South Africa* (Oxford: Blackwell, 1994), 91.

11. Ibid. The information that follows relies on O'Meara's work.

12. Davenport, *South Africa*, 4th edn, 278. Davenport also discusses passage of the 'native bills'.

13. See F.A. Johnstone, 'White Prosperity and White Supremacy in South Africa Today', *African Affairs* 69, no. 275 (1970): 124–40; and Harold Wolpe, 'Capitalism and Cheap Labour-Power in South Africa: From Segregation to Apartheid', *Economy and Society* 1 (1972): 425–56.

14. US companies that invested in South Africa included Mobil, Ford, GM, Goodyear, and Firestone.

15. William Minter, *King Solomon's Mines Revisited: Western Interests and the Burdened History of Southern Africa* (New York: Basic Books, 1986), 83.

16. For more information on the AAC, see Peter Walshe, *The Rise of African Nationalism in South Africa: The African National Congress, 1912–1952* (Berkeley and Los Angeles: University of California Press, 1971); and Tom Lodge, *Black Politics in South Africa since 1945* (London: Longman, 1983).

17. The information on the 1938 election comes from Stultz, *Afrikaner Politics*, 40–59.

18. Davenport, *South Africa*, 4th edn, 297.

19. A considerable amount of scholarship exists concerning the influence of radical right ideas within the National Party during the Second World War. For more information, see Patrick J. Furlong, *Between Crown and Swastika: The Impact of the Radical Right on the Afrikaner Nationalist Movement in the Fascist Era* (Hanover, NH: University Press of New England, 1991) and Patrick J. Furlong, 'Fascism, the Third Reich and Afrikaner Nationalism: An Assessment of the Historiography', *South African Historical Journal* 27 (1992): 113–26.
20. Stultz, *Afrikaner Politics*, 89.
21. J.D. Omer-Cooper, *History of Southern Africa* (London: James Currey, 1987), 182–3.
22. One of the reasons the 1946 strike occurred was the dissatisfaction felt by Africans over the Lansdown Commission's (1943) recommendations that mineworkers' wages did not need to be increased because of the reserve economy. See Dan O'Meara, 'The 1946 African Mineworkers' Strike and the Political Economy of South Africa', *Journal of Commonwealth and Political Studies* 13 (1975): 146–73. For the information that follows, see Pampallis, 156–64.
23. U.G. 28–48. *Report of the Native Laws Commission of Enquiry, 1946–48* (Pretoria: Government Printer, 1948).
24. Dan O'Meara, *Forty Lost Years* (Johannesburg: Ravan Press, 1996), 33.
25. *Verslag van die Kleurvraagstuk Kommissie van die Herenigde Nasionale Party* (Pretoria: Government Printer, 1947).
26. Besides poignant electoral issues, the NP also took advantage of the UP's poor organizational skills, the constitutional weighting of rural constituencies, and higher birth rates among Afrikaners.
27. Kenneth Heard, *General Elections in South Africa, 1943–1970* (London: Oxford University Press, 1974), 42–4.
28. Davenport, *South Africa*, 4th edn, 267.
29. Saul Dubow, *Racial Segregation and the Origins of Apartheid in South Africa, 1919–36* (New York: St. Martin's Press), 142–48.
30. Davenport, *South Africa*, 4th edn, 307. Brookes' position on segregation reveals intriguing developments. Brookes became one of the key proponents of segregation policy in the early 1920s through the encouragement of Hertzog. By 1927, Brookes announced that he could no longer support segregation policy as a result of visits among blacks within South Africa and the United States that convinced him that blacks could achieve high goals within white civilization. See Dubow, *Racial Segregation*, 21–50.
31. To explore these ideas, see Dubow, *Racial Segregation*, 46, 169–71.
32. Dubow, *Racial Segregation*, 15. For more details on Smuts' political perspectives, see W.K. Hancock, *Smuts: The Sanguine Years and Fields of Force* (Cambridge: Cambridge University Press, 1962, 1968); or Kenneth Ingham, *Jan Christian Smuts: The Conscience of a South African* (New York: Martin's Press, 1986).
33. J.C. Smuts, *The Basis of Trusteeship* (Johannesburg: R.L. Esson & Co., 1942), 9. For the information related to Smuts in the next paragraph, see Davenport, *South Africa*, 4th edn, 306–13.

34. Apartheid was used in 1936 for the first time within the *Suid-Afrikaanse Bond vir Rassestudie* – an Afrikaner thinktank.
35. Saul Dubow, 'Afrikaner Nationalism, Apartheid and the Conceptualization of "Race"', *Journal of African History* 33 (1992): 216. Dubow's article provides an excellent overview of the scientific, historical, and scriptural bases of apartheid ideology.
36. L. Thompson, *A History of South Africa* (New Haven: Yale University Press, 1990), 185–6.
37. Deborah Posel, 'The Meaning of Apartheid before 1948: Conflicting Interests and Forces within the Afrikaner Nationalist Alliance', *Journal of Southern African Studies* 14 (1987): 123–39. See also Deborah Posel, *The Making of Apartheid, 1948–1961: Conflict and Compromise* (Oxford: Clarendon Press, 1991).
38. P.J. Viljoen, 'Die Politieke Situasie', *Die Kerkbode* 34 (1934): 232–3. This editorial refers to the outcome of Fusion government and the NGK's cooperative attitude toward it.
39. Hermann Giliomee, 'The Growth of Afrikaner Identity', in *Segregation and Apartheid in Twentieth-Century South Africa*, ed. William Beinart and Saul Dubow (London: Routledge, 1995), 190.
40. Giliomee, 'Growth of Afrikaner Identity', 193. The material that follows is based on Giliomee's chapter, especially pages 195–7.
41. Ibid., 197.
42. For a review of church–state meetings on the 'poor white' problem, see P.J. Perold, 'Samewerking Tussen Kerk en Staat Insake Armeblankedom', *De Kerkbode* 26 (1930): 412–13, 503–4, 590–1, 639–41; or 'Staat en Kerk', *De Kerkbode* 29 (1932): 688–704.
43. J.A. Loubser, *The Apartheid Bible: A Critical Review of Racial Theology in South Africa* (Cape Town: Maskew Miller Longman, 1987), 27–9. See also Dubow, 'Afrikaner Nationalism', 214. I am not a theologian by training, but the theological strands within the NGK, elaborated below, help explain evolving NGK-state relations in the twentieth century.
44. See A.H. Murray, 'Voorwaardes vir Voogdyskap', *Op die Horison* 2 (1940): 7–11; or B.J. Marais, ''n Oproep', *Die Kerkbode* 45 (1940): 645–6. See Jaap Durand, 'Afrikaner Piety and Dissent', in *Resistance and Hope*, ed. Charles Villa-Vicencio and John W. de Gruchy (Grand Rapids: William B. Eerdmans, 1985), 42–5.
45. For the influence of the GK on the development of apartheid ideology, see Irving Hexham, *The Irony of Apartheid: The Struggle for National Independence of Afrikaner Calvinism against British Imperialism* (New York: Edwin Mellen Press, 1981).
46. For a good summary of Abraham Kuyper's ideas, see Loubser, *The Apartheid Bible*, 38–47. Also read Abraham Kuyper, *Lectures on Calvinism* (Grand Rapids: William Eerdmans, 1931).
47. The following work provides the clearest examples of a theological basis of apartheid within a neo-Calvinist framework using Kuyperian-based ideas. H.G. Stoker, F.J.M Potgieter, and J.D. Vorster, eds., *Koers in die Krisis: Artikels Versamel deur die Federasie van die Calvinistiese Studenteverenigings in Suid-Afrika*, 3 vols. (Stellenbosch: Pro Ecclesia, 1935, 1940, 1941).

48. Quoted in Peter Rous, 'The Afrikaner Covenant' (MA, Westminster Theological Seminary, 1980), 39.

49. See Geoffrey Cronje, *'n Tuiste vir die Nageslag: Die Blywende Oplossing van Suid-Afrika se Rassevraagstukke* (Stellenbosch: Pro-Ecclesia Drukkery, 1945); N.J. Diederichs, *Nasionalisme as Lewensbeskouing en sy Verhouding tot Internasionalisme* (Bloemfontein: Nasionale Pers, 1936); and Geoff Eloff, *Rasse en Rassevermenging* (Bloemfontein: Nasionale Pers, 1942). For a succinct explanation of how neo-Fichtean ideas were used within the church's justification of apartheid, see Dubow, 'Afrikaner Nationalism', 209–37.

50. Interview by author, tape recording, Stellenbosch, South Africa, 24 February 1993.

51. Charles Bloomberg, *Christian-Nationalism and the Rise of the Afrikaner Broederbond in South Africa, 1918–48*, ed. by Saul Dubow (London: Macmillan, 1990), 13–23. See also Loubser, *The Apartheid Bible*, 61–64.

52. J.G. Strydom, 'Segregasie of Gelykstelling', *Die Gereformeerde Vaandel* 6 (1938): 306–9; J.G. Strydom, 'Die Naturellebeleid van die Christen Afrikaner', *Die Basuin* 15, no. 1 (1943): 1–2; J.H. Kritzinger, 'Rasse-Apartheid in die Lig van die Skrif', *Op die Horison* 9 (1947): 22–31; and J.D. Vorster, 'Die Rassevraagstuk volgens die Skrifte', *Die Gereformeerde Vaandel* 15 (1947): 4–6. These articles only touch on the multitude of NGK 'theology of apartheid' documents in the 1930s and 1940s. For a further exploration of the NGK's 'theology of apartheid', see secondary works by Johann Kinghorn or A.J. Botha. For example, A.J. Botha's *Die Evolusie van 'n Volksteologie* (Bellville: UWK Drukkery, 1984).

53. Afrikaans text: 'Assimilasie beteken een word van die twee rasse, een in taal, een op sosiaal gebied en een in elke opsig … Ook die ware Christene onder die naturelle wil die suiwerheid van die ras behou. Ons skryf van 'n Christelik-nasionale standpunt en ons glo dat God aparte nasies en tale ens, gewil het en dat die vernietiging daarvan nie tot welsyn van daardie betrokke nasies kan dien nie. Assimilasie is dan 'n oppervlakkige en tewens gevaarlike beskouing … . [Differensiasie] is nie verdrukking nie. Dit erken die aparte rasse en wil hulle elk die regte en voorregte gee wat hulle toekom maar die differensiasie en segregasie is in die werklike belang van beide rasse.' J.G. Strydom, 'Ons Sendingbeleid Nogeens', *Die Basuin* 8, no. 4 (1937): 1–3.

54. *Federale Raad van die Kerken, Agendas en Handelinge*, 16 May 1935, 98. Translated by J. Kinghorn.

55. Dubow, 'Afrikaner Nationalism', 214.

56. 'Die Rassebelied van die Afrikaner', *Inspan* 4, no. 1 (1944): 21–5, 29.

57. J.D. du Toit, 'Die Godsdienstige Grondslag van ons Rassebelied', *Inspan* 4, no. 3 (1944): 7–17.

58. Loubser, *The Apartheid Bible*, 60.

59. Afrikaans text: 'Apartheid strek hom uit oor die hele gebied van die volkslewe … . Die beginsel van apartheid tussen rasse en volke, ook die van aparte sendinge en sendingkerke, is wel in die Skrif voorhande. Uit die ryke verskeidenheid van volke wat almal saam die een Here dien, word sy Naam meerdere eer toegebring (Openb. 7: 9, v.; Fil. 2: 9–11).'

E.P. Groenewald, 'Die Apartheid van die Nasie', *Die Gereformeerde Vaandel* 16 (1948): 9–10.

60. *Federale Sendingraad van die NGK, Notule, Verslae en Memoranda*, 1942–47.

61. To explore these issues further, see Patrick Furlong, 'Improper Intimacy: Afrikaans Churches, the National Party and the Anti-Miscegenation Laws', *South African Historical Journal* 31 (1994): 55–79; Etienne de Villiers and Johann Kinghorn, *Op die Skaal: Gemengde Huwelike en Ontug* (Kaapstad: Tafelberg-Uitgewers, 1984); D.J. Barnard, 'Grondslag en Doel van Onderwys', *Die Kerkbode* 60 (1947): 484–5; D.F. Erasmus, 'Manifes in sake Christelike Nasionale Onderwys', *Die Gereformeerde Vaandel* 3 (1935): 116–17, 362–4; and Peter Kallaway, ed., *Apartheid and Education: The Education of Black South Africans*, 5th edn (Johannesburg: Ravan Press, 1991).

62. Kallaway, *Apartheid and Education*, 1–44.

CHAPTER 4   APARTHEID'S EARLY YEARS (1948–61)

1. The HNP reverted to the *Nasionale Party* (NP) when it brought back into the fold Herzogite and *Ossewa Brandwag* supporters in the early 1950s. In this chapter and the chapter to follow, I will assume a state dominated by the NP. The South African state did include oppositional parties like the UP and the PFP, diverse factions within a variety of state agencies, and serious opposition from groups led by the ANC, but because the NP established extensive control over the rule-making and implementing apparatus of the state, the state was identified primarily with the NP.

2. Afrikanerdom refers to the phenomenon of ethnic unity among Afrikaners encouraged by the consolidation of political-economic power through organizations like the Afrikaner Broederbond, the National Party, the NGK, and the Afrikaner press.

3. For an elaboration of these three categories, as well as the ideas expressed in this description of apartheid, see Hermann Giliomee and Lawrence Schlemmer, *From Apartheid to Nation-Building* (Cape Town: Oxford University Press, 1989), 63–113.

4. See Robert Davies, *Capital, State and White Labour in South Africa, 1900–1960: An Historical Materialist Analysis of Class Formation and Class Relations* (Brighton: Harvester Press, 1979); and Philip Frankel, 'The Politics of Passes: Control and Change in South Africa', *Journal of Modern African Studies* 17 (1979): 199–217.

5. Dan O'Meara, *Forty Lost Years: The Apartheid State and the Politics of the National Party, 1948–1994* (Johannesburg: Ravan Press, 1996), 81, 82.

6. Scholars have debated the significance of apartheid laws which restricted labor movement. Liberals like S.T. van der Horst, D. Hobart Houghton, and F. Wilson argued that influx control laws constrained African employment opportunities and were incompatible with economic growth in the long term because they encouraged labor turnover,

low productivity, and high costs. Revisionists like H. Wolpe and M. Legassick challenged liberals with their 'cheap labour power thesis' which argued that labor controls ware designed to secure the economic and political conditions for capitalist expansion. For works that review these debates and offer a synthesis of the perspectives, see Doug Hindson, *Pass Controls and the Urban African Proletariat in South Africa* (Johannesburg: Ravan Press, 1987); Merle Lipton, *Capitalism and Apartheid: South Africa, 1910–1984* (Totowa, NJ: Rowman & Allanheld, 1985); and Deborah Posel, *The Making of Apartheid 1948–1961: Conflict and Compromise* (Oxford: Clarendon Press, 1991).

7.   Dan O'Meara provides a thorough review of the NP's distinctive rule in the 1950s and the complexity of the NP as a party due to factions found within the Cabinet, the NP parliamentary caucus, and provincial structures. See *Forty Lost Years*, 40–57.

8.   See Merle Lipton, *Capitalism and Apartheid*; Dan O'Meara, *Volkskapitalisme: Class, Capital and Ideology in the Development of Afrikaner Nationalism, 1934–1948* (Cambridge: Cambridge University Press, 1983); and David Welsh, 'The Political Economy of Afrikaner Nationalism', in *South Africa: Economic Growth and Political Change*, ed. Adrian Leftwich (London: Allison & Busby, 1974), 249–86.

9.   See Tom Lodge, *Black Politics in South Africa Since 1945* (London: Longman, 1983); and Shula Marks and Stanley Trapido, eds., *The Politics of Race, Class, and Nationalism in Twentieth-Century South Africa* (London: Longman, 1987).

10. William Nasson, 'The Unity Movement: Its Legacy in Historical Consciousness', *Radical History Review* 46–7 (1990): 189–211.

11. See Gail M. Gerhart, *Black Power in South Africa: The Evolution of an Ideology* (Berkeley and Los Angeles: University of California Press, 1978).

12. Meanwhile, South Africa's relations with the UN were strained. The South African state grew increasingly frustrated with the UN for appearing to side with anti-apartheid protesters. To explore UN pressure on South Africa, see *The United Nations and Apartheid, 1948–1994* (New York: UN Department of Public Information, 1994). For more information on the international pressures on South Africa, see James Barber and John Barratt, *South Africa's Foreign Policy: The Search for Status and Security 1945–1988* (Cambridge: Cambridge University Press, 1990).

13. Deborah Posel, 'The Meaning of Apartheid Before 1948: Conflicting Interests and Forces within the Afrikaner Nationalist Alliance', *Journal of Southern African Studies* 14 (1987): 123. Deborah Posel points to numerous studies which adopt the notion of a 'single policy blueprint'. See works by W.A. de Klerk, Brian Bunting, Dan O'Meara (1983) and Doug Hindson.

14. For an examination of the contested nature of apartheid in the first decade of NP rule, see John Lazar, 'Community and Conflict: Afrikaner Nationalist Politics in South Africa, 1948–61' (PhD diss., Oxford University, 1987); Alan Mabin, 'Comprehensive Segregation: the Origins of the Group Areas Act and its Planning Apparatuses', *Journal*

of Southern African Studies 18 (1992): 405–29; and Deborah Posel, *The Making of Apartheid*.

15. State leaders were not locked within these groups. M.D.C. De Wet Nel, for example, moved between the ideological purists and the purist sympathizers, while H.F. Verwoerd moved between the *baasskap* adherents and purist sympathizers.

16. Afrikaans text: 'Laat ons dan ten slotte die beleid van eventuele algehele skeiding, apartheid, of selfstandige ontwikkeling van die onderskeie rassegroepe bespreek as die enigste alternatief ... Die beweerde besware, nl. dat dit onmoontlike is om die beleid prakties deur te voer, noem dan veral twee onoorkoomlike berge wat die pad versper, t.w. die beskikbaarstelling van genoegsame grond aan naturelle, en die uitskakeling van naturellearbeid uit die blanke ekonomie. Dit sal na die mening van hierdie mense ontsettende ekonomiese verliese beteken en groot offers verg ...' A. van Schalkwyk, 'Beleidsrigtings t.o.v. die Naturellevraagstuk in Suid-Afrika', in *Die Naturellevraagstuk* (Stellenbosch: Pro-Ecclesia, 1950), 20–1.

17. The title moderate pragmatist does not at all indicate that these individuals were progressive or liberal churchmen. People like B.B. Keet and Ben Marais were, in fact, conservative churchmen committed to the Afrikaner's survival and concerned that the NGK establishment was abusing Biblical and church authority to sanction a questionable political policy. See Chapter 3 for an overview of the theological heritage of moderates.

18. B.B. Keet, 'Opening Address', *Christian Principles in Multi-Racial South Africa: A Report on the DRC Conference of Church Leaders* (n.p., 1953), 17–19.

19. B.B. Keet, 'Opening Address', 20–1.

20. The following section relies on David Welsh, 'The Executive and the African Population: 1948 to the Present', in *Malan to De Klerk: Leadership in the Apartheid State*, ed. Robert Schrire (New York: St. Martin's Press, 1994), 137–46. For a more detailed examination of D.F. Malan's views on race policy, see B.M. Schoeman, *Van Malan tot Verwoerd* (Cape Town: Human en Rousseau, 1973) and H.B. Thom, *D.F. Malan* (Cape Town: Tafelberg, 1980). See also O'Meara, *Forty Lost Years*, xxxii.

21. Welsh, 'The Executive', 139. The information that preceeds this quote can also be attributed to Welsh.

22. Ibid., 143.

23. Afrikaans text: 'As Kerk het ons ... steeds doelbewus aangestuur op die skeiding van hierde twee bevolkingsgroupe. In hierdie opsig kan daar met reg gepraat word van apartheid as 'n kerklike beleid.' T.N.H., 'Apartheid as Kerklike Beleid', *Die Kerkbode* 62 (1948): 664. English translation: 'As the church we ... continually aimed purposefully at the separation of the two population groups. In this regard one can rightly talk of apartheid as church policy.'

24. P.B. van der Watt, *Die Nederduitse Gereformeerde Kerk, 1905–1975* (Pretoria: Nasionale Boekdrukkery, 1987), 83–6.

25. N.J. Smith, interview by author, tape recording, Pretoria, South Africa, 29 March 1993.

26. The report was based on E.P. Groenewald's, 'Die Apartheid van die Nasie', *Die Gereformeerde Vaandel* 16 (1948): 9–10 which was discussed at the Council of Churches in 1947 (Chapter 3).

27. Quoted in Johann Kinghorn, 'The Theology of Separate Equality: A Critical Outline of the DRC's Position on Apartheid', in *Christianity Amidst Apartheid*, ed. Martin Prozesky (London: Macmillan, 1990), 67.

28. *The Racial Issue in South Africa* (Bloemfontein: D.R. Mission Press, 1953), 7–8.

29. Kinghorn, 'The Theology of Separate Equality', 66.

30. Afrikaans text 'het die deputasie vriendelik ontvang, maar daarop gewys dat die uitvoering van die beleid van Apartheid tans onprakties is, hoewel dit 'n mooi ideaal behels.' *Federale Sendingraad van die NGK, Notule, Verslae en Memorandum*, 4 Mei 1950, 242.

31. Afrikaans text: 'Daar is egter ernstige besware van die kant van die Boere en Nywerhede dat hul bantoe-werksmense verminder sal word, waar daar reeds 'n tekort is. In die land self is daar nie by benadering genoeg blankes om die werk te doen ...'. Ibid., 239. This quote reflects the government's recognition of the fears of farmers who opposed total apartheid if it meant the elimination of their labor. They did, however, support strict influx control in these years, something purists advocated.

32. *House of Assembly Debates*, 1950, cols 4250–1.

33. The following section relies on Welsh, 'The Executive', 147–52. See also J.L. Basson, *J.G. Strijdom: Sy Politieke Loopbaan van 1929 tot 1948* (Pretoria: Wonderboom, 1980).

34. John Lazar, 'Verwoerd versus the "Visionaries": The South African Bureau of Racial Affairs (SABRA) and Apartheid, 1948–1961', in *Apartheid's Genesis 1935–1962*, ed. Philip Bonner, Peter Delius, and Deborah Posel (Johannesburg: Ravan Press, 1993), 372.

35. Ritner, 'Salvation Through Separation', 231.

36. Welsh, 'The Executive', 148.

37. Lazar, 'Verwoerd versus the "Visionaries"', 362–92.

38. See Posel, *The Making of Apartheid*, 66–8.

39. Ibid., 76–90.

40. Lazar, 'Verwoerd versus the "Visionaries"', 373. The ideas that follow are also attributed to Lazar.

41. O'Meara, *Forty Lost Years*, 71. O'Meara also notes white concerns about apartheid's moral basis.

42. See O'Meara, 73. As Minister of Native Affairs, Verwoerd had never planned on the independence of the reserves. He had envisioned self-governance under Pretoria at the level of Territorial Authority. However, in a 1959 speech in parliament, he mentioned the possibility of independence for the 'Bantu Areas', an idea that was promoted by subsequent governments and achieved in the late 1970s and early 1980s.

43. H.F. Verwoerd relied on the work of N.J. Rhoodie and H.J. Venter in his explanation of separate development. See Rhoodie and Venter's *Apartheid: A Socio-Historical Exposition of the Origin and Development of the Apartheid Idea* (Cape Town: Human en Rousseau, 1959). To

explore further Verwoerd's perspectives on race and other issues, see Alexander Hepple, *Verwoerd* (Harmondsworth, England: Penguin Books, 1967); Henry Kenney, *Architect of Apartheid* (Johannesburg: Jonathan Ball, 1980); and David Welsh, 'The Executive', 152–63.

44.	The inconsistency of separate development policy is that it applied only to Africans. Africans were subdivided into different national groupings, but English-speaking whites and Afrikaners remained politically one 'nation' even though they were culturally distinct. Only Africans were relegated to separate homelands; 'Coloureds', Indians, and whites were exempt from homeland designation.

45.	U.G. 61–55. *Summary of the Report for the Socio-Economic Development of the Bantu Areas in the Union of South Africa* (Pretoria: Government Printer, 1955), 18–19.

46.	Posel, *The Making of Apartheid*, 230.

47.	O'Meara, *Forty Lost Years*, 73.

48.	Lazar, 'Verwoerd versus the "Visionaries"', 362–92.

49.	Ibid., 384. For the ideas represented in this paragraph, see also Posel's and Welsh's work.

50.	Welsh, 'The Executive', 155.

51.	Lazar, 'Verwoerd versus the "Visionaries"', 384.

52.	O'Meara, *Forty Lost Years*, 73–4.

53.	Posel, *The Making of Apartheid*, 236.

54.	See *Christian Principles in Multi-Racial South Africa*.

55.	Ibid., 163.

56.	C.B. Brink, 'The Fundamental Principles of the Mission Policy of the "Nederduitse Gereformeerde" Churches in South Africa' in *Christian Principles*, 34.

57.	'The Dutch Reformed Churches in South Africa and the Problem of Race Relations' in *Statements on Race Relations* (Johannesburg: Information Bureau of the Dutch Reformed Church, 1960), 8, 10.

58.	For an extended discussion of the activities of liberation movements, see Gail M. Gerhart, *Black Power in South Africa*; Tom Lodge, *Black Politics in South Africa Since 1945*; and Francis Meli, *South Africa belongs to Us: A History of the ANC* (Harare: Zimbabwe Publishing House, 1988).

59.	'Statement on the Riots in South Africa' in *Statements on Race Relations*, 13.

60.	Indeed, the NGK churches of the Cape Province and the Transvaal remained loyal to the NGK views, and in a separate statement, made it clear that they felt 'a policy of differentiation can be defended from the Christian point of view, that it provides the only realistic solution to the problems of race relations and is therefore in the best interests of the various population groups' 'World Council of Churches Consultation', *South African Outlook* 91, no. 1078 (1961): 23.

61.	Ibid., 20–2.

62.	Another example of the attempt by pragmatists to influence debate within the NGK at this time was the publication of *Delayed Action* (Pretoria: N.G. Kerkboekhandel, 1960), a collection of articles by eleven NGK leaders who critiqued apartheid's application.

63. Johann Kinghorn, edn *Die NG Kerk en Apartheid* (Johannesburg: Macmillan Suid-Afrika, 1986), 119.
64. Afrikaans text: 'heelhartige onderskrywing van die beleid van ons kerk soos op agtereenvolgende sinodes vanaf 1951–1958 geformuleer is ... 'n beleid van differensiasie of afsonderlike ontwikkeling, wat op die beginsel van Christelike voogdyskap voorgestaan het.' E.P. Groenwald, 'Die Transvaalse Kerk en die Cottesloe-Beraad', *Nederduitse Gereformeerde Teologiese Tydskrif* 2 (1961): 132–3.
65. C.F.B. Naudé, interview by author, tape recording, Johannesburg, South Africa, 8 April 1993.
66. P. Rossouw, interview by author, tape recording, Pretoria, South Africa, 1 April 1993.
67. C.B. Brink, 'The Fundamental Principles', 32.

CHAPTER 5   APARTHEID'S HEIGHT (1962–78)

1. Because of the state's power over the NGK, *an element of* cooptation existed within the relationship. Cooptation refers to a more powerful body or group taking over an independent group and forcing or urging it to cooperate with or follow the dictates of the more powerful group. Some may differ with my description of the NGK–state relationship in these years, arguing that it was an era of cooptation rather than collaboration. I emphasize colloboration over cooptation because the later suggests more independence on the part of the NGK than existed prior to 1962 and more coercion on the part of the state regarding the NGK than existed during the height of apartheid.
2. W.J. de Klerk, an academic at Potchefstroom University who later became a newspaper editor, originally coined these terms in an article written in 1972.
3. Dan O'Meara, *Forty Lost Years: The Apartheid State and the Politics of the National Party, 1948–1994* (Johannesburg: Ravan Press, 1996), 155. See also pages 155–7.
4. Ibid., 155.
5. In many ways, *verligtes* embraced the ideas of the accommodationist segregationists of the 1930s and 1940s.
6. Instead, border industries were encouraged which could take advantage of a cheap labor force. See Nigel Worden, *The Making of Modern South Africa* (Oxford: Blackwell, 1994), 109–11, for the ideas within this paragraph.
7. Ibid., 111.
8. Ibid. The homelands were not recognized as independent nation-states by any other country in the world.
9. Both the military and police force saw dramatic increases in their budgets. O'Meara, *Forty Lost Years*, 109.
10. Ibid., 117–18. For Vorster's continued promotion of the policy of 'white nationalism', see Heribert Adam, 'Survival Politics: Afrikanerdom in

Search of a New Ideology', *Journal of Modern African Studies* 16 (1978): 657–69.

11. For an elaboration of the economic growth of the 1960s, see Stephen Lewis, *The Economics of Apartheid* (New York: Council on Foreign Relations Press, 1990); N. Nattrass and Elisabeth Ardington, eds., *The Political Economy of South Africa* (New York: St. Martin's Press, 1990); Alf Stadler, *The Political Economy of Modern South Africa* (New York: St. Martin's Press, 1987). For a perspective that challenges the perception that the apartheid economy grew rapidly in these years, see Terence Moll, 'Did the Apartheid Economy "Fail"?', *Journal of Southern African Studies* 17 (1991): 271–91.

12. For an elaboration of the ideas in this paragraph and the paragraph to follow, see O'Meara, *Forty Lost Years*, 136–44.

13. Ibid., 151–5. The ideas that follow can also be attributed to this source.

14. Vorster contained early NP tensions through reducing *verkrampte* elements within the Afrikaner Broederbond and through his reliance on the Bureau for State Security (BOSS), which was led by Vorster's confidant General Hendrik van den Bergh. See O'Meara, *Forty Lost Years*, 149–67.

15. See David Dalcanton, 'Vorster and the Politics of Confidence', *African Affairs* 75 (1976): 163–81.

16. O'Meara, *Forty Lost Years*, 169–89.

17. Merle Lipton, *Sanctions and South Africa* (London: Economist Intelligence Unit, 1988), 106.

18. For an elaboration of B.J. Vorster's perspective on race policy and other matters, see O. Geyser, *B.J. Vorster: Select Speeches* (Bloemfontein: Institute for Contemporary History at the University of the OFS, 1977).

19. At the same time as the South Africa state embraced a policy of 'detente' with some African governments, it was involved in an SADF incursion into Angola from August 1975 to March 1976.

20. David Welsh, 'The Executive and the African Population: 1948 to the Present', in *Malan to De Klerk*, ed. Robert Schrire (New York: St. Martin's Press, 1994), 165.

21. O'Meara, *Forty Lost Years*, 201.

22. For more information on the international pressures on South Africa in these years, see Robert Kinloch Massie, *Loosing the Bonds: The United States and South Africa in the Apartheid Years* (New York: Doubleday, 1997) and *The United Nations and Apartheid, 1948–1994* (New York: UN Department of Public Information, 1994).

23. Mulder opposed Defence Minister P.W. Botha, the only other contender for the leadership position. For an intriguing account of the Muldergate scandal and its implications for the ideological stronghold of the NP and the South African state, see O'Meara, *Forty Lost Years*, 210–49.

24. 'Skakeling met die Owerheid', *Die Sendingblad* 9 (1973): 256–8.

25. *Human Relations and the South African Scene in the Light of Scripture* (Cape Town: DRC Publishers, 1976), 74.

26. J.H.P. Serfontein, *Apartheid, Change, and the NG Kerk* (Emmarentia: Taurus, 1982), 77.

27. J.A. Heyns, interview by author, tape recording, Pretoria, South Africa, 30 March 1993.
28. Susan Rennie Ritner, 'Salvation Through Separation' (PhD thesis, Columbia University, 1971), 249–51.
29. Ibid., 249–51.
30. W.A. Landman, *A Plea for Understanding, A Reply to the Reformed Church in America* (Cape Town: DRC Publishers, 1968), 29.
31. Afrikaans text: 'Bostaande toon duidelik dat die Ned. Geref. Kerk se beleid van eiesoortige ontwikkeling wel deeglik rekening hou met die eise van die Skrif en die praktyk.' *Handelinge van die Algemene Sinode van die NGK*, 1970, 180.
32. Previous versions of HR had been rejected because of their 'liberal' emphasis in suggesting some version of united worship. This indicates the pragmatic faction in the NGK was not completely silent.
33. For a critical analysis of HR and the Landman Report, see J.J.F. Durand, 'Bible and Race: The Problem of Hermeneutics', *Journal of Theology for Southern Africa* 24 (1978): 3–11; Brian Johanson, 'Race, Mission and Ecumenism: Reflections on the Landman Report', *Journal of Theology for Southern Africa* 10 (1975): 51–61; and J.A. Loubser, *The Apartheid Bible: A Critical Review of Racial Theology in South Africa* (Cape Town: Maskew Miller Longman, 1987).
34. *Human Relations*, 32, 71.
35. *Human Relations*, 74.
36. See G.J. Kotzé, 'Indrukke en Besluite van die Algemene Sinode 1966', *Die Kerkbode* 118 (1966): 818; *Handelinge van die Algemene Sinode van die NGK*, 1970, 362; and *Handelinge van die Algemene Sinode van die NGK*, 1974, 320.
37. *Human Relations*, 75–6, 73.

CHAPTER 6   APARTHEID'S DEMISE (1979–94)

Portions of this chapter are reprinted, with changes, from the *Journal of Church and State* 38 (1996): 841–72.

1. The paragraphs that follow rely on O'Meara's analysis of the Botha years. See Dan O'Meara, *Forty Lost Years* (Johannesburg: Ravan Press, 1996), 224–393, particularly 254–9 and 224–8. For more information on Botha's rule, see Brian Pottinger's, *The Imperial Presidency: P.W. Botha* (Johannesburg: Southern Book Publishers, 1988).
2. Ibid., 225.
3. Ibid., 226.
4. For a more nuanced description concerning the NP *verligte/verkrampte* camps in the 1970s and 1980s, see Hermann Giliomee, 'Apartheid, Verligtheid, and Liberalism', in *Democratic Liberalism in South Africa: Its History and Prospect*, ed. Jeffrey Butler, Richard Elphick, and David

Welsh (Middletown, Connecticut: Wesleyan University Press, 1987), 363–84.

5. J.B. Knight, 'A Comparative Analysis of South Africa as a Semi-Industrialized Developing Country', *Journal of Modern African Studies* 26 (1988): 475. See also N. Nattrass and Elisabeth Ardington, eds. *The Political Economy of South Africa* (Cape Town: Oxford University Press, 1990); and S. Gelb, *South Africa's Economic Crisis* (Cape Town: David Philip, 1991).

6. Knight, 'Comparative Analysis', 475–81. See also Pampallis, *Foundations*, 298–9.

7. Leonard Thompson, *A History of South Africa* (New Haven: Yale University Press, 1990), 223.

8. O'Meara, *Forty Lost Years*, 259–69. The twelve-point plan or principles of total strategy were revealed at the Natal National Party Congress in August 1979. For an extended discussion of 'total strategy', see Robert M. Price, *The Apartheid State in Crisis: Political Transformation in South Africa, 1975–1990* (New York: Oxford University Press, 1991), 79–189.

9. Ibid., 116–9 and Thompson, *History of South Africa*, 227.

10. See Stanley B. Greenberg, 'Ideological Struggles within the South African State,' in *The Politics of Class, Race and Nationalism in Twentieth-Century South Africa*, ed. Shula Marks and Stanley Trapido (London: Longman, 1987), 389–418; and John Pampallis, *Foundations of the New South Africa* (Cape Town: Maskew Miller Longman, 1991), 279–80.

11. The state's acquiescence of IFP needs, 'third force activity', and the IFP's position on issues like economic sanctions led to the intense political rivalry between the IFP and ANC-affiliated groups like the UDF and COSATU in the 1980s and 1990s. See John Brewer, 'From Ancient Rome to Kwazulu: Inkatha in South African Politics', in *South Africa: No Turning Back*, ed. Shaun Johnson (Bloomington: Indiana University Press, 1989), 353–74; and M. Kentridge, *An Unofficial War: Inside the Conflict in Pietermaritzburg* (Cape Town: David Philip, 1990).

12. O'Meara, *Forty Lost Years*, 273.

13. Mark Mitchell and Dave Russell, 'Black Unions and Political Change in South Africa', in *Can South Africa Survive? Five Minutes to Midnight*, ed. John D. Brewer (London: Macmillan, 1989), 234–6. In the paragraphs that follow, see Thompson, *A History of South Africa*, 224–8.

14. The Black Local Authorities Act of 1982 gave 'local autonomy' to residents of urban areas. But the local administrations associated with Community Councils (later Regional Service Councils) were discredited by many black South Africans.

15. Timothy D. Sisk, 'White Politics in South Africa: Polarization under Pressure', *Africa Today* 36 (1989): 32–4.

16. For a description of the intricate reorganization of South Africa's state structures, see Annette Seegers, 'South Africa's National Security Management System, 1972–90', *Journal of Modern African Studies* 29 (1991): 253–73; and Mark Swilling and Mark Phillips, 'The Emergency State: Its Structures, Power and Limits', in *South Africa Review*, vol. 5, ed. Glenn Moss and Ingrid Obery (London: Hans Zell, 1990), 68–90.

17. For the ideas within this paragraph, see O'Meara, *Forty Lost Years*, 280–7.

18. Frontline states included countries like Angola, Botswana, Mozambique, Zambia, and Zimbabwe. The term not only referred to the independent states bordering South Africa; it came to symbolize a 'terrain of struggle' that separated the apartheid regime from liberation forces/countries.

19. For an elaboration of South Africa's destabilization campaigns, see Joseph Hanlon, *Beggar Your Neighbors* (Bloomington: Indiana University Press, 1986); or Phyllis Johnson and D. Martin, *Destructive Engagement: Southern Africa at War* (Harare: Zimbabwe Publishing House, 1986).

20. For an overview of liberation activity in the 1980s, see John D. Brewer, ed., *Can South Africa Survive?*; Shaun Johnson, ed., *South Africa: No Turning Back*; and Tom Lodge and Bill Nasson, eds., *All, Here, and Now: Black Politics in South Africa in the 1980s* (New York: Ford Foundation, 1991).

21. Mark Swilling, 'The United Democratic Front and Township Revolt', in *Popular Struggles in South Africa*, ed. William Cobbett and Robin Cohen (Trenton, NJ: Africa World Press, 1988), 90–113.

22. Shaun Johnson, 'The Soldiers of Luthuli: Youth in the Politics of Resistance in South Africa', in *South Africa: No Turning Back*, 94–152; and Eddie Webster, 'The Rise of Social-Movement Unionism: The Two Faces of the Black Trade Union Movement in South Africa', in *State, Resistance and Change in South Africa*, ed. Philip Frankel, Noam Pines and Mark Swilling (New York: Croom Helm, 1988), 174–96.

23. On 22 February 1988, the government prohibited seventeen organizations from engaging in politically related activities. The UDF and COSATU were singled out as promoting a 'revolutionary climate' and encouraging civil disobedience and revolt. The State of Emergency was finally lifted by F.W. de Klerk in 1990.

24. Constructive engagement entailed a supportive foreign policy approach to South Africa in an effort to reform apartheid. See George Klay Kieh, 'Beyond the Facade of Constructive Engagement: A Critical Examination of the United States Foreign Policy Toward Southern Africa', *Africa Quarterly* 26 (1988): 1–15.

25. Cosmas Desmond, 'Sanctions and South Africa', *Third World Quarterly* 8 (1986), 81. See also Frene Ginwala, 'The Case for Sanctions', in *South Africa in Question*, ed. John Lonsdale (London: James Currey, 1988); Kenneth Hermele and Bertil Oden, *Sanctions Dilemmas* (Uppsala: Scandinavian Institute of African Studies, 1988); and George Shepherd, ed., *Effective Sanctions* (New York: Praeger, 1991).

26. For a summary of the UN's involvement in apartheid since the late 1940s, see Newell M. Stultz, 'The Apartheid Issue at the General Assembly: Stalemate or Gathering Storm?', *African Affairs* 86 (1987): 25–45; or *The United Nations and Apartheid, 1948–1994* (New York: UN Department of Public Information, 1994).

27. See, for example, Kinghorn, 'Theology of Separate Equality', 69–73 and J.H.P. Serfontein, *Apartheid, Change and the NGK* (Emmarentia: Taurus, 1982).

28. See Craig Charney, 'Class Conflict and the National Party Split', *Journal of Southern African Studies* 10 (1984): 269–82. For a more recent, liberal account of the divisions within Afrikanerdom, see Hermann Giliomee, '*Broedertwis*: Intra-Afrikaner Conflicts in the Transition from Apartheid', *African Affairs* 91 (1992): 339–64.

29. Charney, 'Class Conflict', 270.

30. Ibid., 272–3.

31. Ibid., 277.

32. Interview by author, tape recording, South Africa, 23 February 1993.

33. A. König, interview by author, tape recording, Pretoria, South Africa, 1 April 1993.

34. B. Geldenhuys, interview by author, tape recording, Cape Town, South Africa, 27 April 1993.

35. Jaap Durand and Dirkie Smit, 'The Afrikaner Churches on War and Violence', in *Theology and Violence*, ed. Charles Villa-Vicencio (Johannesburg: Skotaville Publishers, 1987), 31–49.

36. Another reason why the NGK dismissed organizations like the WCC and the WARC was these religious bodies outrightly condemned the NGK's historical support of apartheid. In 1982, the WARC (Ottawa) rejected apartheid as a pseudo-religious ideology. A few months later, the NGSK stated that apartheid was idolatrous and its theological justification a heresy. A *status confessions* was declared. This meant that a church could not differ on the issue because this would endanger the common confession of faith. Such actions put a great deal of pressure on the NGK.

37. W. Nicol, interview by author, tape recording, Pretoria, South Africa, 29 March 1993.

38. See David J. Bosch, Adrio König, and Willem Nicol, eds., *Perspektief Op die Ope Brief* (Kaapstad: Human & Rousseau, 1982) and N.J. Smith, F.E.O'B Geldenhuys, and P. Meiring, eds., *Stormkompas* (Kaapstad: Tafelberg-Uitgewers, 1981).

39. 'Groot Groep Leraars Reik Ope Brief uit oor Kerk se Roeping', *Die Kerkbode* 134, no. 22 (1982): 1–5.

40. See, for example, 'Die Breë Moderatuur se Leiding oop die Ope Brief', *Die Kerkbode* 134, no. 25 (1982): 6; J.A. Heyns, 'Waarom Hierdie Ope Brief 'n Belangrike Gebeurtenis is', *Die Kerkbode* 134, no. 24 (1982): 5; and 'Kyn na Inhoud', *Die Kerkbode* 134, no. 23 (1982): 1.

41. *Handelinge van die Algemene Sinode van die NGK*, 1982, 1986.

42. To repeat, the top echelon of NGK leadership agreed that partial reform was necessary in the 1980s. Leaders like J.A. Heyns, P.C. Potgieter, P.A. Verhoef, P. Rossouw, and D.A. du Toit indicated their acceptance of limited reform (for example, engaging in discussions for structural church unity) if these changes did not disrupt the guidelines of separate development. See P.A. Verhoef, 'Is Etniese Veelvormigheid 'n Bybelse Grondwaarheid?' *Die Kerkbode* 137, no. 4 (1986): 5 and P.C. Potgieter, 'Onsigbare Kerk is die Verborge Inhoud van Sigbare Kerk', *Die Kerkbode* 141, no. 18 (1988): 7. If the opinion of these leaders had influenced the *actions* of the church, the NGK could have represented a civil society institution that actually led the state, or at least supported it enthusiastically, regarding political reforms.

43. The *Afrikaanse Protestantse Kerk* (APK) is an NGK breakaway church that was formed in 1987. It has about 30,000 members.

44. W.A. Saayman, interview by author, tape recording, Pretoria, South Africa, 31 March 1993.

45. 'Groepsgebiedewette', *Die Kerkbode* 142, no. 14 (1987): 4.

46. For excellent background information on mixed marriages legislation, see Patrick Furlong, 'Improper Intimacy: Afrikaans Churches, the National Party and the Anti-Miscegenation Laws', *South African Historical Journal* 31 (1994): 55–79. To explore the historical background, ideological context, and 1980s debates regarding mixed marriages and immorality, see Etienne de Villiers and Johann Kinghorn, *Op die Skaal: Gemengde Huwelike en Ontug* (Kaapstad: Tafelberg-Uitgewers, 1984).

47. *Select Committee on the Prohibition of the Mixed Marriages Act and Section 16 of the Immorality Act*, (Cape Town: Government Printer, 1984), 95–108. Conservative and moderate church positions on these issues are contained in *Handelinge van die Algemene Sinode van die NGK*, 1982, 1109. Liberal dissent within the NGK concerning the church's position on mixed marriages can be found in *Stormkompas*, 139.

48. *House of Assembly Debates*, 1985, cols 3486, 3495.

49. *Church and Society: A Testimony of the Dutch Reformed Church* (Bloemfontein: Pro Christo Publishers, 1986), 47.

50. C.F.B. Naudé, interview by author, tape recording, Johannesburg, South Africa, 8 April 1993.

51. During South Africa's negotiating phase, the major parties differed on the form of democratic governance for the 'new South Africa'. The NP favored a consociational arrangement while the ANC favored majority rule. These differences will be explained below.

52. See Heribert Adam and Kogila Moodley, *The Opening of the Apartheid Mind: Options for the New South Africa* (Berkeley and Los Angeles: University of California Press, 1993); Donald Horowitz, *A Democratic South Africa? Constitutional Engineering in a Divided Society* (Berkeley and Los Angeles: University of California Press, 1991); Johannes Rantete and Hermann Giliomee, 'Transition to Democracy through Transaction: Bilateral Negotiations between the ANC and NP in South Africa', *African Affairs* 91 (1992): 515–42; and Timothy D. Sisk, *Democratization in South Africa: The Elusive Social Contract* (Princeton: Princeton University Press, 1995).

53. See Adam and Moodley, *The Opening of the Apartheid Mind*, Chapter 1 or Steven Friedman, 'South Africa's Reluctant Transition', *Journal of Democracy* 4 (1993): 56–9.

54. John Pampallis, *Foundations of the New South Africa* (Cape Town: Maskew Miller Longman, 1991), 302. The ideas in the next few paragraphs can be attributed to Pampallis.

55. The Broederbond's support for political restructuring was also notable. According to Hermann Giliomee, the AB released two documents in 1989 that recommended a negotiated settlement to protect group rights. The documents even suggested the end to white control of the

government. See Hermann Giliomee, 'The Last Trek? Afrikaners in the Transition to Democracy', *South Africa International* 22 (1992): 113–14.

56. For an in-depth account of the CODESA process, see Sisk, *Democratization in South Africa*, 200–48.

57. Annette Strauss, 'The 1992 Referendum in South Africa', *Journal of Modern African Studies* 31 (1993): 339–60.

58. After this agreement between the ANC and the NP, Buthelezi consolidated leaders from the CP and other conservative groups to form COSAG (Concerned South African Group), an organization established to challenge the ANC and the NP's negotiation gains. COSAG eventually withdrew from negotiations to protest the bilateral dominance of the ANC and the NP. See Sisk's work for details.

59. See Hermann Giliomee and Lawrence Schlemmer, *From Apartheid to Nation Building* (Cape Town: Oxford University Press, 1989); and Arend Lijphart, *Power-Sharing in South Africa* (Berkeley: Institute of International Studies, Policy Papers in International Affairs, 1985). For a critique of consociationalism, see Michael MacDonald, 'The Siren's Song: The Political Logic of Power-Sharing in South Africa', *Journal of Southern Africa Studies* 18 (1992): 709–25; or Rupert Taylor, 'South Africa: A Consociational Path to Peace?', *Transformation* 17 (1992): 1–11.

60. The state became a murky institution in the 1990s. Over time, the Transitional Executive Council, CODESA, and other institutions became part of the state's apparatus. The NGK's relationship with leaders dominating the latter institutions was definitely one of limited engagement. However, I will continue to argue in this section that the main institution 'defining' the state, even in the early 1990s, was the NP because certain actions, for example, the invasion of PAC headquarters in June 1993 and the engagement in 'third force' activity, indicated the NP's dominance within the state .

61. *House of Assembly Debates*, 1991, cols 7271–2.

62. David Welsh, 'The Executive and the African Population – 1948 to the Present', in *Malan to De Klerk*, ed. Robert Schrire (New York: St. Martin's Press, 1994), 196.

63. Ibid.

64. 'The Rustenburg Declaration', in *The Road to Rustenburg: The Church Looking Forward to a New South Africa*, ed. Louw Alberts and Frank Chikane (Cape Town: Struik House, 1991), 277. See also Douglas Bax, 'The Vereeniging Consultation: What Happened?', *Journal of Theology for Southern Africa* 68 (1989): 62 and *Handelinge van die Algemene Sinode van die NGK*, 1990, 46–7.

65. *Church and Society 1990: A Testimony of the Dutch Reformed Church* (Bloemfontein: Pro Christo Publishers, 1990), 39–40.

66. Willie Jonker, 'Understanding the Church Situation and Obstacles to Christian Witness in South Africa', in *The Road to Rustenburg*, 92.

67. P.C. Potgieter, interview by author, tape recording, Bloemfontein, South Africa, 14 April 1993.

68. Christopher Wren, 'For South Africa, A Watershed Vote', *The New York Times*, 16 March 1992, A4.

69. Afrikaans text: 'Die kerk hét 'n taak: ... te vra dat al die betrokkenes die referendum veldtog in 'n Christelike gesindheid en styl sal voer en deurgaans op 'n verantwoordelike wyse sal optree ... Wat die kerk egter nie kan doen nie – nie sy verskillende vergaderings nie en ook nie sy ampsdraers nie – is om vir die lidmate aan te raai om "ja" of "nee" te stem.' 'Die Kerk kan nie sê nie', *Die Kerkbode* 149, no. 8 (1992): 4.
70. P.G.J. Meiring, interview with author, tape recording, Pretoria, South Africa, 30 March 1993.
71. E.M. Tema, interview by author, tape recording, Orlando, South Africa, 7 April 1993.
72. *Human Relations and the South African Scene in the Light of Scripture* (Cape Town: DRC Publishers, 1976), 46.
73. For the diversity–unity debate concerning church structures, see periodicals like the *Nederduitse Gereformeerde Teologie Tydskrif, Op Die Horison*, and *Die Kerkbode*. See also *Raad van die Kerken* and *Algemene Sinode* documents.
74. *Church and Society*, 1986, 12–21.
75. The NGK 'family' included the NGK, the NGSK, the NGKA and the RCA. The term 'family' is ironic in light of the lack of unity and community among the structures.
76. *The Statement of the Vereeniging Consultation*, 1989, 4.
77. *Church and Society*, 1990, 6, 14. 'Indigenous' is synonymous with separate church structures.
78. Ibid., 18.
79. W.A. Saayman, interview by author, tape recording, Pretoria, South Africa, 31 March 1993.
80. F.M. Gaum, interview by author, tape recording, Cape Town, South Africa, 18 March 1993.
81. J.J.F. Durand, 'Church Unity and the Reformed Churches in Southern Africa'. Unpublished paper presented at the WARC conference on Church Unity, 5 March 1993.
82. Adrio König, interview by author, tape recording, Pretoria, South Africa, 1 April 1993.

CHAPTER 7 CONCLUSION

1. Works by D.M. Balia, James Cochrane, John de Gruchy, Albert Nolan, Charles Villa-Vicencio, and Peter Walshe address the historical relationship between English-speaking churches and the South African state before and during the apartheid era. Two of the more recent works analyzing how Christian churches and institutions fostered democracy within South Africa are John W. de Gruchy's *Christianity and Democracy: A Theology for a Just World Order* (Cape Town: David Philip, 1995) and Peter Walshe's *Prophetic Christianity and the Liberation Movement in South Africa* (Pietermaritzburg: Cluster Publications, 1995).
2. 'Discusses Challenges Ahead', FBIS-AFR-94-082-S, 28 April 1994, 24.

3. 'Mandela Interviewed on SABC', FBIS-AFR-94-083-S, 29 April 1994, 13.

4. F.M. Gaum, interview by author, tape recording, Cape Town, South Africa, 18 March 1993.

5. J.A. Heyns, interview by author, tape recording, Pretoria, South Africa, 30 March 1993.

6. Ibid.

7. H.J.D. Brand, interview by author, tape recording, Cape Town, South Africa, 2 February 1993.

8. Afrikaans text: 'die NGK ook in die toekoms so ver dit in sy vermoë is, vir lidmate en hulle belange by die owerheid in die bres sal tree.' 'NGK Weer na Mandela', *Die Kerkbode* 157, no. 28 (1996): 2.

9. Hannes Burger, 'How Gemaak Met Jou Apartheidskuld?' *Algemene Kerkbode* 155, no. 16 (1995): 11–12.

10. 'Kerk en Owerheid in die Nuwe SA', *Die Kerkbode* 159, no. 8 (1997): 13.

11. Afrikaans text: 'Omdat die lidmate van die een in baie gevalle die lede van die ander was, het 'n wisselwerking tussen kerk en party/owerheid ontstaan wat verstaanbaar is, maar meegebring het dat die kerk nie altyd die wenslike kritiese afstand ten opsigte van die owerheid gehandhaaf het nie … Dit is vanweë 'n diepe en geregverdigde vereenselwiging met die lot van die mense vir wie die Ned Geref Kerk in eerste instansie bedien het – die Afrikaners – dat dié kerk dikwels geneig was om sy mense se belange bo ánder mense s'n te stel.' 'Reis met Apartheid' *Die Kerkbode* 159, no. 9 (1997): 7.

12. 'Waarheidspan Kan Versoening Selfs Vernietig', *Die Kerkbode* 156, no. 2 (1996): 1.

13. Freek Swanepoel, 'Presentation to the TRC', C;/algsin/dokument/trc, 14 November 1997.

14. Mark Swilling, 'The Case for Associational Socialism', *Works in Progress*, no. 76 (1991): 20–3; and 'Political Transition, Development and the Role of Civil Society', *Africa Insight* 20 (1990): 151–60.

15. For the ideas expressed in this paragraph, see Blade Nzimande and Mpume Sikhosana, 'Civil Society and Democracy', *African Communist*, 1 (1992): 37–51; and '"Civil Society": A Theoretical Survey and Critique of Some South African Conceptions', in *Democracy, Civil Society and the State*, ed. Lloyd Sachikonye (Harare: SAPES Books, 1995): 20–45.

16. The ideas in this paragraph can be attributed to Steve Friedman and Maxine Reitzes, 'Democratic Selections: Civil Society and Development in South Africa's New Democracy', in *Transformation in South Africa? Policy Debates in the 1990s*, ed. Ernest Maganya and Rachel Houghton (Johannesburg: Institute for African Alternatives, 1996), 230–50. See also Jannie Gagiano and Pierre du Toit, 'Consolidating Democracy in South Africa: The Role of Civil Society', in *Consolidating Democracy: What Role for Civil Society in South Africa?*, ed. Hennie Kotzé (Stellenbosch: Centre for International and Comparative Politics, 1996).

17. See Nicholas Haysom, Firoz Cachalia, and Edwin Molahlehi, 'Civil Society and Fundamental Freedoms'. *Report Commissioned by the*

Independent Study into an Enabling Environment for NGOs, July 1993, 32–3 for related information on a right-based culture in South Africa.

18. Gaye Davis, 'Authoritarian Leadership Alarms ANC Politicians', *Weekly Mail*, 10 October 1996, 12.

19. 'Bitter Inheritance: Overcoming the Legacy of Apartheid', in *Southern African Perspectives*, 1993.

20. I have begun to address the comparative dimensions of state–civil society relations between Zimbabwe and South Africa. Tracy Kuperus, 'Inclusive Democracy: Comparing State–Civil Society Relations in South Africa and Zimbabwe'. Paper presented at the African Studies Association, San Francisco, CA, 23 November 1996.

Select Bibliography

Adam, Heribert. 'Survival Politics: Afrikanerdom in Search of a New Ideology', *Journal of Modern African Studies* 16 (1978): 657–69.

Adam, Heribert and Kogila Moodley. *The Opening of the Apartheid Mind: Options for a New South Africa*. Berkeley and Los Angeles: University of California Press, 1993.

Alberts, Louw and Frank Chikane, eds. *The Road to Rustenburg: The Church Looking Forward to a New South Africa*. Cape Town: Struik House, 1991.

Allen, Chris. 'Who Needs Civil Society?', *Review of African Political Economy* no. 73 (1997): 329–37.

Bax, Douglas. 'The Vereeniging Consultation: What Happened?', *Journal of Theology for Southern Africa* 68 (1989): 61–73.

Bosch, David J., Adrio König and Willem Nicol, eds. *Perspektief op die Ope Brief*. Kaapstad: Human & Rousseau, 1982.

Botha, A.J. *Die Evolusie van 'n Volksteologie*. Bellville: UWK Drukkery, 1984.

Bratton, Michael. 'Beyond the State: Civil Society and Associational Life in Africa', *World Politics* 41 (1989): 407–30.

Charney, Craig. 'Class Conflict and the National Party Split', *Journal of Southern African Studies* 10 (1984): 269–82.

Chazan, Naomi. 'Patterns of State–Society Incorporation and Disengagement in Africa', in *The Precarious Balance: State and Society in Africa*, edited by Donald Rothchild and Naomi Chazan, 121–48. Boulder: Westview Press, 1988.

Christian Principles in Multi-Racial South Africa: A Report on the Dutch Reformed Conference of Church Leaders. n.p., 1953.

Christianity in South Africa: A Political, Social and Cultural History. Edited and compiled by Richard Elphick and Rodney Davenport. Oxford: James Currey, 1977.

Church and Society: A Testimony of the Dutch Reformed Church. Bloemfontein: Pro Christo Publishers, 1986, 1990.

Coetzee, J. Chr. 'Die Volkskongres oor die Armblanke Vraagstuk', *Koers* 2, no. 3 (1935): 13–20.

Cronjé, Geoffrey. *'n Tuiste vir die Nageslag: Die Blywende Oplossing van Suid-Afrika se Rassevraagstukke*. Stellenbosch: Pro Ecclesia-Drukkery, 1945.

Cronjé, Geoffrey, W.M. Nicol and E.P. Groenewald. *Regverdige Rasse-Apartheid*. Stellenbosch: CSV-Maatskappy van Suid-Afrika, 1947.

Davenport, T.R.H. *South Africa: A Modern History*. 4th edn. Toronto: University of Toronto Press, 1991.

De Gruchy, John W. *Christianity and Democracy: A Theology for a Just World Order*. Cape Town: David Philip, 1995.

_____. *The Church Struggle in South Africa*. Grand Rapids: William B. Eerdmans, 1986.

De Gruchy, John W. and Charles Villa-Vicencio, eds. *Apartheid is a Heresy*. Cape Town: David Philip, 1983.

DeLue, Steven M. *Political Thinking, Political Theory, and Civil Society.* Boston: Allyn & Bacon, 1997.

De Villiers, Etienne and Johann Kinghorn. *Op Die Skaal: Gemengde Huwelike en Ontug.* Kaapstad: Tafelberg-Uitgewers, 1984.

De Villiers, René. 'Afrikaner Nationalism', in *The Oxford History of South Africa*, edited by Monica Wilson and Leonard Thompson, 365–423. Vol. 2. Oxford: Oxford University Press, 1971.

Diamond, Larry. 'Civil Society and Democratic Consolidation: Building a Culture of Democracy in a New South Africa', in *Bold Experiment: South Africa's New Democracy*, edited by Lawrence Schlemmer with Sarita Hauptfleisch, 48–80. n.p.: Southern Book Publishers, 1994.

Diamond, Larry, Juan J. Linz and Seymour Martin Lipset, eds. *Democracy in Developing Countries.* 3 Vols. Boulder: Lynne Rienner, 1988–9.

Dubow, Saul. *Racial Segregation and the Origins of Apartheid in South Africa, 1919–36.* New York: St. Martin's Press, 1989.

Du Preez, A.B. *Die Skriftuurlike Grondslag vir Rasseverhoudinge.* Kaapstad: NG Kerk-Boekhandel, 1955.

Durand, Jaap. 'Afrikaner Piety and Dissent', in *Resistance and Hope*, edited by Charles Villa-Vicencio and John W. de Gruchy, 42–50. Grand Rapids: William B. Eerdmans, 1985.

Du Toit, André. 'No Chosen People: The Myth of the Calvinist Origins of Afrikaner Nationalism and Racial Ideology', *American Historical Review* 88 (1983): 920–52.

Du Toit, J.D. 'Die Godsdienstige Grondslag van ons Rassebelied', *Inspan* 4, no. 3 (1944): 7–17.

Du Toit, Pierre. *State Building and Democracy in Southern Africa: A Comparative Study of Botswana, South Africa, and Zimbabwe.* Pretoria: HSRC Publishers, 1995.

Eloff, G. *Rasse en Rassevermenging.* Bloemfontein: Nasionale Pers, 1942.

European and Bantu. Papers and addresses read at the Conference on Native Affairs. Held under the Auspices of the Federal Council of the DR Churches in Johannesburg, South Africa, 1923.

Federale Raad van die Kerken, Agendas en Handelinge (Federal Council of the (NG) Churches: Agendas and Actions). 1915–47.

Federale Sendingraad van die NG Kerke, Notule, Verslae en Memoranda (Notes, Reports and Memos from the Federal Mission Council of the NG Churches). 1942–62.

Foley, Michael W. and Bob Edwards. 'The Paradox of Civil Society', *Journal of Democracy* 7 (1996): 38–52.

Friedman, Steve and Maxine Reitzes. 'Democratic Selections: Civil Society and Development in South Africa's New Democracy', in *Transformation in South Africa? Policy Debates in the 1990s*, edited by Ernest Maganya and Rachel Houghton, 230–50. Johannesburg: Institute for African Alternatives, 1996.

Furlong, Patrick J. *Between Crown and Swastika: The Impact of the Radical Right on the Afrikaner Nationalist Movement in the Fascist Era.* Hanover, NH: University Press of New England, 1991.

Gaum, Frits. 'Kerk en Verkiesing', *Die Kerkbode* 153, no. 4 (1994): 4.

Gerstner, Jonathan. *The Thousand Generation Covenant: Dutch Reformed Covenant Theology and Group Identity in Colonial South Africa, 1652–1814*. Leiden: E.J. Brill, 1991.

Giliomee, Hermann. 'The Beginnings of Afrikaner Ethnic Consciousness, 1850–1915', in *The Creation of Tribalism in Southern Africa*, edited by Leroy Vail, 21–54. London: James Currey, 1989.

_____. '*Broedertwis*: Intra-Afrikaner Conflicts in the Transition from Apartheid', *African Affairs* 91 (1992): 339–64.

_____. 'The Growth of Afrikaner Identity', in *Segregation and Apartheid in Twentieth-Century South Africa*, edited by William Beinart and Saul Dubow, 189–205. London: Routledge, 1995.

Giliomee, Hermann and Lawrence Schlemmer. *From Apartheid to Nation-Building*. Cape Town: Oxford University Press, 1989.

Daryl Glaser. 'South Africa and the Limits of Civil Society', *Journal of Southern African Studies* 23 (1997): 5–25.

Groenewald, E.P. 'Die Apartheid van die Nasie', *Die Gereformeerde Vaandel* 16 (1948): 9–10.

Gyimah-Boadi, E. 'Civil Society in Africa', *Journal of Democracy* 7 (1996): 118–32.

Handelinge van die Algemene Sinode van die NGK. 1962–1990.

Hanekom, T.N. 'Apartheid as Kerklike Beleid', *Die Kerkbode* 62 (1948): 664.

Hanlon, Joseph. *Beggar Your Neighbours*. Bloomington: Indiana University Press, 1986.

Harbeson, John W., Donald Rothchild and Naomi Chazan, eds. *Civil Society and the State in Africa*. Boulder: Lynne Rienner Publishers, 1994.

Heard, Kenneth. *General Elections in South Africa, 1943–1970*. London: Oxford University Press, 1974.

Heyns, J.A. 'Waarom Hierdie Ope Brief 'n Belangrike Gebeurtenis is', *Die Kerkbode* 134, no. 24 (1982): 5.

_____. 'Wir Watter Party Moet Ek Later Vanjaar Stem?' *Die Kerkbode* 153, no. 4 (1994): 4.

Hexham, Irving. *The Irony of Apartheid: The Struggle for National Independence of Afrikaner Calvinism Against British Imperialism*. New York: Edwin Mellen Press, 1981.

Hofmeyr, J.W., J.A. Millard and C.J.J. Froneman. *History of the Church in South Africa*. Pretoria: Promedia Publishers, 1991.

Human Relations and the South African Scene in the Light of Scripture. Cape Town: DRC Publishers, 1974.

Humphries, Richard and Maxine Reitzes, eds. *Civil Society after Apartheid*. Doornfontein: Centre for Policy Studies, 1995.

Huntington, Samuel P. *The Third Wave: Democratization in the Late Twentieth Century*. Norman, OK: University of Oklahoma Press, 1991.

Hutchful, Eboe. 'The Civil Society Debate in Africa', *International Journal* 51 (1995–6): 54–77.

Johnstone, F.A. 'White Prosperity and White Supremacy in South Africa Today', *African Affairs* 69, no. 275 (1970): 124–40.

Keane, John, ed. *Civil Society and the State: New European Perspectives*. London: Verso, 1988.

'Kerk en Owerheid in die Nuwe SA', *Die Kerkbode* 159, no. 8 (1997): 13.

Kinghorn, Johann. 'The Theology of Separate Equality: A Critical Outline of the DRC's Position on Apartheid', in *Christianity amidst Apartheid*, edited by Martin Prozesky, 57–80. London: Macmillan Press, 1990.

Kinghorn, Johann, ed. *Die NG Kerk en Apartheid*. Johannesburg: Macmillan Suid-Afrika, 1986.

Kotzé, Hennie, ed. *Consolidating Democracy: What Role for Civil Society in South Africa?* Papers presented at a conference organized by the Centre for International and Comparative Politics, Stellenbosch, South Africa, August 1996.

Kuyper, Abraham. *Lectures on Calvinism*. Grand Rapids: William Eerdmans, 1931.

Landman, W.A. *A Plea for Understanding: A Reply to the Reformed Church in America*. Cape Town: Dutch Reformed Church Publishers, 1968.

Lazar, John. 'Community and Conflict: Afrikaner Nationalist Politics in South Africa, 1948–1961.' PhD diss., Oxford University, 1987.

Lazar, John. 'Verwoerd versus the "Visionaries": The South African Bureau of Racial Affairs (SABRA) and Apartheid, 1948–1961', in *Apartheid's Genesis 1935–1962*, edited by Philip Bonner, Peter Delius and Deborah Posel, 362–92. Johannesburg: Ravan Press, 1993.

Legassick, Martin. 'The Frontier Tradition in South African Historiography', in *Economy and Society in Pre-Industrial South Africa*, edited by Shula Marks and Anthony Atmore, 44–79. London: Longman, 1980.

Lewis, Peter M. 'Political Transitions and the Dilemma of Civil Society in Africa', *Journal of International Affairs* 46 (1992): 31–54.

Lipton, Merle. *Capitalism and Apartheid: South Africa, 1910–1984*. Totowa, NJ: Rowman & Allanheld, 1985.

Lodge, Tom. *Black Politics in South Africa since 1945*. London: Longman, 1983.

Lodge, Tom and Bill Nasson, eds. *All, Here, and Now: Black Politics in South Africa in the 1980s*. New York: Ford Foundation, 1991.

Loubser, J.A. *The Apartheid Bible: A Critical Review of Racial Theology in South Africa*. Cape Town: Maskew Miller Longman, 1987.

Löckhoff, A.H. *Cottesloe*. Cape Town: Tafelberg, 1978.

MacDonald, Michael. 'The Siren's Song: The Political Logic of Power-Sharing in South Africa', *Journal of Southern African Studies* 18 (1992): 709–25.

Migdal, Joel S. *Strong Societies and Weak States: State-Society Relations and State Capabilities in the Third World*. Princeton: Princeton University Press, 1988.

Moll, Terence. 'Did the Apartheid Economy Fail?' *Journal of Southern African Studies* 17 (1991): 271–91.

Möller, G.S.J. and L. Moolman. 'The Dutch Reformed Church and Separate Development', *Africa Report* (1983): 39–42.

Moodie, T. Dunbar. *The Rise of Afrikanerdom: Power, Apartheid, and the Afrikaner Civil Religion*. Berkeley and Los Angeles: University of California Press, 1975.

Murray, A.H. 'Voorwaardes vir Voogdyskap', *Op die Horison* 2 (1940): 7–11.

Nattrass, Nicoli. 'Controversies about Capitalism and Apartheid in South Africa: An Economic Perspective', *Journal of Southern African Studies* 17 (1991): 654–77.

Nzimande, Blade and Mpume Sikhosana. 'Civil Society and Democracy', *African Communist* 1 (1992): 37–51.

O'Donnell, Guillermo and Philippe C. Schmitter. *Transitions from Authoritarian Rule: Tentative Conclusions About Uncertain Democracies*. Baltimore: Johns Hopkins Press, 1986.

O'Meara, Dan. *Forty Lost Years: The Apartheid State and the Politics of the National Party, 1948–1994*. Johannesburg: Ravan Press, 1996.

O'Meara, Dan. *Volkskapitalisme: Class, Capital and Ideology in the Development of Afrikaner Nationalism, 1934–1948*. Cambridge: Cambridge University Press, 1983.

Pampallis, John. *Foundations of the New South Africa*. Cape Town: Maskew Miller Longman, 1991.

'Die Politieke Situasie', *Die Kerkbode* 34 (1934): 232–3.

Posel, Deborah. *The Making of Apartheid 1948–1961: Conflict and Compromise*. Oxford: Clarendon Press, 1991.

_____. 'The Meaning of Apartheid before 1948: Conflicting Interests and Forces within the Afrikaner Nationalist Alliance', *Journal of Southern African Studies* 14 (1987): 123–39.

Potgieter, P.C. 'Onsigbare Kerk is die Verborge Inhoud van Sigbare Kerk', *Die Kerkbode* 141, no. 18 (1988): 7.

Price, Robert M. *The Apartheid State in Crisis: Political Transformation in South Africa, 1975–1990*. New York: Oxford University Press, 1991.

The Racial Issue in South Africa. Bloemfontein: D.R. Mission Press, 1953.

Rantete, Johannes and Hermann Giliomee. 'Transition to Democracy Through Transaction? Bilateral Negotiations Between the ANC and NP in South Africa', *African Affairs* 91 (1992): 515–42.

'Reis met Apartheid', *Die Kerkbode* 159, no. 9 (1997): 7.

Rich, Paul B. *State Power and Black Politics in South Africa, 1912–1952*. New York: St. Martin's Press, 1996.

Ritner, Susan Rennie. 'Salvation Through Separation: The Role of the Dutch Reformed Church in South Africa in the Formulation of Afrikaner Race Ideology.' PhD diss., Columbia University, 1971.

Rhoodie, N.J. and H.J. Venter. *Apartheid: A Socio-Historical Exposition of the Origin and Development of the Apartheid Idea*. Cape Town: Human & Rousseau, 1959.

Sachikonye, Lloyd, ed. *Democracy, Civil Society, and the State: Social Movements in Southern Africa*. Harare: SAPES, 1995.

Seegers, Annette. 'South Africa's National Security Management System, 1972–90', *Journal of Modern African Studies* 29 (1991): 253–73.

Serfontein, J.H.P. *Apartheid, Change and the NGK*. Emmarentia: Taurus, 1982.

Shubane, Khehla. 'Civil Society in Apartheid and Post-Apartheid South Africa', *Theoria* 79 (1992): 33–41.

Sisk, Timothy D. *Democratization in South Africa: The Elusive Social Contract*. Princeton: Princeton University Press, 1995.

Smith, N.J., F.E. O'Brien Geldenhuys and P. Meiring, eds. *Stormkompas*. Kaapstad: Tafelberg-Uitgewers, 1981.

Smuts, J.C. *The Basis of Trusteeship*. Johannesburg: R.L. Essen & Co., 1942.

Statements on Race Relations. Johannesburg: Information Bureau of the DRC, 1960.

Stoker, H.G., F.J.M. Potgieter and J.D. Vorster, eds. *Koers in die Krisis: Artikels Versamel deur die Federasie van die Calvinistiese Studenteverenigings in Suid-Afrika*. 3 vols. Stellenbosch: Pro Ecclesia, 1935, 1940, 1941.

Stultz, Newell. *Afrikaner Politics in South Africa, 1934–1948*. Berkeley and Los Angeles: University of California Press, 1974.

Strydom, J.G. 'Die Naturellebeleid van die Christen Afrikaner', *Die Basuin* 15, no. 1 (1943): 1–2.

———. 'Segregasie of Gelykstelling', *Die Gereformeerde Vaandel* 6 (1938): 306–9.

Swilling, Mark. 'Political Transition, Development and the Role of Civil Society', *Africa Insight* 20 (1990): 151–60.

Templin, J. Alton. *Ideology on a Frontier: The Theological Foundation of Afrikaner Nationalism, 1652–1910*. Westport: Greenwood Press, 1984.

Thompson, Leonard. *The Political Mythology of Apartheid*. New Haven: Yale University Press, 1985.

The United Nations and Apartheid, 1948–1994. New York: UN Department of Public Information, 1994.

Van der Watt, P.B. *Die Nederduitse Gereformeerde Kerk 1905–1975*. Pretoria: Nasionale Boekdrukkery, 1987.

Van Jaarsveld, F.A. *The Afrikaner's Interpretation of South African History*. Cape Town: Simondium Publishers, 1964.

Van Schalkwyk, A. 'Beleidsrigtings t.o.v. die Naturellevraagstuk in Suid-Afrika', in *Die Naturellevraagstuk*, 12–22. Stellenbosch: Pro Ecclesia, 1950.

Viljoen, P.J. 'Die Politieke Situasie', *Die Kerkbode* 34 (1934): 232–3.

Vorster, J.D. 'Die Rassevraagstuk Volgens die Skrifte', *Die Gereformeerde Vaandel* 15 (1947): 4–6.

Walshe, Peter. *Prophetic Christianity and the Liberation Movement in South Africa*. Pietermaritzburg: Cluster Publications, 1995.

Welsh, David. 'The Executive and the African Population – 1948 to the Present', in *Malan to De Klerk: Leadership in the Apartheid State*, edited by Robert Schrire, 135–208. New York: St. Martin's Press, 1994.

Wilkins, Ivor and Hans Strydom. *The Broederbond*. New York: Paddington Press, 1979.

Wolpe, Harold. 'Capitalism and Cheap Labour-Power in South Africa: From Segregation to Apartheid', *Economy and Society* 1 (1972): 425–56.

Worden, Nigel. *The Making of Modern South Africa: Conquest, Segregation, and Apartheid*. Oxford: Blackwell, 1994.

Index